Class Struggles in Tanzania

Class Struggles in Tanzania

ISSA G. SHIVJI

MONTHLY REVIEW PRESS
NEW YORK AND LONDON

HN
814
T34
S678

Library of Congress Cataloging in Publication Data
Shivji, I G
   Class struggles in Tanzania.
   Includes index.
   1. Social classes—Tanzania. 2. Tanzania—Social conditions.
     I. Title.
HN814.T34S678   301.44'09678   76-1657
ISBN 0-85345-383-7

First Printing

Monthly Review Press
62 West 14th Street, New York, N.Y. 10011
21 Theobalds Road, London WC1X 8SL

Manufactured in the United States of America

Contents

TABLES, APPENDIX TABLES, CHARTS   viii

PREFACE   ix

PART ONE: THE THEORY OF CLASS STRUGGLE
                AND ITS APPLICABILITY TO AFRICA   1

ONE   *The Concept of Class and the Theory of*
      Class Struggle (some aspects)   3
   1.1   Introductory remarks   3
   1.2   The formal definition   4
   1.3   Class and class struggle as dialectical concepts   7
   1.4   Some theoretical lessons of the Cultural Revolution   10

TWO   *The Applicability of the Marxist Theory in Africa*   13
   2.1   Introductory: Marxism as a dogma?   13
   2.2   Skipping the capitalist stage   14
   2.3   Classless Africa!   18

THREE   *Concluding Remarks:*
        The Marxist Orthodoxy and Orthodoxy in Marxism   27

PART TWO: CLASS RELATIONS IN TANZANIA   29

FOUR   *Some Remarks on the Role of the State*   31

FIVE   *Classes in History*   34
   5.1   The colonial (economic) structures   34
   5.2   Ethnic or class relations?   40
   5.3   The class formations   44

SIX   *The Class Content of the Uhuru Struggle*   55
   6.1   Colonialism and the throttling of class struggle   55
   6.2   The class struggle matures   56

PART THREE: CLASS STRUGGLES IN TANZANIA: THE RISE OF THE 'BUREAUCRATIC BOURGEOISIE'   61

SEVEN   *Uhuru and After:*
        The Rise of the 'Bureaucratic Bourgeoisie'   63
7.1   On the 'bureaucratic bourgeoisie'   63
7.2   The class struggle unfolds   66

EIGHT   *Arusha and After:*
        The 'Bureaucratic Bourgeoisie' Forges Ahead   79
8.1   The Arusha Declaration: résumé   79
8.2   The climax of the class struggle:
        the commercial bourgeoisie disintegrates   80

PART FOUR: UJAMAA VIJIJINI AND CLASS STRUGGLE   101

NINE   *Ujamaa Vijijini without Cadres*
        and Class Struggle: The Dilemma of Metaphysics   103
9.1   The policy and the economic rationale   103
9.2   The implementation   107

TEN   *Peasant Differentiation*
        and Class Alliances: Some Thoughts   111
10.1   On peasant differentiation   111
10.2   The worker–peasant alliance   116

PART FIVE: THE BEGINNINGS OF THE PROLETARIAN CLASS STRUGGLE   121

ELEVEN *Background to the Workers' Struggles*
        I: The Mwongozo   123
11.1   Why *Mwongozo*?   123
11.2   The TANU Guidelines: the content   124

TWELVE *Background to the Workers' Struggles*
        II: The Formal 'Industrial Relations Machinery'   127
12.1   The industrial relations machinery: some aspects   128

THIRTEEN *The Post-*Mwongozo *Proletarian Struggles*   134
13.1   The Struggle   134

CONTENTS

APPENDICES: UNDERDEVELOPMENT AND RELATIONS
      WITH INTERNATIONAL CAPITALISM   147

ONE   *The Nature of the Economy*   149
1.1   Sectoral distribution   149
1.2   Export-oriented primary production   151
1.3   Consumption-oriented secondary sector   153
1.4   Disproportionate (non-productive) services sector   156

TWO   *Relations with International Capitalism*
     I: Trade and 'Aid'   158
2.1   Trade and trading partners   158
2.2   'Aid'   160

THREE   *Relations with International Capitalism*
      II: Investments and Partnerships with Multinational
      Corporations   163
3.1   Before the Arusha Declaration   163
3.2   After the Arusha Declaration   165

INDEX   179

TABLES

1 Distribution of ownership of sisal production in Tanganyika in 1964   36
2 Export-orientation: quantum of the total production exported in percentages   39
3 Sectoral distribution of the Gross Domestic Product at factor cost   40
4 Rate of failures in Form IV and Form VI National Examinations   92
5 Changing agriculture structure in some socialist countries   106
6 Industrial disputes involving strikes 1958–73   135

APPENDIX TABLES

A   GDP by industrial sector 1962–72   149
B   Employment by industrial sector 1962–70   150
B.1 Employment by industrial sector in the underdeveloped world 1970   151
C   Value in per cent of main primary exports 1962–72   152
D   Export-orientation in the productive sectors of the economy 1964–72   152
E   The secondary sector by industrial divisions 1964–72   154
F   Employment in the secondary sector by industrial divisions 1962–71   155
G   Value added by category of consumer goods 1970   156
H   The services sector by industrial divisions 1964–72   156
I   Employment in the services sector by industrial divisions 1964–71   157
J   Composition of imports 1962–71   158
K   Sources of imports 1962–72   159
L   Destination of exports 1962–71   160
M   Foreign aid 1962–72   161
N   Source of external loans 1962–72   162
O   Sectoral distribution of direct foreign investments in 1964   163
P   Outflow of international investment income (gross) and inflow of private long-term capital (net) 1961–68   164

CHARTS

1 The colonial economic structures   35
2 The petty bourgeoisie   88
3 Nationally integrated economy   105

PREFACE

Class Struggles in Tanzania was originally conceived as an answer to the various critics of my earlier paper, *The silent class struggle.** Despite its title this did not actually deal with class struggle: rather it concentrated on the analysis of economic structures. Since many of the criticisms revolved around the question of class relations and the identification of specific contradictions in Tanzanian society, it would have been futile for me to answer the critics point by point. Instead I have tried to give an outline sketch of the class struggles in Tanzania since independence. Some of the arguments of the previous paper have been integrated in the Appendix, which also briefly analyses the economy and its integration in the world capitalist system.

The present work is in no way a comprehensive history of class struggles. My aim has been simply to indicate the course of these struggles and hope that further historical research will fill in the many gaps that no doubt exist in the present work.

To analyse the class struggle is very much a *political* task and part of the struggle itself. No doubt therefore this work is likely to tread on the toes of many vested interests, not least the liberal academics who would only want to see 'celebration' of the so-called Tanzanian 'experiment'. Scientific historical analysis is neither to celebrate nor to criticize but to explain. Explanation implies nothing about an author's preference for this or that course of history. In any case, this would be irrelevant; for history cannot be remade, it can only be interpreted and explained.

It is important to emphasize this point, especially in an intellectual climate where celebration and occasional criticism, rather than *consistent explanation*, are the order of the day. Emphasizing explanation does not mean that the author is pleading 'neutrality' as regards the method of analysis or philosophy of history. Nor should emphasis on explanation mean mere 'fascination with ideas': for that is the task of an 'intellect worker or a clown, not of a committed intellectual. A committed intellectual explains and interprets the past to understand and demystify the present with a view to changing it for a rational and human future. As Marx said: 'The philosophers have only interpreted the world in various ways, the point, however, is to *change* it.'

Once again let me thank all those comrades who helped with this work in one way or another: some deciphered my scribble and turned it into a legible form; others read the manuscript and made valuable suggestions.

ISSA G. SHIVJI

* The article together with comments has now been published by the Tanzania Publishing House, Dar es Salaam.

PART ONE

*The Theory of Class Struggle
and its Applicability to Africa*

Without revolutionary theory there can be no revolutionary movement
LENIN

ONE

The Concept of Class and the Theory of Class Struggle (some aspects)

1.1 INTRODUCTORY REMARKS

The Marxist theory of class struggle is perhaps one of the theories least discussed and most distorted by bourgeois academic scholarship. This is understandable. For class struggle is basically about state power, a fact rightly considered subversive and dangerous by the ruling classes and embarrassing by 'objective' academics.

The Marxist concept of class on the other hand has in the last few decades received enormous attention in Western social science, albeit in a typically obscurantist fashion. The political sting has been cleverly removed by reducing the concept to a static, quantitative, and undialectical category. Thus many volumes have been written on social classes and social stratification but a cursory glance is enough to show that they are the work of statisticians rather than social scientists. The mysticism surrounding figures and quantities has claimed victims even among some radical academics.[1]

Nevertheless, there has been progress since the days when even the concept of social class was a taboo. Then, openly against the Marxist concept of class, was pitted the concept of élite. Now that the concept of élite[2] is increasingly losing its previous vigour as an analytical tool in Western countries, it has been exported to the underdeveloped scholarship of the underdeveloped world – especially Africa.

The theories that reign in academic circles are of course not simply of academic interest. The alleged non-existence of classes and class struggles in Africa and the 'élite' substitute therefore serve perfectly the interests of the ruling classes both national and international. The propagation of the non-existence of classes and its theoretical rationalization in the élite theories attempt to exclude by definition the Marxist

---

[1] This is not meant to be a criticism of the use of figures and quantities as such but one must always distinguish *empiricism* as a philosophical outlook which lies at the base of Western sociology from the use of empirical data illuminated by a rigorous social theory.

[2] See *infra* p. 24 for the discussion of the concept of 'élite'.

theoretical tools and therefore the possibility of genuine revolutionary movements guided by scientific methodology. This, and other similar theories, are a most pliable ideological tool in the hands of the unscrupulous African leaders enabling them to harp on the so-called harmonious development and the social homogeneity of the African population. The expounding of the revolutionary ideology as applied to concrete conditions in Africa is at once condemned as un-African; against the harmonious development of African Personality; foreign ideology advocating conflict and hatred between man and man, and so on.

Leaving aside the typical distortions of the Marxist concepts of class and class struggle by bourgeois scholars, there are genuine theoretical and ideological problems surrounding these concepts. It must be admitted that even among Marxists there is anything but clarity about them, especially in their application to the concrete conditions in Africa. Frequently the discussion in this area degenerates into repeating and asserting the commonplaces or taking dogmatic political positions.

In the tradition of Marxist thought and methodology these concepts must be submitted to vigorous scientific inquiry; a creative analysis and application is necessary if Marxism–Leninism is to continue to serve the oppressed classes. Recent events with great historical significance like the debate between the Soviet Union and China, the Cultural Revolution, and the upsurge of a variety of 'socialisms' in Africa and Latin America, have forced Marxists to begin to look at Marxism afresh with some interesting results. This task, however, cannot be left to the academic Marxists* alone: potential revolutionaries must themselves fully appreciate the theoretical problems involved because they have immediate significance and relevance for guiding *revolutionary practice*.

In this part I shall try to discuss briefly the concept of class and the theory of class struggle before applying them concretely to the Tanzanian situation.

1.2   THE FORMAL DEFINITION

The concepts of class and class struggle are probably the most elusive in Marx's writings. Though there have been subsequent interpretations and re-interpretations of his writings, yet academic scholarship remains unsatisfied as to the definition of these terms. Notwithstanding the lack of formal definitions, clear-minded Marxists have not found it difficult to apply the concepts to varied situations and come up with useful results, both theoretical and practical. In fact it will be argued later that

* In any case, recent debates among metropolitan academic Marxists, unlike those of Lenin's time, have often been among those not involved in revolutionary practice and, therefore, of limited value to revolutionaries.

the lack of formal definitions and the relative successes of the Marxist method of historical materialism are neither inconsistent nor accidental: They are built-in to the philosophical back-bone of that world outlook. For the moment, however, let us briefly look at the quotation which comes closest to a formal definition of class.

In Volume III of *Capital*, Marx just begins the discussion of classes before the manuscript breaks off. He says:

> The owners merely of labour power, owners of capital and land-owners, whose respective sources of income are wages, profit and ground-rent, in other words wage labourers, capitalists and land-owners constitute the three big classes of modern society based upon the capitalist mode of production.[3]

This passage is popularly considered to be Marx's definition of class by many Marxists and non-Marxists. That is to say categorization of social groups according to the ownership of the means of production. In itself the idea of the ownership of the means of production needs some analysis.

In the narrower sense, ownership may be looked upon as a *juridical* concept fixed in law and defining the relation of man to thing (man →thing). It is usually a variant of the Roman law concept of ownership meaning the right to 'use, abuse and dispose of property'.[4]

Law is essentially a form which becomes most developed in the society dominated by the production and distribution of commodities, i.e. the capitalist society. Law reflects, as at the same time it facilitates, the commodity exchange-relations and entrenches particular property-relations.

It is true that in capitalist societies, the important aspect of the capitalist social-relations of production is expressed in the *juridical* property-relations. But these juridical property-relations *should not be confused with the social*-relations of production. Rather the very property-relations (i.e. legal-relations) themselves have to be analysed to reveal the real *substance*, that is, the social relations of production. Of course, the *form* and *substance* are not entirely independent of each other; there is a dialectical inter-relationship between them. What needs to be done therefore is to dissect the form so as to lay bare the substantive social relations rather than confuse the form and substance as being one. Thus, for instance, the state-ownership of the means of production, which is essentially a property-relation, does not in itself tell us whether that society has established the *socialist social*-relations of production. It does not even reveal the trends of a transitional – i.e. from

---

[3] *Capital* (Moscow: Foreign Languages Publishing House, 1962), Vol. III, pp. 863–4. Clearly, he does not appear to be satisfied with this definition for in the subsequent passages he raises doubts.

[4] With the development of bourgeois society and various changes in that mode of production – welfarism, state intervention, etc. – even in bourgeois law the right of ownership is not as unlimited as the Roman phrase might suggest.

capitalist to socialist – society. This task can be done scientifically only by an analysis of the class relations which are hidden behind certain legal relations. (For law, as part of bourgeois ideology, partially hides the real relations.) It is this methodology of Marx which makes the analysis dynamic and enables it to discern the trends and tendencies of a phenomenon. Short of that the method would tend to be legalistic and static; it would be robbed of its political and historical dimensions. That would not be Marxist at all.

It is suggested that even where Marx uses the phrase 'ownership' it is meant to convey the idea of the relationship of man to man (man→man), a social relation, and not merely man to object. This is clear from Marx's political and historical writings on class struggles. In what he called the 'guiding principle' of his studies, Marx is categorical on this issue:

> In the *social* production of their existence men inevitably enter into definite relations, which are independent of their will, namely *relations of production* appropriate to a given stage in development of their material sources of production.[5] [Emphasis added.]

Marx is clearly emphasizing the *social* production process and the *social* relations of production. While accepting this in theory, in its application many writers have tended to equate the relations of production with the ownership of the means of production. If ownership as a concept is to be consistent with other Marxist concepts it must include (whatever it means besides) the control and appropriation of the surplus by one social group from another. How, under what conditions, in what historically determined structures, such appropriation takes place, decide the important characteristics of a social formation; the *'form'* and *'manner of disposal'*[6] of the surplus determine the essentials of an economic system. Therefore ownership as a relation to the means of production[7] enables the appropriation of surplus and that is the essential meaning of ownership as used by Marx. For Marx, while it may or may not include juridical ownership, it must definitely include appropriation of the surplus. Appropriation of the surplus itself expresses man-to-man social relations and not man-to-thing or juridical relations. 'The various stages of development in the division of labour are just so many different forms of ownership, i.e. the existing stage in the division of labour determines also the relations of individuals to one another with reference to the material instrument and product of labour.'[8]

---

[5] Preface to *A contribution to the critique of political economy* (London: Lawrence & Wishart, 1971), p. 20.

[6] These phrases are taken from Shigetu Tsuru, ed., *Has capitalism changed?* (Tokyo: Iwanami Shoten, 1961), p. 42.

[7] It is significant that Lenin in his definition of class (see below page 19) uses the phrase 'relation' rather than 'ownership'.

[8] Marx, *The German ideology* in Marx and Engels, *Selected works* (Moscow: Progress Publishers, 1969), Vol. I, p. 21.

It may be concluded from the above discussion that the concept of class cannot be reduced to the question of the ownership of the means of production if ownership is considered in its narrower juridical sense. That ownership itself in the Marxist terminology is a much wider concept and essentially relates to social (class) relation. This brings us to the discussion of 'social relations' and further investigation into the concept of class.

1.3 CLASS AND CLASS STRUGGLE AS DIALECTICAL CONCEPTS

To reduce the concept of class simply to the question of the ownership or the non-ownership of the means of production excludes its integral limb, the concept of class struggle. One need hardly recall that the philosophical back-bone of the Marxist method is dialectical materialism and its analytical categories themselves fully reflect this philosophy. Thus there cannot be an exploited class (for instance) without its opposite nor can motion of development be explained but in terms of contradiction between the opposites. A class society therefore by definition includes struggle of the opposites in whatever forms and, however, 'impure' this may be. Built-in to the concept of class is the inseparable idea of the *political* struggle of classes. 'The separate individuals form a class only in so far as they have to carry on a common battle against another class otherwise they are on hostile terms with each other as competitors.'[9] Thus social class as a category probably remains a theoretical concept and becomes actual and complete only in the political struggle, i.e. when it becomes a class for itself.

> The combination of capital has created for this mass [workers] a common situation, common interest. This mass is thus already a class as against capital, but not yet for itself. In the struggle, of which we have noted only a few phases this mass becomes united, and constitutes itself as a class for itself. The interests it defends become class interests. But the struggle of class against class is a political struggle.[10]

And a political struggle is waged against the instruments of political power of one class over another. Hence political relations are not merely an aspect of class relations but the core of it. Our use of the term *social* relations above covers this important political relation. In fact, in a class analysis political relations should be built into the class relations for the two are inseparable. But when one talks about political relations one brings in the question of state and the state apparatus as the seat of political power and class domination. 'Since the power of the ruling class

---

[9] ibid., p. 65.
[10] Marx, *The poverty of philosophy* (New York: International Publishers, 1963), p. 73.

is always concentrated in the organization of the state, the opposed class must aim directly against the mechanism of the state. Every class struggle is thus a *political struggle* which in its objectives aims at the abolition of the existing social order and at the establishment of a new social system.'[11] To separate the question of state power from that of class struggle is most misleading. Lenin's profound observation that 'politics is a concentrated expression of economics'[12] conveys the important fact that the various class contradictions find their most mature and *condensed* expression in the struggle for state power. As Marx observed: '. . . the political state represents the table of contents of man's practical conflicts. Thus the political state, within the limits of its form, expresses *sub specie rei publicae* (from the political standpoint) all the social conflicts, needs and interests.'[13]

Oliver Cox[14] goes so far as to separate completely the concept of social class from that of political class. This is definitely inaccurate. But otherwise his making of the political struggle an integral part of the definition of class is most important and must be grasped thoroughly.

While class struggle constitutes the motive force in history, it is not always clear and pure as *class* struggle and may take varied forms under different concrete conditions. In non-revolutionary situations much of the class struggle is latent and even unidentifiable as such at any particular moment. Talking about class struggle at such times is really registering the fact of class struggle *ex-post facto*. The development of classes and class struggle can only be talked about tendentially, in terms of historical trends. In fact, classes hardly become fully *class* conscious except in situations of intense political struggle. Class consciousness does not fully dawn upon individuals until they are locked in political battles. It is not surprising to find bourgeois critics of Marx always pointing to the proletariat's lack of class consciousness as an incontrovertible proof of the falsity of his theory. Actually, such conclusions are only too easy to arrive at by interviewing a few hundred workers in the non-revolutionary situations and by computing unfavourable answers as evidence that workers are not class conscious. But this hardly proves anything. From what we have said above it can be readily appreciated that the conclusion is derived from a wrong premise through a wrong method. On the other hand many writers have attested to the fact that in all historical revolutionary situations, contending classes have shown excep-

---

[11] Lewis L. Lorwin, 'Class struggle' in *Encyclopedia of the social sciences*. Quoted in O. Cox, *Caste, Class and Race* (New York: Monthly Review Press, 1970), p. 55 (emphasis in the original).

[12] 'Once again on the trade unions, the current situation and the mistakes of Trotsky and Bukharin', in Lenin, *Selected works* (Moscow: Progress Publishers, 1971), Vol. III, p. 534.

cf. also Mao's call to put 'politics in command', albeit in a different context.

[13] Cited by Lenin in 'What the "friends of the people are" and how they fight social-democrats', *Collected works* (Moscow: Progress Publishers), Vol. I, p. 162n.

[14] *Class, Caste and Race*, op. cit., Ch. 10 on 'The political class'.

tionally high class solidarity and class consciousness.[15] Political struggle, propaganda, and the conscious organization of the potential classes for class struggle are part of the very process of the development of classes: '. . . every movement in which the working class comes out as a *class* against the ruling classes and tries to coerce them by pressure from without is a political movement. For instance, the attempt in a particular factory or even in a particular trade to force a shorter working day out of individual capitalists by strikes, etc., is a purely economic movement. On the other hand the movement to force through an eight-hour, etc., *law*, is a *political* movement.'[16] (Marx.)

Thus the concepts of both class and class struggle are much more complex than has been imagined. They are neither merely sociological nor merely economic but integrated in them are both the Marxist methodology of dialectics and its political philosophy. It is only the complex and varied nature of these concepts that can explain the most perceptive way in which Marx applied them in analysing practical situations like those in France. *The Eighteenth Brumaire of Louis Bonaparate* is, in this sense, a classic of political writing. The use of the concepts of class and class struggle in that work would not fit any of the formal definitions of class propounded by many writers. Given the nature of the concept it is probably not amenable to formal definition at all. What is important for any revolutionary who wants to apply Marxism is Marx's methodology. It is this that needs to be fully grasped.

The dogmatic use of Marxist concepts versus the creative application of the Marxist methodology and further re-appraisal of Marx became most focused in the China–USSR debate of the 1960s and the Chinese Cultural Revolution in the same decade. Deeper analysis of the Cultural Revolution is needed but such discussion as there has been has further enriched the Marxist theoretical apparatus. This further elucidation, in my opinion, is extremely promising if creatively applied to the 'third world'.

While we have touched on some theoretical points rather abstractly, it may be worthwhile here to discuss some of those which the Chinese Cultural Revolution sharply brought into focus.

[15] See for instance the classic by John Reed, *Ten days that shook the world* (London: Penguin Books, 1966).
[16] Marx's letter to F. Bolte, 1871 in Marx & Engels, *Selected correspondence* (Moscow: Progress Publishers, 1965), pp. 270–1.

1.4 SOME THEORETICAL LESSONS OF THE CULTURAL REVOLUTION

Socialist society covers a considerably long historical period. In the historical period of socialism, there are still classes, class contradictions and class struggle, there is the struggle between the socialist road and the capitalist road, and there is the danger of capitalist restoration. We must recognize the protracted and complex nature of this struggle. We must heighten our vigilance. We must conduct socialist education. We must correctly understand and handle class contradictions and class struggle, distinguish the contradictions between ourselves and the enemy from those among the people and handle them correctly. Otherwise a socialist country like ours will turn into its opposite and degenerate, and a capitalist restoration will take place. From now on we must remind ourselves of this every year, every month and every day so that we can retain a rather sober understanding of this problem and have a Marxist–Leninist line.[17] (Mao Tse-tung.)

The present Great Proletarian Cultural Revolution is only the first of its kind. In the future such revolutions must take place. . . . All Party Members and the population at large must guard against believing . . . that everything will be fine after one, two, three, or four cultural revolutions. We must pay close attention and we must not relax our vigilance.[18] (Mao Tse-tung.)

In their theoretical writings the Chinese insist that the Cultural Revolution was not only, scientifically a Revolution; it was also a class struggle between the capitalist readers and the proletariat. Hitherto, the understanding of many Marxists has been that the climax of the class struggle is reached when the proletariat seizes state power from the bourgeoisie, followed by the period of socialism during which there are only non-antagonistic contradictions among friendly strata and classes. Further, that with the ownership of the means of production being in public hands (in practice meaning state-ownership), the bourgeoisie is overthrown as a class. Hence, the question of class struggle receded to the background. This position went further in its dogmatism in the Soviet Union and the East European countries which, in the process of their economic development, built up rigid state and legal structures with the attendant shunning of the question and discussion of political power.[19] The ques-

[17] *Important documents on the Great Proletarian Cultural Revolution in China* (Peking: Foreign Languages Press, 1970).

[18] Quoted in P. M. Sweezy, 'The transition to Socialism', *Monthly Review* (New York), Vol. 23, No. 1, (May 1971), p. 16.

[19] I cannot go into the details of the big debate that is raging as regards how to categorize the Soviet Union and the East European countries. It is not necessary for our present purpose which is only to discuss briefly what light the Cultural Revolution throws on the concepts of class and class struggle. But see Bettelheim and Sweezy, *On transition to Socialism* (New York: Monthly Review Press, 1971).

tion of class struggle then became irrelevant since, in 1936, Stalin declared that there were no classes in the USSR.[20] And in 1962 Khruschev declared that Soviet society had entered the stage of building communism and that the state had become an 'all people's state.'[21] Now, in the Marxist theory, state is essentially a *class* category. To continue strengthening the state as a powerful apparatus isolated and apparently existing above people (which is the case in the USSR), under the guise of it being the state of the 'whole people' is really to gloss over some real contradictions, even class contradictions, existing in the society.

In any case, what is important for our purposes is that the two historical examples – the Soviet Union and China – may enable us to clarify certain theoretical questions. The important theoretical precepts derived from them, and which we have discussed elaborately may be tentatively summarized as follows.

Class relations are essentially *social* relations with the control of the state by the dominating class being one of the most decisive elements. Therefore 'what is decisive – from the point of view of socialism – is not the mode of "regulation" of the economy, but rather the nature of *class in power*'.[22] The institutional set-up of the state apparatus (and other apparatuses: educational, ideological, etc.) and the relation of the state to people becomes decisive. In fact, this is much more so in a situation where state power has been seized from the bourgeoisie by an armed revolution and the private ownership (legal) relations have been changed to state ownership.

The state that is seized by the proletariat and its allies is essentially a bourgeois state. This needs to be smashed. The proletarian state[23] which leads the masses in their further struggle is a different phenomenon both conceptually and as a political and institutional entity. The smashing of the bourgeois state apparatus is a continuous political (class) struggle in which the masses themselves are fully involved. It is not the same thing as the changing of ownership (legal) relations which can be done on the morrow of the seizing of state power.

While the debate mentioned above has been mainly with respect to the transition period between capitalism and socialism, it appears to me to have been important in clarifying the question of class relations generally. It is precisely in the period of transition that the apparent identity between juridical property relations (private ownership) and the

---

[20] For the relevant quotation, see I. Lapenna, *State and law: Soviet and Yugoslav theory* (London: Athlone Press, 1964), pp. 37–9. (I do not necessarily agree with Lapenna's interpretations.)

[21] See the 1961 Party Programme of the Communist Party of the Soviet Union.

[22] C. Bettelheim, 'More on the society of transition', *Monthly Review*, Vol. 22, No. 1 (Dec. 1970) p. 11 (emphasis in the original).

[23] Bettelheim has questioned whether this should be called a *state* at all. In any case, it is this 'state' which withers away with the advance of Communism and *not* the *bourgeois* state which has to be smashed. See Lenin, *State and revolution* in *Selected works* (Moscow: Progress Publishers, 1970), Vol. II, p. 298.

social class relations (private appropriation) is ruptured. The Chinese Cultural Revolution brought this rupture into sharp focus in a concrete way. It is this which has helped to clear the theoretical distortions which had been piled up by revisionist theories on two very important and central aspects of Marxist theory: the question of the *social* relations of production as distinguished from legal property relations; and the centrality of the state in class relations and class struggle. Both these aspects have become crucial in trying to understand two different concrete situations: the period of transition between capitalism and socialism which some of the 'socialist' countries are supposed to be undergoing; and the underdeveloped capitalist countries where state ownership under some variant of 'socialist' ideology have become increasingly dominant. In the former case, the state ownership of the means of production and the importance of the 'political party' have made the political instance most dominant. In the latter case, the embryonic nature of the classes and therefore the importance of the state in buttressing their economic interests, have brought forth the state as a dominant actor on the stage. None of these situations can be understood scientifically without a clear understanding of the Marxist theory of state and class relations.

The current upsurge in the discussion of the theory of state is both a reflection of the concrete situation as well as a most welcome theoretical development. This could not have been possible without a concrete historical event like the Cultural Revolution. This is no place to go into the controversies surrounding the theory of state. Hopefully, the following analysis of the concrete Tanzanian situation, where the central role of the state is in no doubt, will contribute to this important discussion.

At this point it may be useful to discuss the applicability of the Marxist theory to the African situation and try to answer some of the objections raised against it.

TWO

The Applicability of the Marxist Theory in Africa

2.1 INTRODUCTORY: MARXISM AS A DOGMA?

Both among the academic and the ruling circles in Africa, Marxism is shunned as dogmatic; developed in different circumstances for different societies and therefore inapplicable to Africa. More intellectually inclined African leaders put forward more sophisticated arguments against Marxism. Actually, most of these arguments are neither new nor original. They usually come from the second- and third-hand analysis of Marxism by metropolitan bourgeois intellectuals, many of whom have hardly gone into the depths of the methodology of Marxism. It is not surprising therefore that many, otherwise genuine, 'open-minded' commentators on Marxism end up by itemizing the conclusions of Marx they accept and those they don't. This in itself betrays a metaphysical outlook and, *ab initio*, appears to define Marxism as if it was simply a body of conclusions some of which may be accepted and others rejected. This is most unscientific. For Marxism is *not* simply this or that aspect but a whole world outlook with its own philosophical base in dialectical materialism and its own historical method in historical materialism. Applying this methodology to a concrete situation may conceivably produce different conclusions from those reached by Marx. There is nothing un-Marxist about that.

It is true that at times debates among Marxists have sounded like theological disputes in which the scriptures are quoted to prove this or that point. It is true that Marxists have had their share of dogmatists and mechanistic 'Marxists'. But the critics who cite such 'Marxist' writings are either not aware or deliberately omit to refer to those Marxist debates which have contributed to its further development and to the understanding of society generally. The fact that Marxist writers often quote and cite Marx is also understandable. After all, Marx made a fundamental break with his predecessors by expounding a whole world outlook. His contribution and the contribution of his followers have been epoch-making. Even 100 years after Marx's death, debates about

Marxism continue, and its ideology continues to inspire oppressed people all over the world. The struggle between Marxism and bourgeois ideology is the dominating ideological struggle of our time.

Unlike debates among bourgeois writers which are tied to the ideological apron strings of the existing ruling classes, Marxist debates have given hope and provided political philosophy to the oppressed people to wage their struggle in a realistic and scientific way. Above all, Marxists have laid down their lives in the struggle against oppression and the degradation of mankind.

Had Marxists like Mao been believers in the dogma of Marxism, they would today be waiting for the Chinese bourgeoisie to develop a huge proletariat so that they might make a socialist revolution!

2.2 SKIPPING THE CAPITALIST STAGE

In most underdeveloped countries, the arguments under this heading run something as follows. Capitalism has not developed to its advanced stage in these countries. The dominant mode of production is pre-capitalist or feudalist (especially in Latin America) or there is a plurality of modes of production or dualism (especially in Africa). Hence the task of the progressives – and this line of argument was in vogue even among the Latin American Communists [orthodox] – is to support the national bourgeoisie to build capitalism. The struggle therefore is against feudalism and not against capitalism.

The bourgeois version of the argument in Africa emphasizes that Marxism was essentially developed in and, therefore, for highly *developed* capitalist societies: that 'Marxist socialism' (!) essentially refers to that socialism which would develop from the womb of such highly developed capitalist societies. In Africa there is no highly developed capitalism and, therefore, according to Marxism, we would first have to develop capitalism. Of course we can't do that, say the African socialists. We have to skip the capitalist stage and this means that we cannot apply Marxism.[24] (The version of this argument in terms of social classes is stated below.) In other words there is no developed capitalism in Africa and therefore the Marxist analysis of capitalism is *ipso facto* irrelevant. Therefore we must build socialism on the basis of African traditions – hence African Socialism.

Secondly, we are at a very low stage of development and therefore the struggle is against natural conditions and not social or between men and men. The question is not one of *distribution* since there is not much to

[24] The arguments presented here in a nutshell, with variation of details and sophistication are put forward by many writers and can be found in many different places. I have therefore felt it unnecessary to quote any source or any particular author. Since my aim is not to score debating points against any individuals but to clarify issues, the gist of the arguments presented here is sufficient as a peg to hang on my clarifications.

distribute but one of *producing* more. It can be seen how, albeit unconsciously, the authors of this argument have squeezed in the separation between production and distribution, the premise *par excellence* of the bourgeois economic theory, nowadays not taken seriously even by the bourgeois economists themselves.

Having separated the low level of development of technology (productive forces) from the socio-economic organization, it is easy to make the low level of development responsible for the low level of development! Besides being circular the argument does not even pose the correct question: Why is the level of development of the productive forces 'low' – correctly speaking, lopsided – and why does it continue to *reproduce* itself? To answer that question, one would have to look at the social relations of production. This is precisely what the bourgeois writers refuse to do and therefore end up by describing their usual vicious circles. But while they do that the Marxist writers have made important breakthroughs in their attempt to understand the system that is responsible for reproducing the lopsided productive forces in the underdeveloped countries.

In Latin America, recent theoretical writings and practical struggles have all exploded the myth that the real struggle was against feudalists and *not* against capitalists. Stavenhagen, in his 'Seven erroneous theses about Latin America'[25] was among the first to point out the falsity of the dualist theory and to show that the so-called 'modern' and 'traditional' sectors formed an integral part of a single system which in turn was integrated in the global capitalist system: 'first, the relations between the "archaic" or "feudal" regions and groups and the "modern" or "capitalistic" ones represent the functioning of a single unified society of which the two poles are integral parts and second, these two poles originate in the course of a single historical process.'[26] The historical process referred to here is the long historical relation between the *now* developed capitalist countries and the so-called 'third world'. This is the relation which some recent writers[27] have extrapolated into the thesis of the development of underdevelopment and the proposition that under-

[25] *New university thought*, Vol. 4, No. 4 (1966–67), pp. 25 et seq.
[26] ibid., pp. 26–7.
[27] See for instance, A. G. Frank, *Capitalism and underdevelopment in Latin America*, (New York: Monthly Review, 1969). See also T. Szentes, *The political economy of underdevelopment* (Budapest: Akademiai Kidao, 1971) and W. Rodney, *How Europe underdeveloped Africa* (Dar es Salaam: Tanzania Publishing House, 1972). S. Amin, 'Underpopulated Africa', *Maji Maji*, No. 6 (Dar es Salaam: Tanu Youth League, June 1972); S. Amin, 'Underdevelopment and dependence in Black Africa – their historical origin and contemporary forms' (November 1972) (mimeo). Prabhat Patnaik, 'On the political economy of underdevelopment', *Economic and Political Weekly* (February 1973). O. Cox, *Capitalism as a system* (New York: Monthly Review, 1964), P. Baran, *The political economy of growth* (New York: Monthly Review, 1962).

development itself has to be analysed as an integral part of the world capitalist system.

It appears to me that these theoretical developments are fully applicable to the African countries. Though the degree of integration in the world capitalist system may vary, none of them remains outside it. Even the once dominant 'dualist' view which left out large sectors (or regions) like subsistence from being part of the so-called 'modern' capitalist sector and therefore not integrated in the world capitalist system, is being challenged. More and more evidence is being produced to show how these sectors were directly or indirectly integrated as reservoirs of labour or suppliers of food and suffered the universal fate of structural underdevelopment. For instance by 1930s, says Iliffe,

> Tanganyika was divided into three types of economic regions. First, there were regions which specialized in production for export: the sisal estates, the main cash crop areas and the towns. These were surrounded by a second category of regions which supplied the export producing regions with food and other services: Uzaramo, Uluguru and Rufiji, supplying food to Dar es Salaam; Bonde, Ukaguru and Ulanga, supplying food to sisal estates; Kondoa supplying cattle for the Tanga and Korogwe markets; and so on. Finally spreading out beyond the export and food producing regions were peripheral regions which either supplied migrant labour or stagnated in near isolation from the territorial economy. This pattern of regional specialization – all of it focuses ultimately on export production – is one of the main characteristics of an underdeveloped economy.[28]

As a matter of fact the pattern described above could be seen in many African countries.

The capitalist mode of production in fact constitutes the *dominant* mode of production because as was pointed out in the above sections the Marxist notion of the dominant mode of production is inseparable from the idea of the dominant class-ruling class holding state power. The nature of the class holding state power is decisive in categorizing a particular mode of production. This is not to say that there are no other modes of production existing side by side. But they are in subordinate relation to the dominant mode. One cannot escape this by simply itemizing, without going into their mutual and interdependent relations, and without attaching weight to each one of them *vis-à-vis* state power, a number of modes of production in reaching conclusions like those of the 'dualist' theorists or more naïve 'pluralists'.[29]

In few African countries can it be claimed that it is either the feudalists or the 'non-capitalist elements' (whatever that means) who hold state power. In each one of them the state and the ruling class are objectively

---

[28] J. Iliffe, *Agricultural change in modern Tanganyika* (Nairobi: East African Publishing House, 1971), p. 30.

[29] For the embodiment of such *naïveté* see M. Gottlieb, 'Pluralist or unitary systems' (Dar es Salaam: Economic Research Bureau, 1971).

serving the international capitalist system, notwithstanding the moves to disengage from it. In fact in some of them, where the integration was not *complete* during the colonial period, the measures taken after independence – irrespective of the rationalizations – have objectively resulted in further integration[30] within the world capitalist system.

The *peculiar* features (including class features discussed below) to be found in these countries, albeit capitalist – generally summed up in the term 'underdevelopment' – are really the logical and inevitable consequence of their being an integral part of the world capitalist system. Being part of the global capitalist system the question of skipping the capitalist stage does not arise. Therefore building of socialism is *not* skipping or jumping the capitalist stage for we are very much part of the capitalist relations and capitalist milieu. Neither is the option of developing vigorous national capitalisms open to many African countries for, among other things,[31] it would require disengagement from the international capitalist system, a period of primitive capital accumulation (without the slave trade or the colonies!), a vigorous national bourgeoisie to do this and the docile masses to endure a long period of sacrifice. Is there such a national bourgeoisie in Africa? And in this epoch of socialist revolutions and mass struggle, where in Africa would the masses endure such sacrifice? Even the subjugation of the masses by the 'national bourgeoisie' to enable their exploitation for accumulation would require *imperialist* help which would mean the former's subordination to the international bourgeoisie and the acceptance of the role of a junior partner in the international capitalist system. This is the only historical option open to the present African ruling classes: *to develop underdevelopment under imperialist hegemony.*

Secondly, that African countries are at a low stage of development is a fact: it is also a fact that their actual production is low and that they suffer from poverty, ignorance, and disease. But these are not some God-ordained conditions visiting the African people for their past sins! They are conditions resulting from the history of the exploitation of the African people by the advanced capitalist countries. Although the exploitation has changed its forms and has passed through various stages it is one historical process and cannot be separated. The external and internal *production relations* ensure the reproduction of underdevelopment in the African countries. Liquidation of underdevelopment – poverty, ignorance, and disease – therefore requires a social–political struggle against existing relations of production, which are responsible

[30] This may be the case in Tanzania. See the Appendix.

[31] I cannot here go into the whole case, argument by argument, of why it is not possible to build independent national capitalism except refer the reader to some literature on the subject. For this see footnote (27) supra p. 15 and P. Baran's, *The political economy of growth* (New York: Monthly Review, 1968): F. Fanon's, *The wretched of the earth* (London: Penguin Books, 1967). See also J. K. Nyerere, 'The rational choice', in his *Freedom and development* (Dar es Salaam: Oxford University Press, 1973).

for throttling the development of productive forces. Given the initial low level of productive forces the struggle is undoubtedly going to be arduous and calls for new tactics and strategies. It is nevertheless a struggle of classes, a struggle to overturn the existing production relations. The fight against the existing *natural* conditions is inseparably tied with the fight against existing socio-economic organization. Both have their history. This history needs to be fully laid open to conduct the fight in a scientific way. Marxism, as a scientific tool, helps to do this. In fact, the very isolating of the essential features of underdevelopment – and their analysis and conceptually looking at underdevelopment as a system – themselves have resulted from the application of Marxist theoretical tools and methodology.[32] Those who insist on the inapplicability of Marxist theories to Africa may do well to remember that.

2.3 CLASSLESS AFRICA!

One of the other main objections against the application of Marxist theory is that there are no developed classes in Africa as there were in the Europe of Marx's time and therefore one can hardly talk about class struggle. It is true that in Africa there are no classical types of class divisions into bourgeoisie and proletariat with 'middle classes' on the fringes as in Europe. This is precisely what is to be expected. For the two areas of the world have had different though interconnected histories resulting in different socio-economic formations. It would be most surprising if under such a situation one should find similar patterns of class divisions and a similar nature of classes in these two sets of societies. This point needs emphasis because even some Marxists tend to apply the classical Marxian class *categories* to Africa. It is possible that some classes which existed in Europe may not be found in Africa and those that look similar may in fact be different, both in the way they developed historically and in their present relation to other classes, to the state, and to the means of production. For when we talk about Africa today, as emphasized above, we are talking about the countries which have had long historical relations with advanced capitalist countries and which now form part of the world capitalist system.

Classes are inseparable from the system of social production in which

[32] Bourgeois writers who have tried their hand at analysing underdevelopment have only come up with some variation of their metaphysics: either Rostov's a historical 'Stages of Growth' or Parson's psychological pattern–variables or one or the other of élite theories. None of these have thrown light on how and in what direction is social change taking place nor have they provided the exploited masses with a *political* philosophy to struggle for liberation from their wretched conditions. If anything, all of them, without exception, are ideological justification for the *status quo* and the existing ruling classes. For a critique of the bourgeois development theories, see Frank, *Sociology of development or underdevelopment of sociology* (London: Pluto Press Reprint, 1971).

they exist. But the system of social production itself is *historically determined*. Lenin's description of social classes clearly emphasizes this point. Social classes are,

> large groups of people differing from each other by the place they occupy in the historically determined system of social production, by their relation (in some cases fixed and formulated in law) to the means of production; by their role in the social organization of labour, and, consequently by the dimensions and mode of acquiring the share of social wealth of which they dispose.[33]

The historically determined system of social production in Africa is the system of underdevelopment as an integral part of the world capitalist system. The pattern of class divisions and the 'colonial' economic structures are therefore indivisible. They are mutually interdependent and, in my opinion, it is incorrect to dichotomize them. Neither one nor the other should be placed in subordinate/dominant relation.[34] While I fully agree with Arrighi that there is a danger in Frank's thesis which emphasizes the colonial structures at the expense of the specific class contradictions, a warning which is timely, I think Arrighi goes to the other extreme by placing them in *subordinate/dominant* relation. I fail to see how the *'historically determined system of social production'* (colonial or neo-colonial structures) can be placed either in a *subordinate* or a *dominant* position *vis-à-vis* the class structure of *that* system. The class contradictions are nothing but the embodiment of the material contradictions (between the productive forces and the production relations) at the *social* level. That is elementary Marxism! In any case, Arrighi appears to formulate this correctly in one sentence though does not stick to it. 'The analysis of the colonial structure should, so to say, be built into the analysis of the class structure.'

To return to the question of social classes: What we have said above may be illustrated by a brief sketch of the rise of the national bourgeoisies in Europe.

The classical European bourgeoisie had developed and matured as a mercantile class within the womb of the feudal system. Through its mercantile activities (including plunder, slave trade, etc.) it managed to accumulate commercial capital (primitive accumulation) which was channelled into the second bracket, industrial capital – thereby accomplishing the most progressive feat of the era of capitalism – the Industrial Revolution. The struggle between the decaying feudal mode of production (embodied in its dominant class, the landed aristocracy) and the rising capitalist mode of production (embodied in the bourgeoisie) was fought out at social and political levels between the

[33] Lenin, *Selected works*, Vol. 3, p. 248.
[34] See Arrighi, 'The relationship between the colonial and the class structures: A critique of A. G. Frank's theory of the development of underdevelopment' (mimeo).

feudalists and the bourgeoisie culminating in the bourgeois democratic revolutions, with either the overthrow of the landed aristocracy (France, 1789) or with a compromise within which the aristocracy to some degree transformed itself into a bourgeoisie (England).

The ideology of *nationalism* and the cries of 'freedom, equality and fraternity', reflected the objective material conditions. Nationalism was expounded against feudal parochialism and to develop national (and eventually international) markets for the goods of the rising industrial bourgeoisie. 'Freedom' meant freedom of the peasant from land and the freedom of the landless peasant to sell his labour-power (become a proletarian) to the bourgeoisie. Equality meant equality in law (no privileges for the aristocracy!) and equality in the market – for the bourgeois to sell his commodities and buy labour–power with his capital. 'Fraternity' was to signify the bourgeoisie's alliance with other classes against the feudalists.

The so-called 'national bourgeoisies' in Africa, in this sense, are neither national nor bourgeois. They lack both the historical maturity of their metropolitan counterpart and the latter's objective economic base. The natural process of the development of the authentic national bourgeoisies and the national capitalisms in Africa was irreversibly arrested by these countries coming into contact with advanced capitalism. Thus African structures and classes developed in the shadow of formal or informal colonialism. One can therefore hardly talk about a classical type of 'national bourgeoisie' in Africa. The slogans of nationalism and freedom, equality, etc., that the petty bourgeoisie shouted on the eve of independence were merely echoes of the ideology of the metropolitan bourgeoisie without their social or economic content. No wonder none of these countries was able to develop strong bourgeois democratic institutions (parliament, political parties, and so on). Soon after independence, even the pretence of doing so was thrown overboard. Instead of *nationalism*, petty bourgeois squabbles, using ethnicism as their ideological smokescreen, became the order of the day. 'Freedom' found its manifestation in military repression rather than parliamentary democracy. The dust is just beginning to settle down with the reinforcement of the neo-colonial structures and the development of a strong petty bourgeoisie in the protective wing of international capitalism.

How could it be otherwise? From the start the ruling petty bourgeoisie lack an objective independent economic base except the one provided by the colonial economy[35] which was itself an appendage of

[35] It is important to emphasize this point for there is a tendency to dismiss the petty bourgeosie as a class by saying that *it does not have an economic base*. This, in my opinion, is not true. It does have an economic base but its economic base itself is, that of the *underdeveloped* capitalism as part of the international capitalism. The economic base that it lacks is the economic base of a developed capitalist society – that of an authentic 'national bourgeoisie'. It is for this reason that I say in the text *infra* that it may be misleading and conceptually wrong to call it a 'national bourgeoisie'.

the metropolitan economy. The most they could do was to liquidate those *specific* features (where it had not already been done) which tied the economy and the institutions to a particular metropolitan country (mother country) and instead *multilateralize* the imperialist domination thereby becoming authentically part of the world capitalist system. This undoubtedly represents change and motion, enough to satisfy the '*status quo* socialists'[36] and quite in keeping with the objective changes in the international system. As we know, since the Second World War, imperialism itself has become multilateral with its own world-wide social, political and economic institutions (viz. the international corporations; world-wide agencies like the World Bank, the IMF, GATT etc.).

Fanon and other writers have well analysed the characteristics of the so-called 'national bourgeoisie' in the African and other 'third world' countries, some of which have been mentioned above. For these and other reasons, the tendency to identify the so-called 'national bourgeoisies' in Africa with the classical European bourgeoisie is misleading. I wonder, therefore, if it is correct to continue using this term to describe the African ruling classes.[37]

Other writers have used the term 'petty bourgeoisie'. This term, too, has its dangers. While in some countries it may accurately describe a social class, the indiscriminate use of it in other cases may hide some important specific characteristics of the social class in question. What term accurately describes what social phenomenon is a concrete question and therefore cannot be generalized about. All the same, it may be useful to look at the classical use of this term so as to clear the ground for its use in the second part of this paper.

2.3.1 *Petty bourgeoisie*

Petty bourgeoisie in classical Marxian literature refers to those strata which cannot be included either in the bourgeoisie or the proletariat. They exist in the middle 'ranks' and the interstices, so to speak, of a developed capitalist society. This term usually includes such people as small property owners, shopkeepers and small traders, lower ranks of the intelligentsia and liberal professions, etc. In its political attitudes too, this class was divided and ambiguous; now siding with the bourgeoisie, now with the proletariat. The most important characteristic of the petty bourgeoisie in this case is that at no time did it hold the reins of state power – it was *not* a ruling class nor even a stratum of the ruling class.

---

[36] 'Socialists' who hail one and all changes (whether quantitative or qualitative) as part of 'transition' to socialism. More sophisticated among them under the pretext of analysing motion, only end up by *supporting* the *status quo*.

[37] In one public debate I suggested Baran's term – the '*lumpen bourgeoisie*'. For reasons I have never been able to ascertain, it was vigorously resisted. Undoubtedly, I can see the dangers in its use especially because *lumpen* (as in lumpen proletariat) appears to give the idea as if this 'bourgeoisie' was *outside* of the social production process which is of course not the case. Nevertheless, its limited use can be most descriptive.

The petty bourgeoisie in Africa, on the other hand, led the independence struggle and came to control the state apparatus, thus becoming a *ruling class*, albeit in a subordinate place to the international bourgeoisie. This is the most important distinguishing feature of the African petty bourgeoisie. By controlling the state power, its *class* nature becomes fully complete in the real sense of the concept of class discussed above. To borrow Cabral's words, 'in the capitalist countries the petty bourgeoisie is only a stratum which serves, it does not determine the historical orientation of the country; it merely allies itself with one group or another.'[38] In the underdeveloped countries on the other hand, the struggle 'endows the petty bourgeoisie with a function' – the function of ruling.

A closer analysis of a concrete situation would of course call for a deeper understanding of the composition of the petty bourgeoisie. After independence, for example, the interests of the different sectors of the petty bourgeoisie may develop certain contradictions and depending on what functions, besides administration, the state has taken upon itself, even a 'bureaucratic bourgeoisie' may develop, breaking away from its *initial* class base in the petty bourgeoisie. (But more about this in Part Three where we discuss the Tanzanian situation.) It must be remembered that the state plays a crucial role in the underdeveloped countries. Hence the fortunes of the ruling sectors of the petty bourgeoisie are tied up with state power.

After this brief discussion of the petty bourgeoisie, we may now discuss the proletariat, especially the proletariat as the agency of revolution, around which many objections to the applicability of Marxist theory to Africa revolve.

2.3.2 *Proletariat and revolution*

For a number of objective and subjective reasons, into which I need not go, Marx considered the proletariat to be the agency of socialist revolution in developed capitalist societies. Contrary to common belief, however, he did not expect consciousness of their revolutionary role to dawn upon the proletariat spontaneously. Such consciousness comes only through revolutionary practice and in the process of struggle itself.[39] This is an important point to emphasize because many critics of Marx take the lack of consciousness of the proletariat or other revolutionary strata as evidence of the falsity of the Marxist theory.

In many African countries it is true that a proletariat in the classical sense – a large group of wage-earners employed in large capitalist

[38] 'Brief analysis of the social structure in Guinea', in Cabral, *Revolution in Guinea* (London: Stage I, 1969), p. 57.

[39] 'Where the working class is not yet far enough advanced in its organization to undertake a decisive campaign against the collective power, i.e. the political power of the ruling classes, it must at any rate be trained for this by continual agitation against this power. . . .' Marx in his letter to F. Bolte, November 1871, *Selected correspondence*, op. cit., p. 271.

industry and constituting a substantial proportion of the population – did not develop and could not have possibly developed in the conditions of the colonial and, now, the neo-colonial economies. Nevertheless, in all these countries a class of wage-earners did develop. These were employed mainly on plantations, in the docks, in transport and commerce, and in construction, building, etc., i.e. the primary and tertiary sectors. In addition to their widespread sectoral distribution, the system of migrant labour made it still more difficult for them to organize, even for trade union struggles. In spite of this, they played a strategic role in the struggle for independence.

In addition, different structures in the colonized countries have produced their corresponding strata with revolutionary potential. Therefore, depending on actual conditions in the concrete situation of each country, various alliances are possible for revolutionary action. It is instructive to quote an example from a practical situation:

> One important group in the towns were the dockworkers; another important group were the people working in the boats carrying merchandise, who mostly live in Bissao itself and travel up and down the rivers. Those people proved highly conscious of their position and of their economic importance and they took the initiative of launching strikes without any trade union leadership at all. We therefore decided to concentrate all our work on this group. This gave excellent results and this group soon came to form a kind of nucleus which influenced the attitudes of other wage-earning groups in the towns – workers proper and drivers, who form two other important groups. Moreover, if I may put it this way, we thus found our little proletariat.[40] [Cabral.]

What is important is that such potential revolutionary strata are mobilized under the leadership of the *proletarian ideology*. Even the Chinese struggle was based mainly on the peasants and not the proletariat, though given the concrete conditions of China, the peasantry itself, objectively, had revolutionary capacity. The important and decisive point is that the struggle was led by a party expounding proletarian ideology.

This point is truer still in the case of cadres, who may have varied class origins. In fact, the leadership and the cadres may even come from bourgeois and petty bourgeois classes: provided they are imbued with proletarian consciousness, such traitors to their classes are only too common in history. As we have been emphasizing all along, class struggle is a political struggle for state power, and therefore what is important is that potential revolutionary classes and strata are organized for this political conflict under the leadership of the *proletarian ideology* to overthrow the capitalist social order. Again, we cannot resist quoting Cabral on this point:

> We were faced with another difficult problem, we realized that we needed to have people with a mentality which could transcend the

[40] 'Brief analysis . . .', op. cit., p. 54.

23

context of the national liberation struggle, and so we prepared a number of cadres from the group I have just mentioned,* some from the people employed in commerce and other wage-earners, and even some peasants, so that they could acquire what you might call a working class mentality. You may think this is absurd – in any case it is very difficult; in order for there to be a working class mentality the material conditions of the working class should exist, a working class should exist. In fact, we managed to inculcate these ideas into a large number of people – the kind of ideas, that is, which there would be if there were a working class. We trained about 1000 cadres at our party school in Conakry, in fact for about two years this was about all we did outside the country. When these cadres returned to the rural areas they inculcated a certain mentality into the peasants and it is among these cadres that we have chosen the people who are now leading the struggle; we are not a communist party or a Marxist–Leninist party but the people now leading the peasants in the struggle in Guinea are mostly from the urban milieux and connected with the urban wage-earning group.[41]

Thus a *large* developed proletariat is not an essential condition for struggle against capitalism and the building of socialism. There exist in the African situation other strata – for example, lower sectors of the petty bourgeoisie – with revolutionary potential, and these can be mobilized in alliance with the peasantry and the working class under the leadership of the *proletarian ideology*.[42]

Those who argue against the applicability of scientific socialism in Africa because the theory was based on a developed proletariat which does not exist in Africa are therefore only expecting concrete conditions to conform to scriptures! This is not Marxism.

In the concrete situations of the Soviet Union, China, North Vietnam, etc. – and not all of them had large proletariats – Marxism has been applied quite successfully. This has enriched the theory further and sharpened its tools of analysis. That is what science is all about: a scientific theory should be capable of developing in the very process of its application.

2.3.3 'Élites': a critique

Before we leave this section on social classes, it is important to touch very briefly on the alternative élite theories which have been put forward to explain the African situation.

Élite theories, originally developed specifically against Marx's theory of classes, continue to be part of Western sociology and political science. In the last two decades or so, they have come to be widely applied to

---

* This was a group of young people recently arrived from rural areas, who were only intermittently employed, and lived off their petty bourgeois relatives and workers in urban areas (ibid., p. 48).

[41] ibid., p. 55.

[42] See further discussion of this *infra* p. 116 et seq.

the underdeveloped countries and especially to Africa. The fact that in Africa it is difficult to find large social groups with their own mores, customs, social intercourse, intra-group marriages, etc., has apparently lent greater credence to these theories than in Europe.

Implied in the concept of élite is that the members of the élite are what they are because of their superior qualities. Built in to this concept, therefore, is a support for, and an acceptance of, the *status quo*. Secondly, the theories of élite and their corollary, competing élites, to explain political change, are extremely value-loaded ideologically. The ideology and values they imply, needless to mention, are those of capitalism. As one writer put it: '... the theory of élites is, essentially, only a refinement of social *laissez-faire*. The doctrine of opportunity in education is a mere silhouette of the doctrine of economic individualism, with its emphasis on competition and "getting-on".'[43] That the élite theory in its origin and conception is anti-socialist need hardly be stressed. As Bottomore points out: 'Their original and main antagonist was, in fact, socialism, and especially Marxist socialism as Mosca wrote: "In the world in which we are living, socialism will be arrested only if a realistic political science succeeds in demolishing the metaphysical and optimistic methods that prevail at present in social studies. . . ." This "realistic science" which Pareto, Weber, Michele and others in different ways helped to further was intended above all to refute Marx's theory of social classes. . . . As Meisel so aptly comments " 'Élite' was originally a middle class notion. . . . (In the Marxist theory) . . . the proletariat is to be the ultimate class which will usher in the classless society. Not so. Rather, the history of all societies, past and future, *is the history of its ruling classes . . . there will always be a ruling class, and therefore exploitation."* This is the anti-socialist, specifically anti-Marxist, bent of the élitist theory as it unfolds in the last decade of the nineteenth century. Élitist theories also oppose socialist doctrines in a more general way, by substituting for the notion of a class which rules by virtue of economic or military power, the notion of an élite which rules because of *the superior qualities of its members*.'[44]

Thirdly, élite theories are basically anti-masses. The masses are considered passive, inert, the *takers* rather than the *makers* of history. It is only the élites who are actors on the historical stage. This is diametrically opposed to Marx's theory of social classes where masses play the central role and are the main actors on the historical stage. The continuing revolutions in which the masses are rising in their millions prove Marx correct and the élite theorists absolutely wrong. One would like to know from these theorists whether the Chinese Revolution, the Vietnam war, or the national liberation struggles in Africa are being *fought* by élites!

[43] R. Williams, *Culture and society* (Penguin Books edition), p. 236, quoted in Bottomore, *Élites and society* (London: Penguin Books, 1966), p. 17.
[44] Bottomore, *Élites and society*, op. cit., p. 17–18.

Fourthly, as already mentioned elsewhere the élite theories are static, undialectical, and ahistorical. They do not provide any tools for the analysis of social change and social movement. This is its greatest and probably fatal shortcoming *vis-à-vis* Marxist theory. 'Élite theory . . . is at bottom a theory of political inertia, an analysis of the tendency for political power to devolve into the hands of a small, cohesive and relatively closed élite which, notwithstanding democratic "rules of the game" controls all decisions of major importance, is virtually invulnerable to opposition and is capable of forestalling any changes which are potentially threatening to its monopoly of power.'[45]

Finally, what do the élite theorists have (besides looking for modern 'industrializing élites' or conservative 'dynastic élites') to say about getting us out of the quagmire of underdevelopment? What hope or political philosophy do they have to offer to the poverty-ridden masses of our countries to struggle against their internal and external exploiters? None; like their Biblical counterparts, their only prescription would be for the masses to wait passively for some messianic industrializing élite to appear and deliver them from their misery!

[45] Isaac Balbus, 'Ruling élite theory vs. Marxist class analysis' *Monthly Review*, Vol. 23, No. 1 (May 1971), pp. 36, 38.

THREE

Concluding Remarks: the Marxist Orthodoxy and Orthodoxy in Marxism

In my opinion, vulgarization and mechanistic interpretations notwith-standing, there is no scriptural Marxist orthodoxy. If there is any orthodoxy in Marxism, it is the Marxist methodology. That is what makes it a science. The most important concepts of Marxism – like class, class struggle, mode of production, productive forces, relations of production, etc. – are all tied up with his dialectical method and are, therefore, capable of assimilating newer findings and knowledge. For Marx, 'the concept of "class" was inseparably linked to a dialectical theory of social change, "class" was not primarily a category for describing how a particular capitalist society looked at any given point in time, but rather above all an analytical tool for elucidating the sources of structural change within the capitalist system, a theory of the direction in which capitalist societies were developing.'[46] This is true of his other concepts as well and is what explains the dynamism of Marxist theories. The applicability of his method has been creatively shown by Lenin and Mao *in the field* and its use, too, as a theoretical tool for understanding the monopoly stage of capitalism has also been amply demonstrated.[47]

The temptation to dismiss the applicability of Marxism in Africa arises subjectively from a basic misunderstanding or lack of under-standing of Marxist methodology. Objectively, of course, the reason for this is class interests, but then we are only talking about subjective rationalization which does show genuine misunderstanding. Such mis-understanding, especially on the part of those who claim to be Marxists, results in dogmatism and has the effect of repelling some non-Marxists.

In Africa we are prepared to accept the achievements of science, irrespective of from where they come. And rightly so. For scientific knowledge is no monopoly of any one nation or people. The whole of mankind has participated in its achievements – the exploited people probably much more so than the exploiters. If this is true of natural science it is also true of the science of society. The African people cannot

[46] I. Balbus, ibid., pp. 37–8.
[47] See for example, Baran & Sweezy, *Monopoly capital* (London: Penguin Books, 1968).

liberate themselves from their technological backwardness without the modern methods of natural science, nor can they liberate themselves from their oppressive social organization without scientific, social methods.

While Marxism continues to be denounced as 'foreign ideology' our schools, universities, other educational institutions, and mass media continue to disseminate Western, bourgeois social theories on a massive scale – as if they were not foreign!

African intellectuals cannot always echo the voices of others, they have to make original contributions both to natural science and to the science of society. Unlike most bourgeois social theories, Marxism is the only social theory which allows such original contributions, for it is a method which can be continually enriched by the *social practice* of the struggle against the oppression and exploitation of the African people.

The choice therefore is not between 'foreign' and indigenous ideology (non-science). The choice for African intellectuals is not between Marxist and bourgeois theories but between the practice of social struggle which enriches Marxism on the one hand and intellectualizing about bourgeois theories in support of the exploiting ruling classes on the other.

The following is a modest effort to apply Marxist methods in tracing the history of class struggle in Tanzania.

PART TWO

Class Relations in Tanzania

History advances in disguise; it appears on the stage wearing the mask of the preceding scene, and we tend to lose the meaning of the play
REGIS DEBRAY

FOUR

Some Remarks on the Role of the State

Independent Tanzania inherited the colonial economic structures and classes of the colonial era. During the short period of independence these structures and classes have been undergoing rapid transformations – disintegration of some, formation of others, newer re-alignments, and so on. The rapid rate at which social groups see their rise and fall in the underdeveloped world would be unthinkable in an old established capitalist society. But this is historically quite understandable in an underdeveloped country with a very weak petty bourgeoisie.

In a sense, then, the post-independence period has been one in which definite class struggle has made its appearance on the stage with all the 'impurities' and 'distortions' of its colonial history, and which is, hence, not easily identifiable as such. It is from the analysis of the varied and misleading *forms* assumed by the class struggle that one has to identify the *substance* – class struggle.

One thing that stands out sharply is the central, decisive and almost omnipotent role played by the state in these struggles.[1] This is not to say that economic interests have had no effect. But the economic interests of the ruling class have had to be established and buttressed by state power. The ruling class, in Debray's words: 'transforms the state not only into an instrument of political domination, but also into a source of economic power. The state, culmination of social relations of exploitation in capitalist Europe, becomes in a certain sense the instrument of their installation in these countries.'[2]

To be sure, the dominant role of the state does not begin with independence. It goes back to the colonial period itself. The basic divorce of the producer from his means of production and the installation of labour-power as a commodity was *consciously*, and almost exclusively, done by

[1] See Walter Rodney's comment on the first draft of this essay, 'State formation and class formation in Tanzania', in *Maji Maji*, No. 11 (August 1973).

[2] Debray, 'Problems of revolutionary strategy in Latin America', *New Left Review*, No. 45; quoted in J. Saul, 'Who is the immediate enemy?', *Maji Maji*, No. 1.

the state. Various methods like land alienation, taxation, and, virtually, forced recruitment of labour, were used to force the producer to leave his means of production and go to work in the plantations, mines, road-works, etc.[3] Sir Percy Girouard, one of the first Governors of the then East African Protectorate put this very clearly:

We consider that taxation is the only possible method of compelling the native to leave his reserve for the purpose of seeking work. Only in this way can the cost of living be increased for the native . . . and it is on this that the supply of labour and the price of labour depends.[4]

Thus Africans became liable to all sorts of taxes levied on their huts, wives, or even on their mere existence.

The colonial state also played a major role in 'developing' the commercial agriculture sector in Tanganyika. Force, persuasion, fiscal measures, etc., were all used either to create 'free labour' to work on the plantations or force the African peasant to grow cash crops[5] depending on the requirements of the metropolitan economy at the time. For instance, 'the Germans built up a high cost sisal industry because they wanted to have cordage for their navy from an independent supply which they could control. . . . When Britain took over after the war, she discouraged further investments in the industry (as she had no use for the product at this time) only to encourage it during the Second World War when the British Admiralty adopted the use of cordage after her manilla hemp-fibres were blocked by the Japanese.'[6]

In the colonial situation therefore the state was not only the 'regulator' and the 'defender' of the economic system but played an actively dominant role in the very establishment of this economic system. In Tanganyika, the fact that there was no strong *internal* (i.e. within the colony) class opposition (unlike, for example, Kenya, which had politically and economically strong Settler and Asian communities) further reinforced the dominance of the state. Later, after independence it would be because of the relative weakness of the petty bourgeoisie that the state would emerge once more as the dominant factor.[7]

Thus the colonial state was largely responsible for establishing certain economic structures and integrating the colonial economy with the

[3] See J. Woddis, *Africa: the roots of revolt* (London: Lawrence & Wishart, 1960). L. R. Patel, *East African labour régime* (Dar es Salaam: 1972) (mimeo.)·
[4] *East African Standard* (Nairobi), 8 February 1913. Quoted in Patel, op. cit., p. 11.
[5] cf. B. D. Bowles, 'Export crops and underdevelopment in Tanganyika, 1929–1961' Paper presented to the Annual Social Science Conference (1973) of the Universities of East Africa.
[6] J. Rweyemamu, *Underdevelopment and industrialization in Tanzania: a study of perverse capitalist industrial development* (Nairobi: Oxford University Press, 1973).
[7] See *infra* p. 63.

metropolitan economy. In the process it certainly helped or hindered the development of various classes and strata.

So far as the dominance of the role of the state is concerned, there is, therefore, a certain amount of continuity between the colonial and the post-independence state, with one very fundamental break: the post-independence state becomes the instrument for making the hitherto embryonic class a *ruling class* (also helping it to carve out an economic base) and thereby initiating the establishment of certain specific *social* relations within the domestic society.

These arguments will become clearer when we discuss the post-independence class struggles. But before this we must discuss the colonial structure and class formation at the time of independence.

FIVE

Classes in History

5.1 THE COLONIAL (ECONOMIC) STRUCTURES

By the time of independence Tanzanian[8] economic structures had more or less come to be integrated in the world capitalist system. The peculiar feature, however, was that the links – economic and institutional – were mainly with a particular metropolitan power; the United Kingdom. In other words Tanzanian links with imperialism had not yet become fully multilateral. The United States, West Germany, and Japan, for instance, hardly featured as her trade, financial, or cultural partners. This can be easily explained. To international imperialism then, Tanzania was not an important strategic area. Economically it was Nairobi which acted as a sub-metropolis[9] for the whole of the East African region. Dar es Salaam therefore was a sub-satellite. In this sense, when Tanzania became independent it had considerable potential for further integration as an entity in the *world* capitalist system. The ensuing struggle between Nairobi and Dar es Salaam in the East African Community (at international level) may be explained in terms of Nairobi wanting to retain its 'sub-metropolitan' status within East Africa, while Dar es Salaam was fighting against its 'subsatellite' status. This explains the contradictions between the Kenyan petty bourgeoisie and its Tanzanian counterpart.

The Tanzanian economy, being 'peripheral' even to the East African, was an *export economy par excellence*. Thus it is *via* mainly (though not exclusively) the export sector that one finds the vertical links with the metropolitan economy [see Chart 1]. Despite some industrial activity after the Second World War this pattern continued substantially unaltered.[10]

[8] Unless otherwise indicated, Tanzania refers to the *mainland* only.

[9] I am using the metropolis/satellite terminology in Frank's sense. Though I do not wholly agree with his global model, in this case these terms seem to be suitable. cf. Frank, 'The development of underdevelopment', in his *Capitalism and underdevelopment in Latin America*, op. cit.

[10] For a closer analysis of industrial development see J. Rweyemamu, *Underdevelopment and industrialization in Tanzania*, op. cit.

CHART 1
THE COLONIAL ECONOMIC STRUCTURES

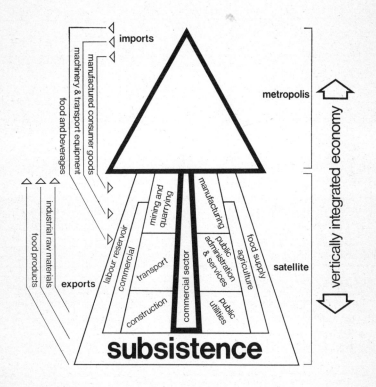

I have tried to show the sectoral division of the colonial, vertically integrated, Tanzanian economy in Chart I. This may be summarized as follows.

We have noted that the main feature of the economy was that it was export-oriented with major economic activities directly or indirectly linked with that sector and therefore directly or indirectly integrated in the world capitalist system.

Firstly, *commercial agriculture, including hunting, forestry, and fishing* (in 1964 46·7 per cent of the GDP)[11] consisting of sisal estates, large plantations growing food and other raw materials for export, and peasant-based cash crop production. Most of these sisal estates and plantations were owned by foreign companies, European settlers, and Tanzanian and East African-based Asian businessmen as illustrated in the case of sisal in the following table:

TABLE 1

DISTRIBUTION OF OWNERSHIP
OF SISAL PRODUCTION IN TANGANYIKA IN 1964

	(tons)	(%)
Greek	70 000	30·5
British	57 600	25·1
Asian	62 250	27·1
Swiss	15 750	6·8
Dutch	13 700	6·0
Italian	150	—
German	1250	0·5
African	9100	4·0
Total	229 800	100·0

Source: C. W. Guillebaud, *An economic survey of the sisal industry of Tanganyika* (3rd edn) (Welwyn: James Nisbet & Co., 1966), p. 134.

Secondly, accompanying this activity, was the urban-based *commercial sector, including finance, insurance, real estate, and business services* (in 1964 this was 22·1 per cent of the GDP) with foreign export–import houses situated in the capital city. These dealt mainly in products for export and imported luxury goods and other manufactured products. Thus the purchasing, transport, warehousing, insurance, and shipping of the most important crop was controlled by Ralli Brothers of Kenya, a subsidiary of Ralli Brothers of London. Coffee and cotton were bought by agents like Tancot Ltd (Tanganyika Cotton), now part of the Lonrho Group, and Brooke Bond. Products like meat and pyrethrum were handled by the Brooke Bond–Liebig Extract of Meat

[11] The figures for the sectoral distribution are computed from *The economic survey*, 1971–72, p. 8. They are at 1966 prices.

Company and Mitchell Cotts respectively. Smith Mackenzie and Dalgety, part of the Inchape Group of London, were the main trading companies.[12]

Immediately linked with these foreign mercantile companies we have a series of concentric circles made up of traders, big Asian wholesalers based in big towns, and smaller wholesalers-cum-retailers in smaller towns, fading into and overlapping with small African retailers in villages and the countryside areas surrounding the towns.

Thirdly, the *Mining and Quarrying sector* (in 1964 this was 2·5 per cent of the GDP) again producing raw materials for export, owned and controlled mainly by South African-based companies.

Fourthly, the *non-monetarized sector* – or what goes under the term 'subsistence' – (in 1964 this was 33 per cent of the GDP) often thought to be parallel to the so-called export enclaves in dualist theories, though not directly integrated in the cash economy, was indirectly linked by supplying food and acting as a reservoir of labour for the above three sectors. The system of migrant labour, for instance, affected this sector substantially and, therefore, it cannot simply be considered as an 'outside' element though it did not *directly* participate in the cash economy.

Fifthly, *construction* (in 1964 this was 3·4 per cent of the GDP), *transport* (in 1964 6·9 per cent of the GDP), *public utilities* (in 1964 0·9 per cent of GDP) etc., provided the necessary infrastructure for the above three sectors. We ought also to mention the 'superstructure', the so-called *public administration* (in 1964 11 per cent of the GDP), and other services built on this economic base.

Sixthly, the *manufacturing industry* (in 1964 7·1 per cent of GDP) occupied an extremely small and almost insignificant role in the economy. What little manufacturing took place was geared to serving the consumer demands of the commercial sector (food, beverages, cigarettes, etc.) or some simple inputs for the first three sectors, like paints, ropes and twine, sawmilling, etc. Even mass-consumed products like textiles were imported. (In 1961, these constituted of about one-sixth, or the single biggest item of imports.)

Let us point out, briefly, some salient features of this type of economy, particularly with reference to the '*form*' the surplus takes and its '*manner of disposal*'.[13]

The *productive* sectors – roughly, (1) commercial agriculture, including hunting, forestry and fishing, (2) mining and quarrying, (3) manufacturing (including construction and public utilities), and (4) the non-monetarized sector – generate most of the surplus. It is these sectors, then, from which the substantial portion of the surplus is extracted. The '*form*' the surplus takes may be placed under three broad categories:

[12] J. Rweyemamu, *Underdevelopment and industrialization*, op. cit., pp. 32–3.
[13] Shigetu Tsuru, *Has capitalism changed?* op. cit., uses this to identify a particular economic system but in my view it is a good working point of departure to identify some features of an individual economy as well.

(*a*) surplus value; (*b*) merchant profits, *stricto sensu*, through unequal exchange and (*c*) surplus labour. Merchant profits are distinguished from commercial profits, the latter being merely the *realization* of the surplus value while the former is through unequal exchange as a result of which value is actually transferred from one trading partner to another. In practice, all these forms are found together and cannot easily be separated, particularly in terms of their quantitative weights and the sectoral spread.

Thus, in the plantation-based agriculture, mining, quarrying and manufacturing, the form that the surplus takes is largely that of the surplus value, extracted by the owners of the means of production. Extremely low wages force the workers to continue to depend on their 'homes' for subsistence: The peasant economy therefore bears part of the responsibility for reproducing the labour power of the workers. This reduces, for the capitalist, the portion of 'necessary labour' in the total product, leaving him an even larger portion as surplus value.

From peasant-based agriculture and other small-commodity producers, the surplus is extracted through unequal exchange taking the form of merchant profits.

The non-monetarized sector provides surplus in two ways: (1) by supplying 'free' (surplus) labour – forced labour, prison labour, so-called 'voluntary' labour, and extremely cheap labour (migrant labour is so cheap, and the conditions of recruited labour are so close to slave labour, that some of it should be included in 'free' rather than paid labour); (2) by supplying food to, for example, the plantation labourers who depend on their 'peasant homes' for food supplies.

As for the '*manner of disposal*' of the surplus: a large portion of the surplus which is extracted in this way is drained into the metropolitan economy through repatriation of the open and hidden profits[14] of foreign owners (and controllers of the means of production) and through unequal exchange of the commodities in the world market. A disproportionate portion of the remaining surplus is used up in the non-productive services sector, e.g. commercial and financial infrastructure; public administration, etc. – only a small portion of which could be regarded as *necessary* through non-productive services.

The repatriated surplus is a permanent loss to the economy. It is accumulated in the metropolitan economy and transformed into industrial capital which aids the metropolitan economy's further development. The accumulation of surplus in large chunks within the colonial economy takes place mainly in the commercial sector. Some of this may find its way to the export-oriented agricultural sector. But the accumulation is basically in the form of commercial capital and is not transformed into industrial capital. This is the single, important characteristic of a vertically integrated export-oriented economy.

[14] Surplus and profits are of course not identical. But for our purposes, since we are only concerned with proportions, this formulation is adequate.

The export-orientation of the Tanzania economy is illustrated by the following figures for five important (including three *main*) agricultural crops:

TABLE 2

EXPORT-ORIENTATION: QUANTUM OF
THE TOTAL PRODUCTION EXPORTED IN PERCENTAGES

YEAR	SISAL	COTTON	COFFEE	TEA	CASHEW NUTS
1964	90·88	81·76	99·26	94·54	76·54
1969	81·89	81·89	100·01	86·94	76·35

Source: (Tanzania) *Statistical abstract*, 1966 and 1970.

The predominantly export-orientation of this type of economy is a result of the colonial economic structures. This must be distinguished from the normal trade, the object of which is to sell surpluses of commodities having substantial home markets to obtain the essential imports. This is not so in the case of the colonial economies. In fact, here, the very production *is* for export. What is produced therefore is not consumed and what is consumed is not produced within the economy. In so far as internal production structures and external relations with the metropolitan economy reproduce themselves so does the form and the pattern of utilization of the surplus. Thus the colonial economy functions as a *system*.

With independence, different sectors may grow quantitatively; the manufacturing sector may show some growth due to the installation of assembly and packaging plants and import-substitution. The basic features of the economy, that is, that of export-orientation without national integration, and the pattern of utilization of the surplus, however, remain largely the same. (See Tables 2 and 3.)

The dominantly export-oriented primary sector; an extremely weak and lopsided secondary sector geared mainly to the production of luxury consumer goods through import-substitution; and a disproportionate tertiary (largely non-productive) sector, are, in fact, the characteristics of the underdeveloped African economies. The basic proportional relationships between these sectors continue well after independence. (This is discussed in greater detail in the Appendix.)

The discussion of the colonial economic system (the production and extraction of the surplus, the form it takes, and the manner of its disposal) constitutes the necessary 'background' to the question of class relations. In fact it is an integral part of the class struggle and was separated here only for the sake of convenience. It is, then, these class formations that we propose to discuss in the next sections.

TABLE 3

SECTORAL DISTRIBUTION OF
THE GROSS DOMESTIC PRODUCT AT FACTOR COST (at 1966 prices)

			(percentages)	
			1964	*1971*
1. Agriculture, hunting, forestry and fishing 2. Mining and quarrying	PRIMARY SECTOR		49·2	40·6
3. Manufacturing and handcrafts	SECONDARY SECTOR	7·1	11·4	15·6 { 9·7
4. Electricity and water supply		0·9		1·2
5. Construction		3·4		4·7
6. Transport, storage communications 7. Wholesale and retail trade and restaurants and hotels 8. Finance, insurance, real estate and business services 9. Public administration and other services	TERTIARY SECTOR		39·0	44·2
10. *Less* imputed bank service charges			0·6	1·4
GDP at factor cost			100·0	100·0

Source: UR of Tanzania, *The economic survey,* 1971–72, p. 8.

5.2 ETHNIC OR CLASS RELATIONS?

An attempt at a class analysis of Tanzanian society runs into the inevitable complexities introduced by a racially structured social organization inherited from colonial times. The purpose of the present discussion is to question the widely accepted view that the relation between Asians and Africans was essentially racial or ethnic. I do not include Europeans here for a number of reasons. Numerically, the European *settlers* involved in the economy constituted a very small group. In 1931, out of 8228 Europeans only 1129 were engaged in agriculture. This hardly varied until independence. In 1957 the number of those engaged in agriculture had gone up by only about 400.[15] The rest would be mainly

[15] A. B. Lyall, *Land law and policy in Tanganyika, 1919–32* (1973). Unpublished thesis presented to University of Dar es Salaam in part fulfilment of LL.M. ibid., p. 4.

state functionaries, representatives of foreign firms, etc. These constituted the 'bureaucratic' representatives of the metropolitan bourgeoisie. The settlers did play a role in the economy, but unlike their counterparts in Kenya or Rhodesia, they were nowhere strong enough to influence the colonial state, let alone control it. Furthermore, the colonial government had no intention to develop a *settler* economy.[16] Rather, they vigorously encouraged the African peasant economy side by side with the *foreign*-owned plantations. Thus, the contradiction between the African masses and the settlers as such did not become a *dominant* one after independence. In contrast, the very fact that the Asians were centrally placed in the predominantly *commercial* economy made 'Asian–African' relations dominant after independence.

Hitherto the analysis of inter-community relations has been essentially in terms of the *ethnic* character of the communities, and their economic functions have only been thrown in to add sophistication. In what follows, we want to reverse the ethnologist's approach and make the place occupied by the actors in the social production process, the centre of the analysis. This is not to belittle ethnic character, for that would be unrealistic. We are fully aware of ethnic consciousness developed over almost three generations of colonial history. This, in itself, needs to be *explained,* rather than be made an independent, but decisive, variable. 'The importance attributed by ethnologists to cultural elements of . . . populations has long concealed the nature of the socio-economic structures into which these populations are integrated.'[17]

Fortunately, we have an excellent model developed by Stavenhagen in his 'Classes, colonialism, and acculturation'.[17] In this article Stavenhagen analyses the relation between Indians and Ladinos in south-eastern Mexico. The thrust of his work is to isolate the *production relations* between the two communities within the context of the whole socio-economic structure. Without describing in detail his model we may use its relevant characteristics to describe the 'Asian–African' relations in the Tanzanian society.

The dominant relation between the majority of the Africans and the majority of the Asians was commercial. The African peasant met the Asian mainly as a producer and a consumer – the Asian being the trader, the middleman, and the creditor. 'The majority of the Indians [read 'Africans'] enter into economic and social relationships with Ladinos [read 'Asians'] at the level of commercial activity, and not at the level of wage labour. It is precisely the commercial relationships which link the Indian [read 'African'] world to the socio-economic region in which

---

[16] ibid.
[17] Rodolfo Stavenhagen, 'Classes, colonialism, and acculturation', revised English version reprinted in J. A. Kahl (ed.), *Comparative perspectives on stratification: Mexico, Great Britain, Japan* (Boston: Little Brown and Co., 1968), p. 31, at p. 33.

it is integrated, and to national society as well as to the world economy.'[18] To be sure, wage labour on the Asian-owned plantations and estates, in commercial establishments and services and as domestic servants was not altogether insignificant. But still the Asian was primarily a *duka-walla*, and only then an employer. Besides, as a producer and a consumer, the African met the Asian trader also as a retailer–buyer. In 1961 it was found that out of 48 535 total traders (including wholesalers but excluding itinerant traders) 34 381 or slightly less than three-quarters were Africans. But the African traders did less than one-third of the total business.[19] Given the African retailer's dependence on the Asian trader as a supplier of goods and particularly credit, the African retailer was more of a 'wage-labourer-cum-consumer', than a retailer in his own right. The colonial administration, while supporting the Asians, discouraged the Africans from getting trading licences. Furthermore, there was a regulation prohibiting wholesalers from giving an African trader goods worth more than sh 600 on credit.[20] This effectively tied the African retailer to the Asian wholesaler and left him at the latter's mercy. Thus, the Asian trader would charge the African retailer extortionate prices and so keep him in permanent debt. Actually, the relations of extreme exploitation of the African could be seen at all levels: as a wage-labourer; as a peasant-producer and as a consumer of simple goods. In other words, owing to his sophisticated knowledge of price mechanisms and the laws of the country, and to the privileged position (in terms of the protection and attention) accorded him by the colonial state, the Asian trader was always a price giver and the African a price taker. To be sure, the Asian only provided an important and indispensable link between the metropolitan and the colonial economies, the major beneficiary of which was the metropolitan bourgeoisie.

Thus the main stimulus behind the formation of the first African co-operatives, whether marketing or traders', was the exploitation by the Asian middlemen as buyers of the African produce.[21] Among the first independent activity of the Tanganyika African Association (TAA), the predecessor of the nationalist political party, the Tanganyika African National Union (TANU) was to supervise and initiate the 'independent weighing' of the peasants' cotton sold to the Asian buyers in Sukuma-land. At the TAA's first provincial conference in May 1947, the 'recurrent theme was that Africans were not able to advance in crop production, marketing, and trade because of legislation prejudicial to African interests and the competition of the non-Africans. Charging collusion between the administration and Asian traders at the expense

[18] Stavenhagen, op. cit., p. 45.
[19] J. Rweyemamu, *Underdevelopment and industrialization*, op. cit., p. 28.
[20] ibid., p. 29.
[21] See generally J. Saul, 'Marketing co-operatives in a developing country: the Tanzania case', in P. Worsley (ed.), *Two blades of grass* (London: Manchester University Press, 1970), Saul and Cliffe, *Socialism in Tanzania*, Vol. II (Nairobi: East African Publishing House, 1972).

of the grower "whose work is forgotten", the meeting asked that Africans participate in decision-making on cotton and food prices. Noting that non-African traders extracted profits from the countryside while effectively blocking African initiative, TAA requested that non-Africans be limited to town trading concerns and barred from villages, that small trade be left entirely to Africans. . . .'[22]

The corrupt business practices – short-weighting, cheating in measuring cloth, lending at extortionate interest-rates, etc. – of the Asian 'dukawalla' which directly affected the African buyers of daily necessities, are legend. Where the Asians were employers – plantations, domestic service, transport – the same exploitative practices repeated. Thus, at all levels the Asian businessman met the African peasant, worker, and retailer in an antagonistic production relationship determined by the Asian's dominance of the commercial sector.

The commercial dominance of the Asian was glaringly manifested in the structure of the Tanzanian cities, towns, and other urban centres. These are essentially commercial centres – the centre of shops and markets – populated by Asians ('Uhindini') with the African urban-dwellers in satellite 'towns' on the periphery of town and city centres. The European residences – mainly of state functionaries – are usually located near the beaches or on the hills ('Uzunguni'). To paraphrase Stavenhagen, this was not merely an ecological relation, an 'urban–rural' conflict, nor only a situation of contact between two cultures, between two ethnic groups with different economic resources, justifying the pre-eminence of one ethnic group over another. 'The city's privileged position has its origin in the colonial period. It was founded by the conqueror to fulfil the very same function it still fulfils; to incorporate the Indian [read 'African'] into the economy which the conqueror had brought and his descendants developed'.[23] It was not only a matter of contact between the two populations: the Asian and the African were both integrated within a single economic system, in a single society. The hub of the system, needless to repeat, was the commercial sector which acted both as a channel through which surplus from the African producer could be pumped, and as the main centre of capital accumulation within the domestic society. This process of accumulation being responsible for reproducing the African as the producer of surplus and the Asian trader as the appropriator on behalf of the metropolitan bourgeoisie. In a developed capitalist economy the main function of commerce is to facilitate the distribution of commodities primarily for the *realization* of the surplus value. *Within* a colonial economy, that is to say, domestically, on the other hand, commerce plays a central role in

[22] G. A. Maguire, *Toward 'Uhuru' in Sukumaland: a study of micropolitics in Tanzania, 1945–59*, Ph.D. Thesis submitted to Harvard University, April 1966, pp. 88–9. The demands are clearly the demands of the African petty bourgeoisie against the Asian commercial bourgeoisie. For more on this see *infra*, pp. 57–8.

[23] Stavenhagen, op. cit., p. 46.

the very relations of exploitation for it is mainly through this that value is transferred from the producers to the non-producers.

The determining characteristic marking off the Asian trader as a 'capitalist' was that a portion of his profits went for capital accumulation.[24] Even the smallest of the Asian retailers, who in practice consumed almost all his profits, always worked with a view and an aspiration to 'save' for accumulation – the specific difference which marks out capitalist ideology. The small African producer, the peasant or retailer, on the other hand, consumed all his 'profits' thus distinguishing him from a typical member of the Asian community.

The essential relationship between the two communities, therefore, is to be found in the sphere of production relations rather than in the area of ethnicity or culture. This is not to deny these latter but only to argue that racial consciousness, etc., was part of the ideological rationalization reinforcing and in turn partially reflecting relations of production. Hence it is justified to employ the framework of class analysis and use the term 'commercial bourgeoisie' for the Asians. To be sure, the Asians were not a homogeneous mass constituting the commercial bourgeoisie. There were important differentiations within the community, to be discussed below. Nor did the Africans constitute an undifferentiated social group. In fact, as far as the intra-African stratification is concerned, the Tanzanian situation substantially departs from the Stavenhagen model. In the Mexican case. Stavenhagen observes that whereas Ladinos have important intra-ethnic stratification, the Indian community is not stratified. The African community in Tanzania, on the other hand, was not only stratified but even the germ of *class* differentiation had already intensified during the colonial period and only needed the formal withdrawal of the colonial state power for the contradictions to break out into the open, as will become clear.

5.3 THE CLASS FORMATIONS

The discussion above was essentially an analytical abstraction to enable us to identify the fundamental aspect of the relations of production. For this reason it was perfectly legitimate to focus on the *cores* of the opposed classes. Having identified the fundamental aspect of the relations of production, an exercise in 'pure' abstraction, one must go back to the *real* social formation and analyse the inter-relationships between the various secondary contradictions and the fundamental contradiction. This involves an analysis of the actual class formations, which is what is attempted in the next section.

[24] The investment-destination of the accumulated capital is, of course, another matter. It was largely ploughed back to expand the business; used in business and real estate speculation and later 'invested' in children's education. The utilization of capital in such a manner is a characteristic *par excellence* of a 'lumpen-bourgeoisie' of an underdeveloped commercial-capitalist economy – a point discussed elsewhere (see *infra*).

5.3.1 *Metropolitan bourgeoisie*[25]

The British bourgeoisie – the ruling class – was physically resident in the mother country. The Tanzanian state, subordinate to the metropolitan state of the colonialists, was run by the state functionaries, most of whom were members of the metropolitan bureaucracy. They symbolized colonial rule by Britain and class rule by the bourgeoisie. The latter's economic interests were taken care of by the local representatives of their companies – import–export houses, sisal estates, etc. And finally, the Asian commercial bourgeoisie provided the necessary link for the domination of the economy as a whole.

Unlike neighbouring Kenya, the European settler farmers – very few in number – did not come to play a significantly independent political role and were not a force for the metropolitan bourgeoisie to contend with.[26]

5.3.2 *Commercial bourgeoisie*

The Asian community could be divided broadly into four strata according to wealth and property, income and status. The upper stratum consisted of the large estate and plantation owners, big wholesalers and produce merchants, and a few really 'successful' professionals such as lawyers, doctors, and accountants. These were the richest of the community, living in expensive bungalows, with chauffeur-driven cars, and their sons and daughters studying in the UK. It was essentially a narrow stratum largely because of the relatively low level of the economy itself but also because an important segment of the industrial enterprises in the country was controlled by the Kenya – and Uganda – based Asians.

The second, a much broader stratum, consisted of prosperous businessmen, well-to-do professionals, highly paid civil servants and managers and executives, etc., employed by foreign companies. The last, strictly speaking, formed the *comprador class*. It is important to note that it was mainly the Asians and not the Africans who comprised this *comprador class* for this would help to explain why there was hardly any opposition from the African petty bourgeoisie against the 1967 nationalization measures affecting the foreign and Asian interests.

The third stratum was composed of the small retailers, self-employed people supplying various services like tailors, shoemakers, etc., middle-level public employees, and the skilled craftsmen.

The fourth level, narrower than the second and third, consisted of mainly 'manual' workers – mostly carpenters, masons, poor retailers in the countryside areas, and self-employed people like pot-makers, repairers, and so on.

---

[25] If capitalism is considered an international system, I submit it is possible to talk about 'classes' at that level of abstraction – provided the level of abstraction itself is always borne in mind.

[26] See supra, p. 40.

It will readily be seen that the stratification is mainly based on *income* and therefore on the standard of living. This was the single most important basis of stratification in the Asian community. Secondly, the broad divisions are extremely vague and rough. This is because hardly any close study has been made of the intra-ethnic stratification system of the Asians. However, for our purposes, the broad sketch derived mostly from observation is adequate.

Some of the important features of this stratification system may be noted in passing:

(1) That in many respects, the communal differentiation complicated the stratification pattern. Thus Asians of the same stratum but belonging to different communities would hardly ever intermarry. There was some social intercourse but mostly at a business level.

(2) Social mobility among these strata, especially among the first three, was rather high, thus blurring the divisions.

(3) As an immigrant community, occupying a *class position* in relation to the Africans (as argued above), it was not the differences resulting from stratification but the class unity manifested in ethnic consciousness that was predominant. Lack of mutual antagonism and hostility among these strata made them part of a *complementary* system of co-operating 'status entities' to use Cox's phrase,[27] rather than classes in conflict. Internally these 'status entities' could remain complementary only given a particular state of class relations in the society as a whole. Given an appropriate change in these class relations the complementary 'status entities' would in fact develop into classes resulting in class antagonism. It is conceivable, for instance, that after independence, a state led by oppressed classes could, through *discriminatory* measures against different strata of the Asian community, mobilize the lower strata as allies of the workers and poor peasants against the core of the class. But this is not what happened in Tanzania. Indiscriminate building takeovers and continued harping on the *Asian* as an exploiter, in fact reinforced ethnic solidarity, which worked in favour of the *core* of the commercial bourgeoisie.

There is a further interplay, discussed below, of the objective and subjective conditions which justifies including the Asians within a single class of the commercial bourgeoisie.

Firstly, within the production process, we find that the stratum (the fourth in the above categorization) which includes workers in the strict sense of the word was numerically very small. In view of the fairly high rate of social mobility, this small group could hardly coalesce into a separate class. They tended to be on the *fringes* of the class rather than a separate class. Again, in terms of the standard of living it was not this group but the 'lumpen' elements living off the communal welfare

[27] O. Cox, *Class, caste and race*, op. cit., p. 154.

services and the philanthropy of the rich, who constituted the poorest of the community.

The Asian 'petty bourgeoisie' might be divided into two groups: the professionals (doctors, lawyers, architects, etc.), and the small shop-keepers and small commodity producers (craftsmen, shoe-makers, tailors, etc.). A substantial number of these professionals were the sons, daughters, and other relations of the core – the traders. They continued to provide their services to the commercial group. Thus, both because of their origin but more particularly because of the role they played, this group could not be said to be a separate class. (The only exception to this appears to be the higher Asian civil servants – most of whom came from a particular ethnic group, the Goans.) Later on, in fact, it was some of the members of this group who articulated the interests of the commercial bourgeoisie and its 'comprador' industrial wing.

The small shopkeepers, by acting as a conduit pipe for draining off the surplus from the African producer bore an antagonistic relation to the African producer but a complementary one to the Asian big business-man.

The small commodity producer (not including those who employed labour and became businessman in their own right) like the tailors or shoemakers, constituted a very small group numerically. Many of the observations made earlier about the workers apply to this group as well. Therefore, like the workers, they occupied the fringes of the class and were not an independent class.

It can be seen, therefore, that the members of the Asian 'petty bour-geoisie' were either very much part of the core of the commercial bourgeoisie (like the professionals), or acted as its complementary group (like the shopkeepers), or simply occupied the fringes of the class (small commodity producers). Hence none of them constitutes a separate class from the commercial bourgeoisie.

Secondly, these strata and groups, encouraged by the colonial state, shared common values and the dominant values were those of the com-mercial milieu. Although in terms of numbers, not more than half the total Asian working population derived their livelihood from commerce (i.e. retail and wholesale trade),[28] even those in other sectors funda-mentally shared the commercial milieu, not simply because of the dominance of commercial values but more because of the important *economic* and familial ties between them and the commercial core of the class.

Thirdly, and probably this is the most important point, none of these strata or groups could even potentially put itself in a *class situation in relation to* other strata or groups by political control, i.e. control of state power. The domination of the community by the upper stratum derived

[28] D. P. Ghai, 'An economic survey', in Ghai (ed.) *Portrait of a minority: Asians in East Africa* (Nairobi: Oxford University Press, 1965), p. 94.

its legitimacy not from the control of the state but from historical and ethnic reasons. It is true that the upper stratum dominated the Asian communal organizations but this was not because it shared in the 'national political power'. The relation of the colonial state to each separate stratum was not qualitatively different. Rather it was the Asian community as a whole which occupied a particular place in its relation to the colonial state. For this same reason hardly any Asian stratum had the potential to be organized as a 'political conflict group' and therefore could never become a 'class' for itself.[29] By the same token, on the other hand, the commercial bourgeoisie *as a whole* by accepting the protection of the colonial state (besides its role in the social production process already discussed) occupied a class position *vis-à-vis* the African community.

The Asian commercial bourgeoisie could be considered a subordinate partner of the metropolitan bourgeoisie, the latter being the ruling class in the real sense of the word. This must be distinguished from a situation (for instance in the advanced capitalist countries) where there may be two sections of the ruling bourgeoisie, for example industrial and commercial. In that case, each one of them may be organized as a political faction, ready to seize political power to serve its interests and the interests of the capitalist class as a whole. The Asian bourgeoisie was not such a faction of the ruling class. It did not, nor could it expect to, take part in political rule.[30] It was only protected, and therefore politically it was a *ward* under the guardianship of the metropolitan bourgeoisie.[31] Economically dependent and politically servile, this bourgeoisie occupied the historically curious position of controlling an important sector of the economy without ever hoping to protect it with political power. Power and property were *apparently* divorced, but only in a unique historical situation which was to give way to a 'purer' form of class struggle after independence.

5.3.3 *Petty bourgeoisie*

The African petty bourgeoisie at the time of independence may be broadly divided into three social groups as follows:

upper layer   intellectuals, teachers, higher civil servants, prosperous traders, farmers, professionals, higher military and police officers.

[29] This is the most important reason (among others) why I describe the incipient division in the African community as class formations and not merely intra-ethnic stratification. In fact in the case of the African community each 'class' – either alone or in alliance with others – was a potential bidder for state power.

[30] This probably explains the unique political apathy of the Asians in Tanzania.

[31] The most it could do was to get this or that favour from the colonial state either legally by protest, or illegally by corrupting the state functionaries. The latter being easier, convenient and safer was the more predominant than the former method.

middle layer	middle government salariat, junior clerks, soldiers, etc.
lower layer	shopkeepers, lower salariat in the services sector, and generally lowest grades of the salariat.

The petty bourgeoisie therefore did not form a homogeneous mass though in its fight for *Uhuru* it presented a common front. The national leadership positions in the party (TANU), the trade unions, and the co-operatives were generally occupied by those in the upper and middle layers of the petty bourgeoisie.[32] Even in the co-operatives the urban-based intelligentsia and the traders played important roles in the leadership positions.[33]

One of the outstanding features of the petty bourgeoisie was that they overwhelmingly came from urban-based occupations, and had some education and knowledge of the outside world. In a colonial situation, such a section was the only one well-placed to lead the *Uhuru* struggle.

The petty bourgeoisie were subjected to important contradictions from the commercial bourgeoisie, for the latter blocked and circumscribed the former's limited economic aspirations. These contradictions could not be resolved while the commercial bourgeoisie continued to get political protection from the colonial state. Nor could the African petty bourgeoisie economically fight the commercial bourgeoisie without the state's assistance.[34] The *objective* economic interests of the petty bourgeoisie therefore called for a struggle against the colonial state. In this their interests coincided with those of the broad masses. Thus it was 'destined' to become a ruling petty bourgeoisie, unlike its counterpart in Europe where the petty bourgeoisie could hardly play any historical role. Furthermore, unlike neighbouring Kenya, where the 'yeomanry', almost consciously created by the colonial power, constituted an important sector of the petty bourgeoisie that came to power, in Tanzania the kulak farmers did not dominate either the economic or the political struggle. This, it is submitted, has had a lot to do with the subsequent developments of class struggles in Kenya and Tanzania. Whereas in one (Kenya) the petty bourgeoisie consolidated itself as a ruling class, in the other (Tanzania) its ruling section gradually but definitely began to

[32] This can be gleaned from the biographies of the leaders. See, for instance, Bienen, *Tanzania: party transformation and economic development* (Princeton: Princeton University Press, 1970), pp. 133–9.

[33] For some evidence of this see Saul, 'Marketing co-operatives in a developing country: the Tanzanian Case' in P. Worsley (ed.), *Two blades of grass* (London: Manchester University Press, 1970), pp. 351–3. The most successful co-operative, VFCU, for instance, originated from the Mwanza African Traders' Co-operative Society. ibid., see also *infra* p. 57.

[34] For instance, the Asian commercial bourgeoisie vigorously resisted the rise of the co-operative movement and the up-coming African commercial ventures had to face stiff competition from the Asian traders. See Saul, ibid.

transform itself into a 'bureaucratic bourgeoisie', as at the same time by its intermittent ideological hostility to 'kulaks', continued to maintain its popular peasant base. (These questions will occur again in a subsequent section.)

5.3.4 Kulaks

There is enough evidence to show that rural stratification in the countryside intensified during the colonial period.[35] With the introduction of commercial agriculture, this was inevitable. The existence of a small number of kulak farmers at the time of independence can easily be documented. But what is important for our purposes is that the kulaks *as a class* did not develop to the extent where they could become an important political force at the national level. There are a number of reasons for this: Firstly, land as such, owing probably to the absence of settler farmers, never became a dominating political issue. Land alienation on a scale comparable to that of Kenya was not among colonial government policies.[36] The colonial government's interests lay mainly in encouraging peasant-based cash crop farming since there was no threat of competition with white settler farmers, a constant factor in Kenyan colonial policy. Secondly, until the 1950s, the colonial government continued supporting 'dual' land tenure régimes – customary laws and rights of occupancy granted under the Land Ordinance 1923. The idea of creating a class of yeoman farmers through individualization of land tenure was not officially broached until 1958 by which time TANU had become strong enough to resist it. Thus individualization of land tenure never really succeeded in Tanzania. In Kenya, on the other hand, this policy was vigorously pushed in the wake of the Mau Mau uprising of the 1950s. There is no doubt, as Sorrensen has documented, that this was a political strategy on the part of the colonial government 'to create a stable middle class built around the Kikuyu loyalists, regarded by many officials as the "natural" Kikuyu leaders of the future. Such a class, it was hoped, would be too interested in farming to be seduced by Kikuyu politicians into further subversion.'[37]

The first effort at a local level to create a yeomanry in Tanzania was made through the formation of the Tanganyika Agricultural Corporation (TAC) in 1953. Its stated aim was to promote *a healthy, prosperous yeomen farmers class, firmly established on the land, appreciable of its*

[35] See Iliffe, *Agricultural change* . . . , op. cit., pp. 39–41. See also the discussion of peasant differentiation in Part Four, *infra* p. 111.

[36] The principles which generally governed the land tenure system during the colonial period were basically: (*1*) strict regulation of transference of land from an African to a non-African and also among Africans, and (*2*) land security being made dependent on land use. Details of this and subsequent discussion in the text can be found in my (as yet unpublished) paper: *Land tenure and agricultural development in Kenya and Tanzania*.(1969).

[37] P. Sorrensen, *Land reform in the Kikuyu country* (Nairobi: Oxford University Press, 1967), p. 201.

fruits, jealous of its inherent wealth, and dedicated to maintaining the family unit on it . . .[38][emphasis added]. This class was seen as 'one of the most stabilizing influences on the African community' and would thus help to maintain the *status quo*. But the settlement schemes under TAC, except for that in Urambo, were not very successful in terms of creating such a class.

In any case, the Tanganyika African National Union (TANU) was formed in 1954 and by 1958 had become an important political force. Thus, in 1958, when the colonial government published its paper[39] proposing individualization of the customary land tenure, TANU successfully opposed it. President Nyerere, the president of TANU argued:

> If people are given land to use as their property, then they have the right to sell it. It will not be difficult to predict who, in fifty years' time, will be the landlords and who the tenants. In a country such as this where generally speaking the Africans are poor and the foreigners rich, it is quite possible that within eighty or a hundred years, if the poor African were allowed to sell his land, all the land in Tanganyika would belong to wealthy immigrants, and the local people would be tenants. *But even if there were no rich foreigners in this country there would emerge rich and clever Tanganyikans*[40] [emphasis added].

The ideological underpinnings of the above argument must be emphasized, for it lay at the basis of much of the land legislation that was passed in the post-independence period. The argument is not necessarily against capitalism as such but against the rise of a landed bourgeoisie. We shall return to this point in our later discussion.

The third reason for the absence of a strong kulak class was the general lack of capital accumulation and investment in agriculture. Such capital on a large scale could only come from the commercial sector which was dominated by the Asians. There is some evidence that even for the African kulaks the initial capital came from their trading activities[41] and was supplemented by kulak farmers branching out in other activities – like transport, real estate and services – which in time would often become more important than farming itself.

To sum up; it is suggested that the kulaks *as a class* as opposed to the urban-based petty bourgeoisie, were relatively not a strong force. This is not to say that they did not dominate local activities in some areas, nor that they would not stand up for their rights. At this point, I am only suggesting that there is evidence for important contradictions at the time

[38] Quoted in Cliffe and Cunningham, 'Ideology, organization and the settlement experience in Tanzania', in Saul and Cliffe, *Socialism in Tanzania*, op. cit., p. 131 at p. 134.

[39] 'Review of land tenure policy', Government Paper No. 6 of 1958.

[40] J. K. Nyerere, 'Mali ya Taifa', reprinted in his *Freedom and unity* (Dar es Salaam: Oxford University Press, 1967), p. 55.

[41] Iliffe, *Agricultural change . . .*, op. cit., p. 23, cites Ismani in Iringa as an example of the 'application to agriculture of capital drawn from urban trade'.

of independence between the emerging 'bureaucratic bourgeoisie' and the kulaks.[42]

The consequence of the relative weakness of the kulaks was that they could not press even the colonial state to act in their interests. Their potential for a bid for power on their own or in alliance with other classes (especially the masses of peasants) was weak. The kulak class was therefore 'destined' to be led by other sectors of the petty bourgeoisie who could command mass peasant support.

5.3.5 Workers

The wage-earning population in Tanzania was very small given the narrow industrial base of the country (411 538 in 1961).[43] The small working class was mainly employed in the sisal plantations, mining and quarrying, services, commerce, construction, and public utilities. The other most important characteristic of the working class was that a large percentage was migrant. Forced to leave his land temporarily to pay the poll and hut tax, the peasant became a temporary worker. But the conditions of employment and low wages did not allow him to cut off all his links with land. He had thus to go back to cultivation once he had collected enough cash to pay his taxes. The migratory system was, for obvious reasons, fully supported by the colonial government. Lack of stability at the work-place discouraged any organization and cohesion of the working class. This was mainly responsible for there being virtually no organization of the workers until after the Second World War. By 1947, some five trade unions, among which the Stevedores and Dockers' Union claimed a membership of some 1500, had been established.[44] After that, despite the efforts of the colonial government to stave off its development, trade unionism began to move fast. The Tanganyika Federation of Labour (TFL) was registered in 1955 with 17 registered trade unions affiliated to it. By 1958, the sisal workers had formed a 30 000-strong National Plantation Workers' Union. By this time, TANU too, had been formed and from the beginning the TANU–TFL alliance was forged. The workers had thrown in their lot with the nationalist movement and the wave of strikes during the 1950s was probably instrumental in bringing about independence.[45]

Thus, despite their numerical smallness, the workers' contribution, given their strategic role in the economy, cannot be belittled. TANU

[42] Incidentally, it does not exclude the forging of links and alliances between these two classes as a possible method of resolving the contradictions.

[43] 'Employment and earnings in Tanzania' (Dar es Salaam: Central Statistical Bureau, 1966).

[44] Annual Report (1947) of the Labour Department.

[45] In the five year period (1955–60), there was a total of 771 stoppages involving 298 161 workers with 2.40 million man-days lost, 1.5 million being in 1960 alone. See Patel, 'Trade unions and the law in Tanganyika', in Singhvi (ed.), *Law and the Commonwealth* (1971).

fully recognized this and President Nyerere called the trade unions the 'industrial wing of the nationalist movement'.[46]

Notwithstanding the workers' role in the *Uhuru* struggle, TANU never came under the influence of proletarian ideology nor were the workers considered the leading force in the struggle. The trade union movement itself was basically structured on traditional (English) lines led by some elements from the petty bourgeoisie. If anything, the TANU ideology was essentially peasant-biased.

It is true that the small working class in the African countries cannot be considered to be the same as the European proletariat or *ipso facto* revolutionary. At the same time, there is a tendency to emphasize the quantitative aspects and forget the strategic position the workers occupy even in the African countries. While the peasantry is a large physical force, it is only in alliance with the working class under the proletarian ideology that it can play a revolutionary role.[47]

Secondly, even among the working class itself there are certain sections which tend to be more conscious than others. These small sections can form the nucleus to influence others. In each concrete situation, revolutionaries have to find, in Cabral's words 'our little proletariat'.

5.3.6 *Peasantry*

The peasantry in Tanzania, unlike some Asian countries, does not have a long tradition of violent struggle against authorities, either 'feudal' or colonial. In the first place, feudalism in Tanzania was not developed to a very high level and, secondly, as we have seen, the sacrosanct possession of a peasant – land – was not radically interfered with by the colonialists.[48] Thus peasant protest was generally confined to written petitions, organized demonstrations, protracted negotiations, and legal fights[49] against such colonial measures as the levying of taxes or regulations on dipping cattle. The peasantry, which provided a mass physical force for TANU, also set the pattern for the way the struggle for independence was waged.

Despite the fact that a strong class of yeoman farmers did not develop, yet, as already noted, the peasant differentiation was substantial. Besides a small group of rich, labour-employing farmers, some writers have also noted the existence of middle and lower peasants, including the 'rural

---

[46] I. Davies, *Trade unions in Africa* (London: Penguin Books, 1966), p. 110.

[47] For a more comprehensive discussion of this point see *infra* p. 116 et seq.

[48] Where the colonial government did try land alienation, the peasants rose in opposition, for example, the famous 'Meru land case'. This case is discussed in K. Japhet and E. Seaton, *The Meru land case* (Nairobi: East African Publishing House, 1967).

[49] For one such example see, Kimambo, *Popular protest in colonial Tanzania* (Nairobi: East African Publishing House, 1971).

proletariat'.[50] This differentiation was to become much more pronounced after independence.

The differentiation itself originated from the introduction of cash crops. It was thus that the peasantry in Tanzania – besides supplying food and labour to the plantations – became integrated in the world capitalist system.[51] Thus also the seeds of substantial inequalities among the peasantry were laid: '. . . commercial agriculture for a territorial or international market offered new opportunities for inequality within African societies. This can be seen very clearly in the large-scale, mechanized farming of Ismani and Mbulu, but it took place on a smaller scale wherever cash crops were grown.'[52] The normal pattern of differentiation that emerged in cash crop areas was, 'a mass of small growers among whom a few larger producers had emerged as actual or potential employers of labour'. 'The beginnings of a capitalist agriculture were becoming apparent in several areas where the market economy had stimulated African commercial farming.'[53] It must, however, be re-emphasized that the capitalist agriculture that was becoming apparent was integrally tied to the international capitalist system, both in its origin and in its continued existence. This is an important point to bear in mind when evaluating subsequent agricultural and especially land tenure policies of the independent government. Changes in the land tenure system may facilitate further integration in the capitalist system or may retard it but by itself, without radical overall structural changes, it cannot be against the capitalist system.

Finally, the peasantry as a political force. As observed elsewhere in this book, the peasantry, except for the kulaks, formed the mass base of the independence movement led by the petty bourgeoisie. It was not their revolutionary capacity (or absence of it) that was important in this struggle but their sheer physical force. Coalescence of a number of factors[54] objectively enabled the *Uhuru* struggle to be waged as a 'peaceful mass struggle' for which the peasantry – both by the pattern of the struggle it had already set and its numerical strength – was immediately responsive.

The class content of the *Uhuru* struggle and the way it was waged would have important implications for the subsequent development both of the class struggle and ideology. This forms the subject matter of the ensuing chapter.

[50] See for instance the recent study of the Ismani area in Iringa by Awiti, 'Class struggle in rural society of Tanzania', *Maji Maji*, op. cit., No. 7 (October 1972). See also Cliffe, 'Rural class divisions – the realities'. (mimeo.)

[51] See generally Iliffe, *Agricultural change in modern Tanganyika*.

[52] ibid., p. 26.

[53] ibid.

[54] See below p. 57.

SIX

The Class Content
of the Uhuru Struggle

6.1 COLONIALISM AND THE THROTTLING OF CLASS STRUGGLE

Colonialism 'mutes' the class struggle and creates, so to speak, different phases through which it should pass in its course of development. Colonialism not only arrests the development of productive forces but sets it on a different trajectory, the trajectory of underdevelopment. It is *this* that constitutes the history and the past of the present class struggles. The class struggle itself matures within the womb of colonialism. The ideology of anti-colonialism and the struggle for political independence are themselves, therefore, at one level, part of the class struggle and at the other level an objective necessity to 'clear the ground' for its development. The struggle for *Uhuru* is hence linked with class struggle. The failure to understand such a link, especially in an epoch of international class struggles, would be: (*a*) to make the colonial history *foreign* and not the history of colonized people and, (*b*) to render the 'colonial epoch' in the history of colonial people *without* class struggles. Such an approach would neither explain history nor help to identify trends in the onward historical process. We would end with a singularly useless 'history'; celebrating individuals, narrating their biographies and heroic acts or, at the most, erecting monuments for 'valiant tribes'. These would leave the large mass of our people *out of history, without history!*

I therefore find it difficult to agree with Cabral wholly when he says:

> We consider that when imperialism arrived in Guinea, it made us leave history – our history. We agree that history in our country is the result of class struggle, but we have our own class struggles in our own country; the moment imperialism arrived and colonialism arrived, it made us leave our history and enter another history. Obviously we agree that the class struggle has continued, but it has continued in a very different way: our whole people is struggling against the ruling class of the imperialist countries and this gives a completely different aspect to the historical evolution of our country.

55

And later:

> What commands history in colonial conditions is not the class struggle. I do not mean that the class struggle in Guinea stopped completely during the colonial period; it continued, but in a muted way. In the colonial period it is the colonial state which commands history.[55]

Its implication is that the whole colonial period was one long 'history-less' period in the lives of the people and that they 'return to' (Cabral's term) history only after independence.[56] That if there was history at all, it was that of the colonial country – *commanded by the colonial state*. This is unacceptable. It comes uncomfortably close to colonial history as written by bourgeois historians – which is nothing but the history of the colonial state!

Throughout the colonial period different sections of the people in one way or another were engaged in making history: by their anti-colonial struggles, peaceful and violent. These struggles at international level were part of the class struggles but they were also a *phase* of the class struggle at the territorial level, in so far as they were aimed at liquidating the colonial condition which *throttled* the class struggle – which made the class struggle continue 'in a muted way' (Cabral's phrase). Muted or not, it meanwhile continued making history, not 'foreign' or that of the colonial state. 'Colonial history' itself is an integral part of 'our' history.

As regards the whole people fighting against the ruling class of the imperialist countries there is nothing particularly unique in this. Successful struggles against ruling classes have always been waged by the unity of all remaining classes and strata. Even the classical bourgeois revolutions of Europe were made by the large mass of the people against the landed aristocracy. Nevertheless, it was the bourgeoisie that provided the leadership and the ideology and they were fought for *their class* interests. Similarly, the independence struggles, though supported by the broad masses were led by the petty bourgeoisie under petty bourgeois ideology. At best, therefore, they were petty bourgeois 'political revolutions'.

6.2   THE CLASS STRUGGLE MATURES

The petty bourgeoisie was, for various reasons, the only class in a position to lead the *Uhuru* struggle against the colonial state. Its very origins and continued growth lay in the colonial socio-economic structure, including its educational system. Large sections of the petty bourgeoisie came from urban-based occupations – the creation of colonialism *par*

---

[55] A. Cabral, *Revolution in Guinea*, op. cit., p. 56.

[56] To quote Cabral fully: 'The moment national liberation comes and the petty bourgeoisie takes power *we enter, or rather return to history*, and thus the internal contradictions break out again' [emphasis supplied] (op. cit., p. 57).

excellence. It had thus come into closest contact with the colonial state. The colonial education system itself had created its own grave-diggers in the form of the intelligentsia – teachers and civil servants – who provided the necessary leadership.

The most interesting section and that which supplied the petty bourgeoisie with its *economic* kernel was the up-and-coming group of African traders. So long as the Tanganyika African Association (TAA), the predecessor of TANU, remained an organization of the intelligentsia it was no more than a social club.[57] It was the traders who provided the material base for it to transform itself into a political organization. The teachers and the civil servants could become the successful ideological spokesmen of the class only when linked with the traders and neither would be able to achieve their material interest without a mass base: the peasants. The traders provided the necessary bridge between the urban-based intelligentsia and the rural peasants to forge a mass nationalist movement.

In the Lake Province, the strongest TANU area, where decisive battles for independence were fought, the traders managed to get the peasant base through the co-operatives. In fact it was the leaders of the Mwanza *African Traders'* Co-operative Society who initiated the formation of the first co-operatives in this area.[58] The African traders' dominant antagonism was of course to the commercial bourgeoisie – the Asians. But they were too weak to fight the Asians successfully. No wonder the Traders' Co-operative failed in a number of its commercial ventures. It was not until one of their leaders, Paul Bomani, took up the promotion of the peasant-based co-operatives that they began to deal decisive blows to the commercial bourgeoisie. Meeting after meeting of the producers addressed by Bomani and other local traders agreed: 'We want unity; we are tired of doing our work for the (profit of) Asians.'[59]

Iliffe[60] notes that in its first phase of 'spontaneous growth', Sukumaland was the only area where TANU managed to get mass rural support. This is precisely because it was here – given a weak kulak class – that the coalition of the urban intelligentsia, the traders, and the peasants was possible. Sukumaland, being a latecomer on the commercial scene compared to Kilimanjaro and Bukoba, had not yet developed a strong kulak class.[61] It 'grew up' as a small, peasant, cotton-growing area. On the

[57] cf. G. Bennet, 'An outline history of TANU', *Makerere Journal*, No. 7 (1973).

[58] See J. Saul, 'Marketing co-operatives . . .', pp. 351–2 and A. Maguire, *Towards Uhuru . . .*, op. cit.

[59] Quoted ibid., p. 126.

[60] 'Nationalism and the commercial economy in Tanganyika, 1954–61' (University of London: 1971) (mimeo).

[61] Iliffe, in the essay cited above, notes this point but fails to link it with the development of classes and the question of the class base of TANU. Thus he remains wondering why TANU in its first phase of development received massive rural support in the Sukumaland and not the Kilimanjaro and Bukoba, all of

other hand, in areas like Kilimanjaro and Bukoba, the strong kulak elements who controlled the co-operatives and the local political unions, *cut off* (so to speak) the urban intelligentsia from the mass peasant base.

The kulaks' opposition to TANU is illustrated in the case of Bukoba. 'Most of TANU's support in Bukoba came from the underdeveloped Karagwe chiefdom (which provided a third of the members in 1957) rather than from the commercial farmers.'[62] The leaders of TANU in Bukoba were themselves coffee *traders* who were at loggerheads with the *kulaks* based in the co-operatives 'which threatened to put them out of business'.[62]

The pattern described above repeated itself even in the less-developed areas. Thus 'large numbers joined TANU in the remote southern area of Mbulu district in 1956–57 at a time when the party had very little success among the prosperous wheat farmers of Northern Mbulu.'[63]

In kulak-dominated areas like Kilimanjaro and Bukoba, the political organization tended to take the form of tribal unions.[64] These tribal unions could not make the necessary 'transition from local to national politics' (Iliffe) (a precondition for a nationalist mass struggle for independence) for three inter-related reasons: (1) being tribal they could not of course mobilize support from other tribes; (2) the kulaks, who dominated these unions did not form a strong class at the territorial level to provide a *national* leadership to the independence movement. Their strength was essentially local; (3) such an independence movement would have to get its mass support from the peasants, whose fundamental contradiction with the kulaks would make the 'kulak–peasant' alliance difficult if not impossible. It is not surprising therefore that the support for the kulak-based organizations was based on a tribal ideology rather than the nationalist one.

Thus it was that the 'intelligentsia–traders–peasant'[65] 'coalition' together with the support of the trade unions formed the mass movement for the independence struggle under the leadership of the urban-based petty bourgeoisie.

In a limited sense, the petty bourgeoisie was a 'rising class' whose

---

them being commercial areas. The only explanation he can come up with is that Kilimanjaro and Bukoba got involved in the commercial agriculture long before Sukumaland. 'But so what?' Having no *class* analysis as such Iliffe does not even raise let alone answer this question.

[62] Iliffe, 'Nationalism . . .', op. cit., p. 6.

[63] ibid., p. 8.

[64] Iliffe, 'Tanzania under German and British rule', in Saul and Cliffe, *Socialism in Tanzania*, op. cit., p. 15.

[65] In 1955, TANU's Secretary-General for instance reported that 'the Party had succeeded in gaining mass support in only three areas of the country: Dar es Salaam [intelligentsia; traders; workers] Sukumaland [traders; peasants] and Arusha (presumably referring to the Meru Citizens' Union.) [peasants].' (Words in square brackets are my additions – I.G.S.) Iliffe, 'Nationalism . . .', op. cit., p. 4–5.

interests coincided with those of the broad masses and hence was progressive. The African petty bourgeoisie, unlike the classical national bourgeoisie, was incapable of a national bourgeois revolution to build an independent national capitalism. This would require disengagement from world capitalist system, a task which the petty bourgeoisie could hardly accomplish. It would, among other things, in fact, mean its own liquidation. There were therefore strong objective reasons for the only paltry economic ambitions of the petty bourgeoisie. It could only aspire to stand in the shoes of the Asian commercial bourgeoisie. But this could not be accomplished without seizing state power. Hence the contradiction with the colonial state became primary; it had to be solved before the contradiction between the petty bourgeoisie and the commercial bourgeoisie could come to the fore.

In mobilizing the masses, the TANU activists themselves spelt out the important contradictions in surprisingly clear terms. Addressing a meeting in Ujiji, a month after the formation of TANU, S. A. Kandoro, a leading Party activist and himself a trader, described the aims of TANU as follows:

> Its objectives are many: (a) to defend or fight for our rights; (b) to do everything possible with the object in mind for a self-government; (c) to fight for equal pay where the work and skill or experience is the same; (d) to see that the government fulfils her duty towards its subjects and vice versa; (e) to further trading spirit among Africans with a view to ousting Indian traders. . . . What sort of people are we Africans? We watch Indians come from acute poverty to rich and well to do traders! We ourselves are the people who make them rich by offering them our labour and goods. They buy our crops at very meagre prices and send them to be sold at markets at distant places where they will yield good profits. All the time we lazy Africans do nothing to compete with these traders but just watch and help them to become wealthy at our expense. Well, cannot the African send his crops and fish to be sold at the same markets where Indian traders make such good profit? You will never get better prices for your crops and fish simply because you have no unity of action.[66]

One of the aims of TANU, provided in its 1954 Constitution in fact was:

> . . . to encourage co-operatives and trade unions; urge that producers get the best price and that consumers buy in the best market; help Africans establish an increasing share in the running and owning of business; establish a minimum wage and a system of assisted farming; and oppose alienation of land.[67]

[66] Report on the meeting by D. Amri, 12 August 1954, typewritten from the personal papers of Mr Daudi Amri, Senior Superintendent of Police. Quoted in D. E. McHenry, *Tanzania: the struggle for development* (1971). Unpublished Ph.D. Thesis in the University of Dar es Salaam Library.

[67] Quoted in Bieren, *Tanzania party transformation*, op. cit., p. 128.

This aim is neither anti-capitalist nor anti-imperialist. It caters absolutely for the interests of the different sections of the petty bourgeoisie.[68] The petty bourgeoisie was interested in political freedom as an end in itself or at most to facilitate its own struggle against the commercial bourgeoisie, not as a weapon in the fight for the total emancipation of the whole society. Therefore, as Cabral says: 'there is something wrong with the simple interpretation of the national liberation movement as a revolutionary trend'. '[To] hope that the petty bourgeoisie will just carry out a revolution when it comes to power in an underdeveloped country is to hope for a miracle although it is true that it could do this.'[69]

With the gaining of independence, however, the internal contradictions within the petty bourgeoisie itself broke out into the open. In an underdeveloped country, there is a strong tendency for the ruling section of the petty bourgeoisie to become cut off from its general petty bourgeois base. Depending on the concrete conditions and especially the extent to which the state – controlled by the ruling sector – participates in the economy, the ruling sector may develop into a 'bureaucratic bourgeoisie', thus giving rise to contradictions within the rest of the sections of the petty bourgeoisie. It is these contradictions among others which'shape the subsequent history – the subject of our next section.

In this section, we had a brief look at the class formations at the time of independence. We did not deliberately go into the details of how these classes came to be what they were at the time of independence; this would have taken us too far afield. Admittedly, therefore, the picture is a little static – deriving from a particular point in time. This forms the point of departure for the next sections where the dynamics of the class struggle are considered.

[68] Fight for higher prices for peasants is not inconsistent with the interests of the petty bourgeoisie – both to support the co-operatives and an ever-growing state bureaucracy. Minimum wage for workers was absolutely necessary if the system of migratory labour was to be stopped.

[69] Cabral, *Revolution in Guinea*, op. cit., p. 58.

PART THREE

Class Struggles in Tanzania:
the Rise of the 'Bureaucratic Bourgeoisie'

And as in private life one differentiates between what a man thinks and
says of himself and what he really is and does, so in historical struggles
one must distinguish still more the phrases and fancies of parties from
their real organism and their real interests, their conception of themselves, from the reality.   MARX

SEVEN

Uhuru and After: the Rise of the 'Bureaucratic Bourgeoisie'

The facts of history are indeed facts about individuals, but not about actions of individuals performed in isolation, and not about the motives, real or imaginary, from which individuals suppose themselves to have acted. They are facts about the relations of individuals to one another in society and about the social forces which produce from the actions of individuals results often at variance with, and sometimes opposite to, the results which they themselves intended.[1]   E. H. CARR

7.1   ON THE 'BUREAUCRATIC BOURGEOISIE'

In an underdeveloped African country with a *weak petty bourgeoisie*, its ruling section which comes to possess the instruments of state on the morrow of independence, relatively commands enormous power and is therefore very strong. This was precisely the case in Tanzania. The situation becomes much clearer when contrasted with that in Kenya. In Kenya, there were important sections of the petty bourgeoisie – yeoman farmers and traders, for example – besides the urban-based intelligentsia, which had already developed significant 'independent' roots in the colonial economy. Thus the petty bourgeoisie as a class was itself strong and different sections within it were more or less at par. This considerably reduced the power of the 'ruling clique' irrespective of its immediate possession of the state apparatus, and kept it 'tied' to its class base – the petty bourgeoisie. The Kenyan situation comes closer to classical class rule in an advanced bourgeois country where, although there may be different contending groups or 'cliques', it is the bourgeoisie as a whole which continues to be the ruling or 'governing class'. Moreover, the group or 'clique' immediately in possession of the instruments of state power, cannot in normal circumstances cut itself off from its class base.

[1] *What is history?* (London: Penguin Books, 1964), p. 52.

63

PART THREE: CLASS STRUGGLES IN TANZANIA

The Tanzanian scene, on the other hand, comes closer to the
'Bonapartist' type of situation where contending classes have weakened
themselves thus allowing the 'ruling clique' to cut itself off from its class
base and *appear* to raise the state above the class struggle. Of course, it is
not that the contending classes had weakened themselves in the independence struggle. But a somewhat similar situation resulted from the
fact that the petty bourgeoisie was weak and had not developed deep
economic roots. This allowed the 'ruling group' a much freer hand. In
other words the control of the state became the single decisive factor.
For these and other reasons to be discussed later, it is proposed to
identify the 'ruling group' as the 'bureaucratic bourgeoisie'. Before the
Arusha Declaration, this would consist mainly of those at the top levels
of the state apparatus – ministers, high civil servants, high military and
police officers, and such like. In so far as the state has not yet gone into
the economy in a major way this group still, strictly speaking, constitutes
a bureaucratic stratum of the petty bourgeoisie. It has not yet acquired
an economic base, hence the major turning point in its development
was the nationalizations of the Arusha Declaration.

The immediate question that arises is whether the 'bureaucratic
bourgeoisie' is a class *as distinct* from the petty bourgeoisie. To answer
the question, we need a longer discussion than is convenient at this
point in our exposition. Suffice it to say that the post-independence class
struggles (including the Arusha Declaration) were themselves a process
leading to the emergence of the 'bureaucratic bourgeoisie'. The process
may not be complete. For the purposes of our present section, therefore,
we shall use the term to describe the actually ruling section of the petty
bourgeoisie and not as a class distinct from the petty bourgeoisie. The
latter term will be used, unless otherwise indicated, to refer to the whole
class, including the 'bureaucratic bourgeoisie'.

One important feature of the 'bureaucratic bourgeoisie' is its extremely 'nationalistic' outlook. Being in possession of the state, it sees
itself as the saviour of the 'nation' and identifies what are objectively its
own or the interests of the petty bourgeoisie or even the interests of
other classes, as the interests of the whole nation. To be sure, this is true
of all ruling classes but much more true of petty bourgeois rule. The
social-democratic and nationalistic outlook was further facilitated by
the fact that the *Uhuru* struggle was essentially a 'coalition' between the
petty bourgeoisie and the peasantry. The latter, with its small-property
consciousness, reinforced the petty bourgeois ideology of social
democracy. The characteristics of social democracy have been well-
described by Marx:

> The peculiar character of the social-Democracy is epitomized in the
> fact that democratic-republican institutions are demanded as a means,
> not of doing away with two extremes, capital and wage labour, but of
> weakening their antagonism and transforming it into harmony. How-
> ever different the means proposed for the attainment of this end may

64

be, however much it may be trimmed with more or less revolutionary notions, the content remains the same. This content is the transformation of society in a democratic way, but a transformation within the bounds of the petty bourgeoisie. Only one must not form the narrow-minded notion that the petty bourgeoisie, on principle, wishes to enforce an egoistic class interest. Rather, it believes that the *special* conditions of its emancipation are the *general* conditions within the frame of which alone modern society can be saved and the class struggle avoided. Just as little must one imagine that the democratic representatives are indeed all shopkeepers or enthusiastic champions of shopkeepers. According to their education and their individual position they may be as far apart as heaven from earth. What makes them representatives of the petty bourgeoisie is the fact that in their minds they do not get beyond the limits which the latter do not get beyond in life, and that they are consequently driven, theoretically, to the same problems and solutions to which material interest and social position drive the latter practically. This is, in general, the relationship between the *political* and *literary* representatives of a class and the class they represent.[2]

The anti-capitalism of the petty bourgeoisie is that of a small-property-owner. In the concrete conditions of Tanzania this meant anti-kulakism. On the other hand, there was hardly any conception of *structural* change and struggle against the international capitalist system.

The 'bureaucratic bourgeoisie' saw anti-imperialism primarily at two levels: (1) at the level of anti-colonialism in the classical sense, i.e. strong opposition in world councils to continued foreign rule in Southern Africa, condemnation of powers supporting colonialism as imperialist, support to the national liberation movements, etc. Secondly, anti-colonialism as opposition to a particular imperialist country which happened to be the former metropolitan colonizing power. It is surprising how often, both in the leaders' and in popular consciousness, imperialism is identified with the former colonial power.[3] (2) At the level of foreign policy resulting in support for Vietnam, the Arab states, and other progressive countries.

This shows that there is no consistent appreciation of the collective imperialism led by the United States, as a global system of capitalism functioning in a most sophisticated way through structural links with underdeveloped countries reinforced by international institutions. Hence, many of the economic measures taken immediately after independence objectively resulted in a further integration of the economy in the world capitalist system.

[2] Marx, *The Eighteenth Brumaire* ..., in Marx and Engels, *Selected works*, Vol. I, op. cit., pp. 423–4.
[3] To cite only one example: As progressive a document as the *Mwongozo* (TANU Guidelines) observes:
   'For Tanzania, it must be understood that imperialist enemies we are confronting are British imperialism, Portuguese colonialism, the racism and apartheid of South Africa and Rhodesia.' (p. 3).

Objectively, the national economic policy of the 'bureaucratic bourgeoisie' was directed against the specific metropolitan bourgeoisie and in favour of the international bourgeoisie. Thus, links with Britain were gradually diminished and relations with the United States, the US-dominated international agencies, West Germany, the Scandinavian countries, Canada – and to a lesser extent with the socialist countries – were expanded, especially in terms of financial and technical aid[4] and also in terms of training and expertise.

Foreign investment was to be encouraged for it did not appear to conflict with the commitment to 'African socialism'. This socialism was both anti-capitalist and anti-communist, it aspired to a 'mixed-economy'!

It is unnecessary for us to go into the details of the pre-Arusha economic policy. We have discussed that in *The Silent Class Struggle*. Suffice it to say that there was nothing in it to show that the 'bureaucratic bourgeoisie' was objectively anti-imperialist in the revolutionary sense of the word and for complete political and economic independence. But even the 'anti-imperialism' of the 'bureaucratic bourgeoisie' discussed above would frequently bring it in open conflict with some of the imperialist countries. Rejection of West German aid when this was tied to the question of East German representation in Tanzania; a virtual break with the Commonwealth over Rhodesia and the straining of relations with Britain over the same question, etc. Support for liberation movements in Southern Africa also mean sharp clashes between Tanzania and some imperialist countries in the world councils. However, these incidents are the reflection of *secondary* contradictions within the relations between the 'bureaucratic bourgeoisie' and the metropolitan bourgeoisies.

7.2   THE CLASS STRUGGLE UNFOLDS

Power and property may be separated for a time by force or fraud – but divorced never. For so soon as the pang of separation is felt . . . property will purchase power, or power will take over property. And either way, there must be an end to free government – Benjamin Watkins Leigh[5] (nineteenth-century Virginia Statesman).

[4] See, for instance, the 'Annual Economic Surveys' for the rise of financial borrowings from the US aid agencies, US dominated World Bank and its agencies; Scandinavian countries; Federal Republic of (West) Germany, etc. The latter, by accepting to build and staff (all West Germans) the Faculty of Engineering have made a substantial inroad in the country's educational system. They have also shown interest in the iron ore deposits in the South.

For a detailed discussion of the international links of the Tanzanian economy see the Appendix.

[5] Quoted in the *Monthly Review*, Vol. 20, No. 10 (March 1969), p. 19.

The situation Tanzania found itself in after independence was precisely where power and property were separated. They simply could not remain separated for long. The incipient 'class struggle' between the petty bourgeoisie and the commercial bourgeoisie could not be waged without state power.

To be sure, the contradictions between the commercial bourgeoisie and the petty bourgeoisie had manifested themselves long before independence, as we noted in Part Two. The various efforts made by the African petty bourgeoisie to form co-operatives – in some cases with the assistance of the colonial state – had faced vigorous resistance from the Asian 'middle-man' and was successfully sabotaged. As early as 1936, the Chamber of Commerce section of the Indian Association passed the following resolution at their Conference in Dodoma:

> The association records its appreciation of the assurance of the Government of Tanganyika that they have no intention to press for the general adoption of a system of co-operation in the Territory . . . (but) this Federation is further of the confirmed opinion that the Government is moving too rapidly towards the augmentation of the co-operative system. . . . It also reiterates its strong belief that the system of co-operation is quite premature in the infant economic circumstances of the Territory. Wherefore it urgently requests the Government to stop the advancement of the co-operative system until the Territory is placed on a basis of intensive and extensive protection and industrial development so that the trading population which might be displaced by the co-operative institutions might be suitably absorbed in other spheres of economic fabric of the territory.[6]

Thus although the Co-operative Ordinance was first passed in 1932 the government's interest in the co-operatives dwindled because of, among other things, the opposition from the Asian traders. The co-operatives, outside Moshi area, did not really become a force until after the Second World War and particularly in the 50s when encouraged by the nationalist movement and the independent government respectively.[7] Under the leadership of Paul Bomani, the Victoria Federation of Co-operatives (VFCU), one of the biggest African-owned co-operatives, was formed in 1955 in Sukumaland. 'Arising out of discontent with the Asian-controlled monopoly buying system, which both exploited the grower by legal means and cheated him through corrupt and illegal methods, the co-operatives had captured 13 per cent of the total crop by 1953, 60 per cent by 1956, and 100 per cent by 1959. In 1956 the Victoria Federation opened its first ginnery, it completed a second in 1958, and opened four more in 1960. After 1962 the Federation launched

---

[6] Extract from a Resolution at First Annual Session of the Federated Chambers of Commerce section of the Indian Association, held at Dodoma on 11, 12, 13 and 14 April, 1936. (?) TNA: 19005. Quoted in D. E. McHenry, *Tanzania: the struggle for development*, op. cit., p. 101.

[7] See generally, Maguire, *Towards Uhuru* . . . , op. cit.

all out at privately owned Asian ginneries. By 1965, it ginned about 65 per cent of the total crop.'[8]

Once the petty bourgeoisie *formally* acceded to the state power after independence, the contradiction with the commercial bourgeoisie became dominant. But the 'alliance' between the various sections of the petty bourgeoisie also began to crack down on the questions revolving around the main contradiction: how and under what ideology would the struggle against the commercial bourgeoisie be waged?

There were important sections of the petty bourgeoisie – for example the African traders – whose only aspiration had been to step into the shoes of the commercial bourgeoisie after independence. This section found its spokesmen, paradoxically, in the petty bourgeois leadership of the trade unions. When the government presented its Citizenship Bill to the Legislative Council in 1961, prominent trade union leaders vehemently opposed it. They were proposing that the citizenship be based on race. One of the speakers on the Bill neatly summarized the 'sentiments' of the opposition when he said:

> I think 75 per cent of the non-African population still regard an African in Tanganyika as an inferior human being. Why is it so? It is because the white population has been dominating us, both economically and politically, and their neighbours, the Asians, have been economically dominating us, we Africans. . . . Do you think the individual African forming the vast majority of the population will agree to have equal rights with the Europeans and Asians? My answer is no. . . . All foreigners who are living in Tanganyika now and have transferred their money to their home countries or to other countries should within this period of five years bring their money back. I repeat . . . they must bring it back. From now on those foreigners who are rich . . . should contribute at least 15 per cent of their money to us, the Tanganyika National Fund.[9]

The trade union-based opposition resulted in a number of strikes. The government retaliated by passing legislation virtually banning the strikes.[10] In early 1963, two trade union leaders were deported to the Sumbawanga District.[11] Finally, in 1964 the government banned the Tanganyika Federation of Labour (TFL) and formed a single union (the National Union of Tanganyika Workers – NUTA) under its own auspices.

The opposition to the government found its expression in a number of splinter groups (parties) as well.[12] All of them had one demand in common: Africanization of the economy. Thus they were basically

[8] Maguire, ibid., pp. 118–19.

[9] Quoted in Bienen, *Tanzania: party transformation* . . . , op. cit., p. 162.

[10] See the Trade Dispute Act, 1962.

[11] A detailed account of the TANU/TFL split is found in Patel, 'The political role of trade unions in Tanzania', (mimeo).

[12] Bienen, *Tanzania: party transformation* . . . , op. cit., pp. 58–9.

representing the interests of the African traders and to some extent kulaks. (A number of them, for example, opposed the government land Bills.) The name of one such splinter group candidly sums up the interests that lurked behind the opposition: It was called the '*Nationalist Enterprise* Party'!

But the ruling sector of the petty bourgeoisie ('bureaucratic bourgeoisie') would not yield. While recognizing the truth in the argument of the opposition, it did not agree with the methods proposed. It was going to use different methods (Africanization of the civil service and the cooperatives) and a liberal not racial ideology. President Nyerere had vigorously attacked the opposition during the Citizenship Debate, describing them as 'potential Verwoerds'.

> I have said sir, because of the situation we have inherited in this country, where economic classes are also identical with race, that we live on dynamite, that it might explode one day, unless we do something about it. But positively not negatively.[13]

If the 'bureaucratic bourgeoisie' had 'opted' to wage its struggle within the confines of a liberal ideology, the commercial bourgeoisie was not capable of even that. It could not see beyond the colour of its skin. Two-and-a-half generations of the colonial racial structure had completely internalized racial consciousness in the Asian community. Having always been under the guidance of the metropolitan colonial state as its political mentor, it was ideologically bereft. Besides, the use of the racial ideology in resistance to the 'bureaucratic bourgeoisie' was objectively necessary for the leading sectors of the commercial bourgeoisie if the intra-class stratification was not to exacerbate into class divisions. It was this intense ethnic consciousness, however irrational, that kept its different strata together as complementary without becoming antagonistic. Politically and economically dependent on the metropolitan bourgeoisie, and with the political vision of a prosperous shopkeeper and a real estate speculator rather than that of an industrial captain, the Asian commercial bourgeoisie was not even capable of bourgeois liberalism. Thus it viewed almost every measure taken by the post-independence government through its racial lenses.

The 'Africanization' of the civil service was seen as a necessary political move, for the civil service could not go on having a completely disproportionate racial composition. As President Nyerere explained: 'the composition of the civil service should broadly reflect the racial pattern of the territory's population as a whole and thus that the great preponderance of posts should be held by indigenous Africans. Indeed anything else would be artificial and unhealthy. . . .'[14] In practice, it meant the Africanization of all political and top civil service posts with

---

[13] Nyerere, *Freedom and unity*, op. cit., p. 129.
[14] 'Africanization of the Civil Service', Address of the Chief Minister, 19 October 1960, *Hansard*, 36th Session reprinted in his *Freedom and unity*, p. 97.

the former incumbents, mostly British, retained as advisers. This move did not hit the commercial bourgeoisie very hard. It was mostly the Indian 'professional' civil servants who were affected and who in any case were not intending to take up Tanzanian citizenship. So they simply emigrated.

The more important side of the 'Africanization' process was, what may be called, the 'Africanization' of the economy. It is interesting that the state did not come out openly in favour of supporting the African traders. As we shall see its main thrust was on the co-operatives.* Indirectly, however, the state posts provided the bureaucrats with an opportunity to 'accumulate' necessary initial capital to go into commerce. Admittedly, salariat posts could hardly provide substantial capital for investing in commerce in a big way and in sectors with a relatively long gestation period. Thus the thrust of the petty bourgeoisie was mainly in such 'enterprises' as real estate, bars, transport, petrol stations, business, farms, etc. With a strong resistance – effected through sabotage, superior manipulative skills, and bribing of the bureaucracy – the commercial bourgeoisie very successfully warded off the incipient competition from the petty bourgeoisie. Frequently, the commercial bourgeoisie was urged to branch out into the industrial sector and make way for Africans (petty bourgeoisie) in commerce. This was the advice of some of the leaders of the commercial bourgeoisie as well. Though this happened to some extent, the dependent commercial bourgeoisie could not mobilize enough capital to channel it into the industrial sector on a large scale.† In fact, this is precisely what makes this bourgeoisie *dependent*. As Baran has explained:

> Important as it is that the 'lumpenbourgeois' element of the mercantile class eats up a large share of the economic surplus accruing to the class as a whole, even more portentous is the fact that such capital as is accumulated by its wealthier members is typically not turned into the *second* bracket of the non-agricultural economy; industrial production. Existing for the most part in small morsels, it can find profitable application only in the sphere of circulation where relatively small amounts of money go a long way, where the returns on the individual transactions are large, and where the turnover of the funds is rapid. And merchants in possession of larger resources find even better opportunities for gain in buying up land yielding rent revenue, in various undertakings auxiliary to the operation of western business, in importing, exporting, money lending, and speculation. Thus to the extent that a transfer of capital and business energies from mercantile to industrial pursuits is at all possible, the transfer price becomes inordinately high.[15]

* It is this which allowed the Tanzanian petty bourgeoisie, unlike its many African counterparts, to retain its mass peasant base.

† The relative weakness of the Tanzanian commercial bourgeoisie as compared to the Kenyan and Ugandan is a further reflection of Tanzania's sub-satellite status in East Africa during the colonial era. See *supra* p. 34.

[15] Baran, *The political economy of growth*, op. cit., p. 173.

The commercial bourgeoisie directed their attention to such 'industrial' activities as biscuit and sweet manufacture, garment production, hotels and tourism, and most important of all, real estate speculation. Not even foreign capital, albeit for different reasons, to which the 'bureaucratic bourgeoisie' looked upon for 'national' development lived up to the expectations.

The foreign enterprises did some window-dressing by Africanizing a few posts. Most of the likely African candidates were absorbed by the government. Many foreign enterprises only had branches in Tanzania with their headquarters in Nairobi, and the few local posts, in any case, were occupied by the Asians and European employees who conducted the local operations.

In spite of the considerable inroads made by the petty bourgeoisie into the commercial sector and in spite of the rise of rich African traders, it can safely be concluded that before 1967, the petty bourgeoisie was not on the whole radically successful in the commercial ventures. Firstly, because of the initial economic weakness of the petty bourgeoisie compared to the commercial bourgeoisie; which did not hesitate to use all its economic power – legally and illegally[16] – for its survival as a class; a typical case of property buying power. Secondly, the state did not come out openly and forcefully to support African penetration of the commercial sector. Rather, it firstly concentrated on its mass peasant base – the co-operative movement, the villagization scheme etc. and on expanding the 'territorial'[17] economy with the help of foreign capital – the international bourgeoisie. As can be seen, these two are not mutually exclusive. In fact, they are in accord with the rule of the 'bureaucratic bourgeoisie'. We may recall our discussion on the 'nationalistic' outlook of the 'bureaucratic bourgeoisie'. Its field of operation is the whole territory and the territorial economy, as opposed to the parochial outlook of say, kulaks or traders. Its very base lies, through the state (up to 1967 indirectly and after 1967 directly), in the territorial neo-colonial type of economy. Thus facilitating the further integration of peasants in the cash economy, raising their production for export, raising of the productivity of workers, encouraging and attracting foreign capital (private, state, and from international agencies) became the preoccupations of the state. This should not be confused with the building of an independent nationally integrated economy because for the proponents of the development of the territorial economy there is no perspective whatsoever which would enable them to confront the international bourgeoisie and imperialism. In fact, the ideological rhetoric vigorously and almost exclusively harps on the

---

[16] The Asian businessman as a 'corruptor' is legion in East Africa.

[17] I am using the term 'territorial' – as opposed to 'national' – advisedly. The first is more of a geographical phenomenon, the second a concept of political economy – national as opposed to *colonial* economy.

'dukawalla'[18] (the businessman – mainly retailer) as the supreme exploiter. Foreign investment, on the other hand, is depicted as part of development. The former fits in with the stereotype of popular consciousness and helps to obscure the real issues – the neo-colonial structure of the economy, the objective alliance of the 'bureaucratic bourgeoisie' with the international bourgeoisie.

The businessman involved in the sphere of circulation is, no doubt, an essential link in the chain of exploitation. He fully participates in the exploitation. But to identify a link with the chain is absolute obscurantism. In so far as it does not control the state, it is not even a *decisive* link. To confine attention to circulation without even touching production has been a past-time of bourgeois ideologues. To confine exploitation to circulation without linking it with production is a political gimmick of the petty bourgeoisie. For to expose the chain of exploitation would mean exposing the ruling classes – both internal and external. Objectively, therefore, this obscurantism does not arise from mere ignorance but from basic class interests. It is class obscurantism!

Coming back to the mechanisms of the struggle: The *co-operative front* was looked upon as an important movement both for the marketing of the peasant's produce and a convenient way for the state to appropriate the surplus: strictly, the latter function was performed by the marketing boards. Thus it was the most important form against the commercial bourgeoisie. As the *Presidential Commission on the Establishment of a Democratic One Party State,* stated: 'The remarkable success of the Co-operative Movement in Tanganyika has been a decisive factor in the economic development of our country since the Second World War. It has been decisive because the steady expansion of co-operative enterprise *has enabled Africans to participate in and obtain control of certain sectors of the economy, which would otherwise have remained in the hands of immigrants or foreign companies.*'[19] [Emphasis supplied.]

The *Special Committee of Enquiry into Co-operative Movement and Marketing Boards* (1966) (hereinafter 'Committee') was quite clear and forthright as regards the role of the co-operative in the struggle against the commercial bourgeoisie.

Tracing the history, the committee stated: 'When Tanganyika achieved independence in 1961 some important decisions were taken by the Government vitally affecting the movement. It was decided to embark on a crash programme for the organization of co-operatives in vast sections of the country which until then were largely untouched by the movement: the central and coastal parts, Mtwara and Ruvuma in the South, and the western areas. It was decided that the co-operative

---

[18] It is interesting that the upper echelons of the commercial bourgeoisie are not usually included within the notion of 'dukawalla' exploiter which refers to middle and lower level retailers. For the upper stratum is expected to participate in 'development' – tourism, hotels, sweets manufacture, etc.

[19] Dar es Salaam: Government Printer, 1968, p. 27.

form was well suited to the African setting and to the achievement of independence in the economic sense: *Control of the economy by the indigenous people rather than by expatriates and others non-African in origin.*[20] [Emphasis supplied.] One does not expect the Committee to talk in terms of *class struggle*, but it pulls no punches as regards the motives of encouraging the co-operative movement. Thus the number of registered co-operatives increased from 857 in 1961 to 1 533 at the end of April, 1966. The volume of produce handled by them increased from 145 000 tons in 1960 to 496 000 tons in 1965.[21] 'To help bring about this great expansion the Co-operative Societies Ordinance was changed in 1963 so that the Registrar of Co-operative Societies no longer had the final power to refuse to register a co-operative because he was not satisfied as to its viability; in the future such decisions were to be *subject to reversal by a Minister carrying out a political policy. The political pressures were considerable. Societies were organized from "on top", without genuine local demand or even understanding but in their enthusiasm in the first flush of freedom, people went along.'*[22] [Emphasis supplied.]

The 'bureaucratic bourgeoisie' rationalized the co-operatives as a 'national' movement serving the producer, the consumer and the public at large. The ideological rhetoric sometimes took its own toll in terms of excessive 'political interference'[23] – to use the Committee's phrase – from the government bureaucrats. The more experienced heads of the co-operatives, on the other hand, kept their economic perspective and were not taken in by the political rhetoric of their bureaucratic counterparts. What they wanted from the state was its assistance to crush the commercial bourgeoisie, not to interfere in *their* organization.[24]

Apart from the agriculture marketing co-operatives, wholesale, consumer, and transport co-operatives were also organized. Accumulation of the surplus by the agricultural co-operatives enabled some of them to branch out into some processing as well.

Again it is interesting to note that the Committee is forthright on the motives behind the formation of a wholesale co-operative Co-operative Supply Association of Tanganyika (Cosata)[25] in 1962 and establishing

[20] *Report of the Special Committee of Enquiry into Co-operative Movement and Marketing Boards*, (Dar es Salaam: Government Printer, 1966), p. 5.
[21] ibid.   [22] ibid., para. 28, p. 5.   [23] ibid., para. 51, p. 11.
[24] The manager of the TNT (Tanganyika National Transport Co-operative Ltd), for instance, clearly saw his organization as a commercial, profit-making transport enterprise rather than that of 'a servant of the public, devoted to rendering the best possible service at the lowest possible cost consistent with the payment of responsible compensation to its workers'. (The formulation in the quote is that of the Committee.) See the Committee's Report, op. cit., p. 50.
[25] Cosata was set up and run with the help of the Israelis. Thus the bridgehead of imperialism in the Middle East and increasingly in Africa was considered a suitable 'partner' by the 'bureaucratic bourgeoisie' against the commercial bourgeoisie. [For Israel's economic and military interests in Africa see *David and Goliath collaborate in Africa* by the Africa Research Group (1969)].

of consumer co-operative shops. 'It must be emphasized that the motivation for this decision was not that the profit margins were excessive; on the contrary the available evidence is that competition had kept them very low indeed. The *political decision* was a consequence of the fact *that the bulk of the retail trade in Tanganyika was in the hands of Asian merchants* who had not identified themselves with the aspirations of Tanganyika nationalism *and whose commercial dominance appeared to be an obstacle to the full development of the Africans*, who made up some 98 per cent of the population. The hostility was compounded by the fact that many Asian commercial enterprises were linked by family and caste ties, and by the failure of most of the Asian merchants to bring Africans into their firms in any meaningful way.'[26] [Emphasis supplied.]

The co-operative, therefore, was an important front in the class struggle between the commercial bourgeoisie and the petty bourgeoisie. The preponderance of the state, however, meant that the hand of the emerging 'bureaucratic bourgeoisie' would be strengthened. Furthermore, in the consciousness of the 'bureaucratic bourgeoisie', the successes or failures of the struggle would be identified with those of the 'nation'. All this meant that the struggle was pregnant with the potential of its further intensification and possibly greater state 'intervention'. The latter automatically implying further strengthening and consolidation of the 'bureaucratic bourgeoisie' even at the expense of other sections of the petty bourgeoisie and exacerbation of the intra-petty bourgeoisie stratification.

Next we need to consider briefly the resistance of the commercial bourgeoisie. Lacking political weapons, it resorted to economic sabotage, corruption and bribery of the bureaucrats – to 'buy power' – business and financial manipulation. This is difficult to document, but there is no doubt that it played an important role in causing losses and failures of the co-operatives, especially the consumer co-operatives. Dishonesty on the part of the bureaucracy itself is just another side of the coin. Without such dishonesty, corruption cannot take place and corruption itself breeds more dishonesty. Economic sabotage by the commercial bourgeoisie and the dishonesty of the bureaucrats are interlinked and cannot be separated.

The Special Committee noted:

> Apart from the basic defects within the movement, it must be appreciated that the co-operatives have enemies outside the movement – the private traders and others who have lost business. These enemies have not given up hope of running the co-operatives and they use devious tricks to bring about their downfall. Regretfully we must report that some TANU officials, Members of Parliament, and Regional Commissioners have allowed themselves to be used as tools by these enemies of the co-operatives, accepting directorships and financial

[26] ibid., pp. 46–7.

participations in their firms, and using their influence to harm the interests of this national movement.[27]

The Committee also noted the 'accusations that the private trading community, naturally hostile to co-operatives and especially to Cosata, has engaged in deliberate campaigns to destroy them by withholding wholesale supplies at prices available to private competitors, and by underselling.'[28] The Committee, however, regarded underselling as a 'traditional practice in competitive trade'. Actually, though again it is difficult to document, the economic sabotage went much further than the so-called traditional practices. The problems of consumer co-operatives, especially Cosata, were in no small measure a result of the economic warfare waged by the commercial bourgeoisie.

Almost on every page of its Report, the Committee speaks of losses incurred by the co-operatives; mismanagement and corruption of the Union Committee men and the co-operative employees; failures, petty thievery, and so on. On the whole it appeared from the Committee Report that there was a general 'failure' on the part of the co-operative movement. This is not to say that the co-operative movement has no achievements to its credit. In fact, since colonial times it was a very significant and one of the most successful movements in Africa. In absolute terms it was probably an economic 'success'. But in this book we are not talking about absolute 'failures' and 'successes'; but relative: relative in the sense that they became harbingers of further movement. They spur further class struggles and propel historical motions. It is only in this sense that we are talking about 'failures'. In that sense the co-operative movement was a 'failure' for the petty bourgeoisie as a whole. There was a need for change. For the 'bureaucratic bourgeoisie', there were additional reasons calling for change. The territorial economic development was not impressive; foreign capital on which so much hope was pinned – the First Five-Year Development Plan had allocated something like 80 per cent to foreign investments – did not appear to oblige. The villagization scheme was clearly unsuccessful.[29] With falling prices – especially that of the main export, sisal[30] – the economy was in a bad shape – which affected large sections of the population.

Peasants had vigorously complained against the bureaucratic corruption in the co-operatives:

'We regret that after having achieved *Uhuru* in this country,' they said, 'we, the farmers, have been deprived of all blessings of *Uhuru*; our incomes have been dwindling, and what is worse, we are continually being overtaxed. For example, we pay two types of Development Levy: the Local Council cess and the National Development

[27] ibid., pp. 11–12.
[28] ibid., p. 12.
[29] See Cliffe & Cunningham, 'Ideology, organization . . . , op. cit.
[30] The price of sisal fell from £103 per ton (average price in 1960–62) to £70 per ton in 1967 – almost 33 per cent.

Levy. Under these circumstances, we feel ourselves to be the forgotten children, and we can see nothing better than the total ruin of this country and our children in the long run. . . . [Whilst] we assure the President that we appreciate the desirability of substituting co-operatives for the private traders, so far we strongly object to the way in which this is being done.'[31]

Different sections of the petty bourgeoisie, too, were disgruntled: the soldiers had openly demonstrated their grievances in the 1964 Army Mutiny; the University students had opposed the National Service Scheme in October, 1966. Workers, too, despite the government's call for restraint (which sounded meaningless where the enterprises were privately owned), were asking for wage increases which in many cases they managed to get. The cultural exclusivism of the commercial bourgeoisie and, sometimes, abominable public behaviour, continually attracted criticism and condemnation in the public media giving credence to the restlessness of some sections of the petty bourgeoisie who were calling for decisive action. Thus both subjectively and objectively the country was ready for change.

As we have seen, while the members of the 'bureaucratic bourgeoisie' had made some inroads into the economy, they had not been successful in developing a substantial economic base. This could not go on. The only alternative, both for further struggle against the commercial bourgeoisie and for further penetration of the economy, was state intervention. To a limited extent, this coincided with the interests of substantial sections of the population. It *also* followed from *Ujamaa* – the policy of TANU, which until then was only a paper declaration.

President Nyerere succinctly explained the motivations behind securing majority ownership in the private enterprises: '. . . We decided to secure majority ownership in these industries because they are key points in our economy, and because we believe that they therefore be under the control of Tanzania. *Our purpose was thus primarily a nationalist purpose:* it was an extension of the political control which the Tanzanian people secured in 1961'[32] [emphasis supplied]. Such 'economic nationalism' was common to all countries and universal: 'As I have said,' the President continued, 'this economic nationalism has nothing to do with the ideologies of socialism, capitalism, or communism. It is universal among nation states . . . whatever economic system the peoples of different African countries eventually adopt, it is quite certain that sooner or later they will demand that the key positions of their economy are in the hands of their own citizens.'[32]

It was thus that the Arusha Declaration was born in 1967. It marked the end of one phase of struggle between the petty bourgeoisie and the

[31] Quoted in the Special Committee's Report, op. cit., p. 4.

[32] Speech at the opening of the extension of the Tanzanian Breweries plant in Dar es Salaam, reprinted in his, *Freedom and socialism* (Dar es Salaam: Oxford University Press, 1968), pp. 262–3, under the title 'Economic nationalism'.

commercial bourgeoisie and the beginning of the second, probably the decisive phase. It also marked an important historical turning point in the development of the 'bureaucratic bourgeoisie' and possible contradictions among the petty bourgeoisie itself. Moreover, by using the rhetoric of socialism it marked the beginnings of debates and discussion of the proletarian ideology as well.

Before we discuss further the 'bureaucratic bourgeoisie' it is appropriate at this point to review briefly the attitude of the petty bourgeoisie towards workers.

7.2.1 *Workers as exploiters?*

We have already seen the immediate post-independence struggle between the government and the trade union leaders on the questions of Africanization and citizenship. This was undoubtedly a power struggle between two sections of the petty bourgeoisie.[33] The government had passed legislation virtually banning strikes[34] and bringing the trade union movement more under government control.[35] The rationalization was that now that there was a 'people's government' (to use President Nyerere's phrase), there was no need of an independent trade union movement: 'The same people are members of the trade union and of the political wing of the labour movement. How then can these two wings be separate? We believe that the institutions of society must bring into harmony all the different interests of man, and we do not understand how it helps a worker if the Trade Union he belongs to regards itself as independent from, and in conflict with, the political movement he himself helps to control'.[36]

To stabilize the work force, the government passed minimum wage legislations,[37] Security of Employment Act,[38] and established the National Provident Fund. With this, the government expected the workers to make 'sacrifices', raise productivity and thereby contribute to 'national development'. The idea that somehow workers had gained

[33] See *supra* p. 68.
[34] The Trade Disputes (Settlement) Act, No. 43 of 1962 makes strikes virtually impossible. This was opposed by the then TFL leader, Mr Mkello.
[35] The National Union of Tanganyika (NUTA) (Establishment) Act, No. 18 of 1964. This came in the wake of the Army Mutiny, of which some trade union leaders had tried to take advantage. (See Patel, 'The political role . . .' op. cit., pp. 8–9). See also *infra* p. 69.
[36] Address to the First Annual Congress of NUTA, quoted in Patel, *Trade Unions, Labour and Law in Tanganyika*, op. cit., p. 13.
[37] It was expected that this would result in the fall of employment but the aim was to have a small number of workers employed at 'higher' wages rather than a big number at a lower wage (see the 'Report of the Territorial Minimum Wages Board' – or 'Chesworth Report' – appointed on 4/8/1961 by G.N. 281/1961, para. 91). The 'high wage' policy had in fact been agreed upon by other East African countries also at the Tripartite Labour Conference of East Africa held in Dar es Salaam on 15 and 16 November 1962.
[38] No. 62 of 1964. See also *infra* p. 128.

77

from independence at the expense of the peasants came to a head when Professor Turner, an International Labour Office expert, produced his report on 'Wages, Incomes and Prices Policy'.[39] One of his main contentions was that workers had managed to get increases in wages at the expense of the peasants and that employment had fallen because of this. Incidentally, he noted that during the same period the *profits* of the enterprises had in fact increased. Notwithstanding, his recommendation was that measures should be taken to restrict wage increases. The government's comments on the paper more or less accepted Turner's recommendations and even hailed the spirit of the ILO Report as being in close accord with the socialistic principles of the Arusha Declaration.[40] But 'sacrifices'; rises in productivity, restraint in wage demands, etc., were asked of workers when the profits of the capitalists continued to increase. At least formally, therefore, this contradiction had to be resolved. The characteristic method, a result of the Arusha Declaration, was to obtain majority shareholdings in the private enterprises. This would now allow a further period in which to exort workers to work hard for the enterprises which were now 'theirs'. However, the *Mwongozo* (TANU Guidelines) and the subsequent 'downing of tools' showed that the workers did not wholly accept this interpretation. We shall return to this point in Part Five.

The workers as a class did not play a leading role during the first phase of the struggle. In fact banning of strikes without workers' participation in the control of the enterprises and the state, meant that objectively it was *capital* rather than *labour* which was being assisted. Accepting Turner's Report with its implied theses that workers were 'exploiting' peasants – a notion which is not uncommon among the petty bourgeoisie – had the danger of driving a wedge between these potential allies in the fight against capital. In any case, given the historical past that we have described at length, the contradictions that were being ironed out during this phase were between the petty bourgeoisie and the commercial bourgeoisie. Objectively, the workers and poor peasants had limited interest in this struggle as a means to 'clear the way' for *their* struggle which could only be carried out under their leadership guided by scientific socialist ideology. The struggle between the petty bourgeoisie and the commercial bourgeoisie was not only an inevitable but a necessary phase.

[39] Government Paper No. 3 of 1967 (Dar es Salaam: Government Printers 1967). For a critical analysis and political implications of this paper see, J. F. Rweyemamu, 'Some aspects of the Turner Report', Economic Research Bureau (ERB) Paper 69.20. He rightly points out: 'Professor Turner would have us believe that wage increases have been at the expense of the rural workers. The implication of such a conclusion is clear: to antagonise the working class and the peasantry, who should ally themselves in fighting counter-revolutionary forces.' (p. 5).

[40] Government Paper No. 4 of 1967. (Dar es Salaam: Government Printer, 1967), p. 1.

EIGHT

Arusha and After: the 'Bureaucratic Bourgeoisie' Forges Ahead

8.1 THE ARUSHA DECLARATION: RÉSUMÉ

We have seen the constellation of objective conditions and social forces which led to the party, TANU, adopting the policy of 'socialism and self-reliance' enunciated in the Arusha Declaration. For the first time the party took *concrete* measures describing them as 'socialistic'.

The Arusha nationalizations constituted the first open attempt on the part of the bureaucratic sector of the petty bourgeoisie to carve out an economic base for itself.

Together with the Declaration the party also adopted the 'leadership code'. The code is supposed to prevent those in the leadership positions in the government, the party, and the parastatals from holding shares or accepting directorships in private enterprises, from receiving two or more salaries, and from owning houses which are rented to others.[41]

The Arusha Declaration was the most decisive turning point in the struggle between the petty bourgeoisie and the commercial bourgeoisie, leading to the latter's disintegration, as we shall see in a moment.

The bureaucracy controlling the state had provided the leadership in the first phase of the struggle of the petty bourgeoisie against the commercial bourgeoisie by supporting vigorously, for instance, the co-operatives. But in the process it had antagonized some sectors of the petty bourgeoisie who would have liked the state to support them to *replace* the commercial bourgeoisie by straightforward Africanization of the economy. This opposition, as we saw, found its spokesmen in the

---

[41] Leader is defined as: 'Members of the TANU National Executive Committee; Ministers, Members of Parliament, Senior Officials of Organizations affiliated to TANU, Senior Officials of Parastatal Organizations, all those appointed or elected under any clause of the TANU constitution, Councillors, and Civil Servants in high and middle cadres.' (Arusha Declaration, p. 20.)

The Code was the first act of *class self-restraint* imposed on the *individual* members of the class in the long-term interests of the class *as a whole*. It was also an objective recognition of the fact that a new class with its particular conditions of reproduction was emerging. (For further discussion see the text *infra* p. 95).

petty bourgeois leadership of the trade unions. With the banning of the Tanganyika Federation of Labour, the opposition appeared to have had gone 'underground' though did not disappear completely. For in the very adoption of the Declaration and the post-Arusha period it resurfaced in the form of an opposition to these measures and especially the Leadership Code.[42] So there had been intra-petty bourgeois contradictions since Independence. But they became more intensified when the bureaucratic sector attempted to control the very economy through the state.

To recapitulate: There are three inter-related trends which would dominate the post-Arusha period until the 'Mwongozo'.

(1) Attempts at consolidating the 'bureaucratic bourgeoisie';
(2) The intensification of the intra-petty bourgeoisie contradictions;
(3) The disintegration of the commercial bourgeoisie.

It is the discussion of these that we turn our attention to in the ensuing sections.

8.2 THE CLIMAX OF THE CLASS STRUGGLE: THE COMMERCIAL BOURGEOISIE DISINTEGRATES

The Arusha Declaration, by initiating the penetration of the state into the export–import and wholesale trade, milling, and other light industries, directly and substantially affected the upper echelons of the commercial bourgeoisie. The nationalization of foreign firms too, though to a smaller extent, affected its 'comprador' section. The professionals – private doctors, lawyers, etc. – had begun to feel the pinch of the high licensing fees while the expanding 'public sector' held a threat of reduced private litigation and the reduction of legal business. The only professional cadres, whose relative position may, in fact, have improved as a result of the nationalization, are those employed in the private banks. As a result of the nationalization, the European employees of the banks immediately left and this opened up promotion opportunities for the Asians who were urged to stay on.[43]

---

[42] One of the strongest opponents to the Citizenship Bill, Mr S. Mtaki, was also one of the first to 'drop out' from the leadership after the Arusha Declaration.

[43] It is interesting to note that even the post-Mwongozo exodus does not appear to have affected substantially the Asians employed in the Banks. I may suggest one possible explanation: The large majority of Asians employed in the Banks happened to be Hindus, etc. – i.e. non-Ismailis. The exodus, on the other hand, was mainly among the Ismailis, a business community *par excellence*. Even the Ismaili *professionals* had close familial ties with their commercial counterparts: in fact, most of them had their education in Tanzania and were sent for higher education overseas, as part of the 'investment' of their merchant-fathers: (Most of them, for instance, have British rather than Indian qualifications). The non-Ismaili professionals on the other hand, were educated in India and came to

One opportunity that the Arusha Declaration and the Leadership Code opened up for the commercial bourgeoisie was in real estate, since it heavily restricted the freedom of their possible rivals – members of the 'bureaucratic bourgeoisie' – to engage in it. This was fully and conspicuously exploited by the commercial bourgeoisie. Real estate speculation had always been a good source of income but now it became a real money-spinner.[44] 'Key money' and extortionate rents became the order of the day.[45] Increased bureaucracy and the expanded public sector provided further opportunities to the commercial bourgeoisie to practise corruption and black marketeering – another source of quick money-making. But the commercial capitalist had lost 'confidence' in the country, and gradually but definitely they began to restrict their business activities, and instead of saving, accumulating, and investing, they began to *export* capital. The post-Arusha period witnessed continual reports in the newspapers of breaches of the foreign exchange controls and the flight of capital. The continued *reproduction* of a capitalist class – be it commercial or industrial – depends on its ability to accumulate. To reproduce itself as a class, the capitalist must reproduce and continually expand his capital; this is an essential condition. The restricting of the activity of saving and accumulation[46] within the territorial economy, selling off businesses, running down of stocks, etc., marked the beginning of the trend towards the disintegration of the commercial bourgeoisie as a class. The stream of the Asian emigration, which became an exodus after the Buildings Acquisition Act, marked the beginning of its actual, physical disintegration.

These trends reached their zenith with the acquisition of buildings in April 1971. Fimbo's calculation shows that out of some 2908 buildings acquired as at 16 November 1972, only about 97 belonged to the

---

Tanzania as *professionals*. This is one possible explanation though difficult to authenticate with figures.

[44] In 1967–68, the growth rate of buildings by household/enterprise (private sector) was 12·3 per cent, 5·1 per cent points higher than the average growth rate (7·2 per cent) between 1960/2–68. (1968), *The Annual Economic Survey*, Table 5, p. 9.

[45] See, for instance, the *Sunday News Opinion* of 14 September 1969.
'The profit demanded by many traders on items such as motor cars, accessories, essential household equipment and foodstuffs, as well as the rental being charged by landlords, not to mention the practice of key money, which still thrives, all show that it takes much more than independence and the Arusha Declaration to end exploitation.'

[46] Accumulation here must be understood in a wider sense, including 'diversification' – i.e. branching out of commerce *stricto sensu* into transport, small industries, like repairs, engineering, textiles, garment manufacture etc., which had become important outlets for the surplus generated in the commercial sector. This type of expansion, too, appears to have stopped and the surplus generated in the already existing private small industries may be finding its way to outside countries rather than being reinvested. (I am indebted to John Loxley for drawing my attention to this point.)

members of the commercial bourgeoisie.[47] Not only the buildings of the landlords (i.e. those who had rented their houses) but also those of the owner-occupants (in many cases, small flat-owners) were initially taken over. This provided the upper echelon of the commercial bourgeoisie with an excellent propaganda opportunity to whip up racism and appear to 'speak' for the 'poor' Asian.[48] Thus instead of the intra-class stratification becoming exacerbated, it became (probably only temporarily) solidified. Hence, the resulting exodus was almost universal, from the upper echelons of the commercial bourgeoisie, to professionals and even retailers and retired people! In a few cases, those without ready money took loans to 'get out of the country'.

The foreign exchange scandals, illegal buying of foreign currency (including forged ones!), export of capital goods, running away of Asian professionals, including the undergraduates from the university and the post-secondary students – in breach of their formal contracts – became almost everyday occurrences. The amount of capital flight[49] during this period is difficult to estimate but it must have been substantial, especially when one includes the loss of qualified manpower.

Cultural exclusivism, tight-groupism, and racial prejudice among Asians may, today, probably be more intense – for now their vital class interests had been destroyed. No amount of appeal to morality or patriotism or loyalty could affect them as a *class*. Class morality ('it is right and moral to send out your hard earned money'!), class patriotism, and class loyalty come first: that is the objective law of class struggle.[50] This is an important point and needs emphasis. The popular image (created by newspapers and demagogic leaders) of the Asians as unpatriotic simply because they are Asians, hardly explains anything and tends to blur the *class nature* of the Asian community.

8.2.1 *The commercial bourgeoisie as a declining class*

The commercial bourgeoisie is a dying class. The essential condition of its reproduction – accumulation of capital – has been eroded. Sav-

[47] See the Appendix to G. M. Fimbo's, 'Land, socialism and law in Tanzania', in G. Ruhumbika (ed.), *Towards Ujamaa* (East African Literature Bureau, 1974).

[48] It was utterly disgusting to hear in private conversations one-time big landlords, now more or less feeding on 'exported' Tanzanian resources in a foreign country, arguing that they did not really mind the taking over of their buildings but were hurt to see the flats of 'poor people' being taken over! Incidentally, 'poor people' here refers to 'poor Asians'!

[49] 'Asian businessmen adopted the simple technique of carrying large quantities of bank notes into Kenya where they could be freely converted and then either saved in Kenya or repatriated, taking advantage of Kenya's comparatively easier exchange control system. In all some £T7m. are estimated to have been lost to the Tanzania reserves in this way.' Alan Rake, 'Brave economic experiment', *Financial Times*, 9 December 1971.

[50] To be sure, patriotism, loyalty to one's country, morality, etc., may radically affect *individuals* but these cannot explain the rise and fall of whole classes and the historical motion resulting therefrom.

ing may have been further cut by an upsurge in discretionary consumption that is apparent even to an untrained observer; exceptionally large groups of Asians in bars, cinemas, and restaurants; Asians' expensive gadgets and clothes, etc., are all signs of this conspicuous consumption.[51] I do not think this can be explained simply by increased incomes. Even if there were increased incomes and 'quick money-making', the point is that it is not saved but largely consumed.

Another interesting aspect of a dying social class is the way its old moral order, always thought to be an unassailable fortress, begins to crumble. The thrift and accumulative zeal inculcated even in children;[52] abhorrence of ostentatious living and apparent Victorian sexual morality; respect for parental authority, school, and religious authorities; and slavish acceptance of irrationalities like religion, show visible signs of disintegration. And this is not confined to the 'younger' generation only. Surprisingly, though obviously to a much lesser extent, it has affected the older generation as well. There is not much generation gap here! Of course, this may be part of the general influence of Western cultural trends, but it is difficult to believe that these trends could have gained legitimacy with such ease *at the time* if it had not been for the objective conditions described above.

Paradoxically, the incomes of the commercial bourgeoisie since the nationalizations and the setting up of wholesale parastatals like the State Trading Corporation (STC) and the National Textile Corporation (NATEX), may have, in fact, increased. Much of this income accrues from outside the normal established channels, the so-called unaccounted money. The virtual breakdown in the distribution system has opened up numerous avenues for quick money-making, from which the various groups of the Asian community have benefited: from the 'lumpen' elements – retired people and the unemployed – to the established merchants.

First there is the group of, what one may call NATEX-men, the counterpart of the Soviet 'tolkachi' ('pushers') of the industrialization period.[53] A retired person or a school-leaver or even a former businessman, who is prepared to stand in long queues at the NATEX shops to obtain goods and supply them at a mark-up to the established businessman. His basic function is to fish out and do economic intelligence for

[51] One often hears the Asian businessmen saying since there were no 'prospects for investment', there was no point in saving.

[52] 'Every good child must have a savings account', was almost a religious prescription.

[53] The Russian *tolkachi* were involved in semi-legal deals between enterprises to ensure supplies; to get allocation certificates; string-pulling through powerful Party and government officials and to work out arrangements to get necessary supplies and dispose of surpluses. cf. A. Nove, *The Soviet economy* (London: George Allen & Unwin, 1965), p. 38.

the various established distributors: to find out which goods are obtainable, where, etc. He has neither an established business nor premises; his deals are conducted in tea shops and restaurants; the only thing he receives is the 5 or so per cent, but he never sees the goods himself. He keeps no books, no accounts, and pays no tax. Even the deals and the transactions in which he is involved know no specialization. Today he is negotiating the sale of a dozen cartons of soap; tomorrow he is 'making' a passport for someone or exchanging local for foreign currency; the day after he is using his 'influence' to get a car permit for his principal.

Then there are the professional racketeers; passport and currency rackets being very common.

Finally, there are the top established merchants whose relations, acquaintances, and friends have woven their way into the state distribution organizations. Thus, through bribery and corruption they continue getting supplies even when there are shortages and rationing. In this way these businessmen have made enormous amounts of money in the last four or five years. As they say: the times have never been so good – but there is no future in Tanzania! Large amounts of this sort of money are sent out to other countries, and substantial amounts are used in conspicuous consumption. The fact is that very little is invested within the territorial economy because 'there is no future in Tanzania'!

In practice, the various groups we have outlined above overlap and even merge. Thus, a NATEX-man may own a shop as a *front* while the big merchant's real business may, in fact, be his shady deals rather than his normal business. The truth is that much of the trade and professional specializations within the commercial bourgeoisie have become things of the past. Unofficial and illegal means have taken over. Bourgeois standards of 'honesty', fair play, etc. ('Honesty is the best policy'!), have been completely eroded. There has been a spectacular decline in respect for bourgeois law and bourgeois business ethics. The question that a typical member of the commercial bourgeoisie asks today before doing something illegal has little to do with the 'ethics' of legality as such or *even* the fear that he might be caught. Rather he asks how much he would have to pay in terms of bribery if he is caught: And that becomes part of the 'cost'!

The crumbling of established business channels and the conspicuous decline in 'business morality' are themselves some of the signs of the declining nature of the commercial bourgeoisie.

Classes take long to die – and they do not die in one stroke either. Their death and disintegration are themselves processes, especially when the class struggle itself, as I have described, was 'peaceful', subtle, and smooth. We are not saying, therefore, that the disintegration of the commercial bourgeoisie is an accomplished fact. In fact, it may have just begun. It is submitted, however, that the commercial bourgeoisie is definitely disintegrating as a class and that it is unlikely that it can reconstitute itself.

8.3 ON THE 'BUREAUCRATIC BOURGEOISIE' II

Up until the Arusha Declaration, the 'bureaucratic bourgeoisie'[54] cannot be said to have really become a *bourgeoisie*. Rather it was a politico-administrative bureaucracy. Although the state played an important role in the economy, it was mostly a regulatory one. With the Arusha Declaration the state and state institutions (including the parastatals) became the dominant factor in the economy. Thus a new and the most important wing of the 'bureaucratic bourgeoisie' was created. Political power and control over property had now come to rest in the same class.

At this point, let us remind the reader of the thesis of *The silent class struggle*. The 'bureaucratic bourgeoisie' that arose from the struggle described above and to be analysed further in this section, is *not* an independent class; otherwise it would be a national bourgeoisie. In so far as the economy remains structurally linked with the capitalist world and within the world capitalist system, the 'bureaucratic bourgeoisie' is a *dependent* bourgeoisie – dependent on the international bourgeoisie.[55] This is not to say that the 'bureaucratic bourgeoisie' would throw up no contradictions within the international bourgeoisie, or that the 'alliance' is perfect. In fact, in the very attempt to create for itself an internal economic base, this class may come into conflict with the interests of a *particular* metropolitan bourgeoisie. Thus, the nationalization of the banks and some other British interests after the Arusha Declaration created 'tension' between Britain and Tanzania. However, since the 'bureaucratic bourgeoisie' is incapable of restructuring the internal society and thereby disengaging from the world capitalist system, their objective class interests in the long run converge.

Admittedly, it is a wrong formulation to say that the 'bureaucratic bourgeoisie' has an *economic* base in the international bourgeoisie.[56] Their economic base is, no doubt, within the territorial economy but the territorial economy itself is, as is shown in the Appendix, an *under-*

---

[54] Ngombale-Mwiru uses the term 'politico-bureaucratic bourgeoisie' – which is more descriptive but rather cumbersome; hence, my use of the term 'bureaucratic bourgeoisie' (See Ngombale-Mwiru, 'The Arusha Declaration of *Ujamaa na Kujitegemea* and the perspectives for building socialism in Tanzania', in Saul and Cliffe, *Socialism in Tanzania*, Vol. II, op. cit.

[55] Different imperialist countries of course, have their own bourgeoisies and they have their own inter-class secondary contradictions. But with the rise of world capitalism and world imperialism under US hegemony, the general and fundamental interests of the ruling classes of the imperialist countries coincide while their particular interests are hierarchical rather than *equally* important. The so-called international institutions, including the global corporations, dominating the world social economic and political scene as part and parcel of this *system*, provide the institutional links between these various imperialist bourgeoisies. For these reasons, and at that level of abstraction, we are justified in talking about the 'international bourgeoisie'. See further, Cox, *Capitalism as a system* (New York: Monthly Review, 1964).

[56] This was pointed out by some of the critics of *The silent class struggle*.

developed part of the world capitalist system – a neo-colony. Let us hasten to add that the neo-colonial economic structures and class contradictions are mutually reinforcing; inseparable. They do not have a unilateral cause–effect relationship – rather they have *dialectical* and *historical* relationship. It is for this reason that the struggle against imperialism is at the same time, a class struggle; in fact, in two senses: (1) as a part of the *world-wide class struggle* in so far as the breaking away of every territorial unit from the world capitalist system is a blow to the system and to its defenders, the international bourgeoisie with its allies the local dependent bourgeoisie; (2) as a *territorial class struggle* in so far as it is aimed at smashing the *territorial capitalist* system and therefore directed against its defenders, the local dependent bourgeoisies and their ally, the international bourgeoisie.[57]

It is wrong and misleading to talk in terms of the international struggle being between the 'proletarian nations'[58] and the bourgeois nations; between the 'Rich North' and the 'Poor South'; between the whites and the non-whites ('a world-wide conflict of races'[59]) – or simply as the struggle being 'anti-imperialist'.[60] It is always necessary to penetrate the surface and look at the substance of the struggle.

To come back to the 'bureaucratic bourgeoisie': When discussing the

---

[57] There is a third sense of the international class struggle – i.e. between the 'World Socialist System' and the 'World Capitalist System'. I do not think that this is its most important sense. In so far as there is such a struggle to prevent the expansion of the socialist system, the theatre of the struggle is the 'third world' and therefore covered by my sense (1) in the text. Direct confrontation between the two systems – mainly verbal exchanges and 'economic competition' – governed by the rules of 'peaceful co-existence' should not therefore be made the *only* or even the most important sense of the international class struggle. Secondly, there is a long-term potential danger in conceptualizing the international class struggle as between the two existing *Systems*. Since, the existing 'socialist' countries themselves are in a transition stage between capitalism and socialism, there is a constant danger of some of them (due to their specific contradictions) slipping back, eventually developing their ruling classes and even allying with the international bourgeoisie. So long as there is no world socialism, this danger should not be discounted.

Incidentally, none of these senses imply that there should be a *simultaneous* world revolution or a world war. That is nonsensical! The first time I came across such a notion was in Szentes's Paper ('*Status quo* and *socialism*'), who attributes it to 'those who put the *status quo* into the centre of their analysis'!

The problem, however, is that the advocates of 'peaceful co-existence' invariably hinder the revolutionary activities of the 'third world' people with the threat of a world war. The threat of the 'third world war' has become their pet argument against the revolutionary activities of the oppressed people.

For T. Szentes's paper, see *The silent class struggle*, (Dar es Salaam: Tanzania Publishing Houe, 1973).

[58] See the way in which Dia uses this notion in his book, *The African nations and world solidarity*.

[59] The sub-title of Ronald Segal's book, *The race war* (London: Penguin, 1967).

[60] Anti-imperialism itself needs to be concretely defined and analysed, otherwise the verbal condemnations of imperialism and neo-colonialism by the Emperor of Ethiopia and the Shah of Iran would all pass under the label 'anti-imperialist'!

petty bourgeoisie in Part Two, we mentioned its different divisions. Since the time of independence, the petty bourgeoisie, as would be expected, has expanded, with the internal differentiation becoming more varied. This may be roughly represented as in Chart II.

The chart on page 88 is admittedly a very rough indication of differentiation among the petty bourgeoisie. A more precise one would have to be supported by quantitative data. Nevertheless, it is sufficient for our purposes, various overlappings between the different categories notwithstanding. But a brief mention of the criteria that are implied in (1) marking off the petty bourgeoisie from the other classes and (2) intra-class divisions, is appropriate. These may be grouped as follows though not in terms of their importance:

(a) income; (b) education;
(c) standard of living and life-style (the urban milieu);
(d) control of or potentially effective participation in the decision-making bodies;
(e) the role occupied in the production process;
(f) control of or proximity to state apparatuses.

These criteria are interlinked,[61] reinforcing each other, and sometimes inseparable, for example, (d) and (f). However, the last one needs special emphasis, and will be discussed in connection with the 'bureaucratic bourgeoisie'.

Standard of living and life-style of the petty bourgeoisie – especially its upper echelons – are very much part of the 'urban milieu'. Urban-rural divisions in underdeveloped countries are not merely geographical or economic but inform the whole superstructure of social values, mores, and patterns of consumption. It is primarily for this reason that, for instance, a well-to-do peasant at the same income level as a member of the petty bourgeoisie, cannot easily be integrated with the differentiation of the petty bourgeoisie. In any case, such a peasant, given his income and mobility, eventually forges links with firstly the urban economic activities (transport, ownership of a bar or a hotel, a house in 'town', etc.) and later urban 'culture' and life-style. In this case, he would fall within our 'farmer' category. Secondly, for the reason that state power is made the centre of our class analysis and given the historical fact of pre-ponderant domination of the urban-based petty bourgeoisie in the *Uhuru* struggle and the post-*Uhuru* rule in Tanzania, it appears more useful to first analyse separately the intra-petty bourgeois and intra-

---

[61] A machine-operator, involved fully in the production process (a *productive* worker), may be earning as much as or probably more than a clerk (*unproductive* worker) coming close to the life-style and consumption pattern of the 'lower salariat' – the lower levels of the petty bourgeoisie. Should he therefore be included in the petty bourgeoisie? Undoubtedly, the Chart raises many such difficult questions for *precise* class demarcation. But such demarcation is not absolutely necessary for the analysis of class struggle. There are overlaps between classes and there are 'fringes' around the 'cores' of the classes. The problem therefore is statistical rather than political.

CHART 2

THE PETTY BOURGEOISIE

'BUREAUCRATIC BOUROISIE'	**POLITICO-ADMINISTRATIVE** ↑	political heads of government ministries and departments (central and local) and their top civil servants; heads and top functionaries in the judiciary, police and security; and the top leadership of the party.
	↓ **ECONOMIC***	heads and higher functionaries of parastatals, public corporations, and other quasi-economic, either state-run or state-supervised institutions (co-operatives, marketing boards, higher educational institutions, included).
	MILITARY	top military officers (majors, colonels, captains, and lieutenants).
UPPER SECTOR	**GENERAL INTELLIGENTSIA**	intellectuals, teachers, higher civil servants, professionals;
	OTHERS	prosperous traders, farmers, transporters, businessmen, executives in private firms, etc.
MIDDLE SECTOR		middle-level government and parastatal salariat; middle level salariat in the private sector; teachers; urbanized rich farmers; soldiers; police and other security cadres and middle-level bureaucracy of the Party.
LOWER SECTOR		small shop-keepers; self-employed craftsmen including mechanics, tailors, shoemakers, etc.; lower salariat in the tertiary sector and generally the lower grades of the salariat.†

* The term 'economic bureaucracy' was used for this category in *The silent class struggle*.

† It is very much in the *formal* sense that this category is included under the petty bourgeoisie, otherwise for all practical purposes the 'lower level' is much closer to workers.

peasantry differentiations and then try to investigate any linkages between them – similarity in political behaviour, control over the state power, etc. Therefore, in my opinion, indiscriminate assimilating of the peasant differentiation within the petty bourgeois differentiation without clarification and qualification, could be misleading and *politically* not very useful. Furthermore, peasant differentiation is a very concrete question and needs to be investigated in different parts of the country before generalization can be made at the national level.[62]

The various sections of the 'bureaucratic bourgeoisie' are self-explanatory. What must be emphasized is the inter- links- familial, marriage and cultural – among these three sections. In fact, the politico-administrative and economic sections are marked by considerable identity of the top personnel. The first appointments to the leaderships of the parastatals were invariably from the government top ranks. Ministers, principal secretaries, etc., sit on the boards of directors of the various parastatals and a small group of the members of the 'bureaucratic bourgeoisie' share among themselves a large number of directorships of the parastatals and even government posts.

This is illustrated below in the case of a few principal secretaries of some government ministries and departments.[63]

MINISTRY   PARASTATAL POSTS HELD ON 22 APRIL 1971

	Directorships (or representatives)	Chairmanship	Total
1. CENTRAL ESTABLISHMENT (Mr D. A. Mwakosya)	13	3	16
2. COMMERCE (Mr O. M. Katikaza)	17	10	27
3. TREASURY (Mr C. D. Msuya)	24	–	24
4. NATURAL RESOURCES (Mr G. J. Kileo)	6	2	8
5. RURAL DEVELOPMENT (Mr A. Mushi)	6	–	6
6. LANDS (Mr E. P. Mwaluko)	8	–	8
7. DEVPLAN (Mr E. A. Mulokozi)	8	10	18
8. EDUCATION (Mr J. D. Maganga)	1	1	2
9. COMWORKS (Mr I. A. Kaduma)	6	–	6
	89	26	115

(* Boards and Committees not directly dealing with the economy are excluded but Marketing Boards are included.)

[62] See infra p. 111 for the discussion of the peasant differentiation.
[63] *Hansard*, 22 April 1971.

Thus nine principal secretaries shared among themselves 89 director-ships and 26 chairmanships, in all 115 top posts in the parastatals. On average therefore each one of them had 13 leadership posts in the parastatals.

These links considerably minimize the internal contradictions between those running the state and those running the economy. It also gives – besides the sharing of common cultural and social values and educa-tional backgrounds – a close identity of interests[64] to the different sections of the 'bureaucratic bourgeoisie' and a self-identification with the system itself.

Recruitment of the new members of the 'bureaucratic bourgeoisie' from the upper sector of the petty bourgeoisie, overlapping in terms of functions and closer cultural and social ties (and involvement in the private business regardless of the leadership code) mean that there is a very close integration between the 'bureaucratic bourgeoisie' and the upper sector of the petty bourgeoisie. This marks off the last two sectors of the petty bourgeoisie. Although in the early days of independence higher bureaucrats were recruited more from the last two sectors, with the increasing saturation of the high bureaucratic jobs, this has dimin-ished drastically. The relative privileges, political power (in terms of decision-making), institutional control – all resulting in bureaucratic arrogance – have given rise to *important contradictions between the 'bureaucratic bourgeoisie' and the upper sector of the petty bourgeoisie on the one hand, and the lower sectors (middle and lower in the chart on page 88)* on the other. One of the manifestations of these contradictions has been the widespread student unrest in the secondary schools.[65] At the University the contradictions exploded in 1971 with the boycott of lectures which led to the use of the paramilitary Field Force Unit and the rustication of the student leader, Mr Akivaga.[66]

[64] It is necessary to point out that this observation does not fully apply to the inter-links with the military – which are, to date, mostly familial. Given the professional nature of the army, and its youthfulness, such links have not yet developed. We have as yet to get the first group of retired army officers, who would then be avail-able for political and economic leadership. With recent changes in the army this appears to be happening already: The Major-General of the army was appointed Minister of Culture and its Chief of Staff was appointed the General Manager of the Sugar Development Corporation. See the *Daily News*, 12 February 1974.

[65] cf. Karim Hirji, 'School education and underdevelopment in Tanzania', *Maji Maji*, op. cit., No. 12 (September 1973). See also 'Crisis at Pugu School', by A Sixth Former, *Maji Maji*, No. 4.

The following extract from a letter by a student of the Njombe Secondary School describes the typical way in which the authoritarian bureaucracy reacted:

(After some conflict with the teachers) . . . pupils were ordered to have a shower while in school uniform then commanded to roll on gravel or clay soil, then forced to enter the class without changing clothes. The barbarity they also launched was to beat pupils with clubs on any parts of their bodies.'

(*Daily News*, Letter to the Peoples' Forum, 5 February 1973. Quoted in K. Hirji, op. cit., p. 22).

[66] For the whole episode see 'The University Echo', the news bulletin published

Students as such do not belong to any social class (since they do not participate in the production process) but are in preparation to join one. However, in a neo-colonial African situation, an educational certificate is invariably a licence to join the petty bourgeoisie. The question before an ex-secondary school or an ex-University graduate therefore is: Which sector of the petty bourgeoisie? The incumbents of the high-level posts in the state and economic bureaucracy are relatively young people. Therefore, the natural process of upward mobility for a University graduate to fill the top posts is rather slow. On the other hand, given the neo-colonial nature of the economy, there is a limit to the extent of expansion of the 'bureaucratic bourgeoisie', the proliferation of the public corporations notwithstanding. Thus a fresh University graduate finds that his middle-level civil service or parastatal job falls far short of his aspirations. In contrast, he finds his 'boss', who probably does not have as good qualifications, occupying the top post perhaps because he participated in the independence struggle – enjoying the 'fruits of independence'! Hence considerable potential hostility on the part of the students towards the members of the 'bureaucratic bourgeoisie'.

It was such potential hostility that the leadership of Akivaga, the president of the University Students' Union, made actual in 1971 by using the left anti-bureaucracy slogans. Though students do not belong to any class as such they may adhere to a particular class ideological position: this, in the large majority of cases, is petty bourgeois. In the university incidents it was therefore this ideological position that finally triumphed. In fact within a matter of some nine to twelve months, the student mass had swerved from the left to the extreme right. In December 1972, the re-elected, but now extremely moderate Akivaga, was overthrown on the basis of national-chauvinistic slogans.

The best post-mortem of the so-called students' struggle was done by none other than the workers themselves. Reminding the students of their past mistakes the workers said: 'In the University crisis of 1971 which resulted in the rustication of the students' leader . . . one of the most important things that the radical students did was to shout in the name of workers and peasants. But not a single worker answered their call even though some of us – the workers – were fighting against the same enemy. The principal reason of this has been that this institution of higher learning in Tanzania, a country which is trying to build *Ujamaa*, has continued to be the vehicle of neo-colonialism. Can these radical students really claim that this was due to the refusal to co-operate on the part of the workers and peasants? No, not at all. It could not have been possible for the workers and peasants . . . to co-operate when the students discriminate against workers and think that they are a separate class with different interests; especially when the students themselves did not

by the Dar es Salaam Students' Organization: Particularly the following Special Issues, 16 July 1971; 4 August 1971 and 21 August 1971.

see any need to co-ordinate their struggle with that of their allies – workers and peasants.'[67]

The secondary contradiction between the students and the 'bureaucratic bourgeoisie' may have been eased lately to some extent through the recent decentralization measures affecting both the state and the parastatal organizations.[68] A number of fresh graduates have found themselves in high-level positions of the Regional and District bureaucracy, with its attendant high salaries and privileges.

But this is only a temporary palliative: the contradiction may have been eased but it is far from resolved.

The position of the ex-secondary school students is rather different. An ex-Form IV student finds himself in the lower sector of the petty bourgeoisie with a salary not very different from that of a minimum wage-earner. On top of such 'bleak' future prospects he is also a victim of a very authoritarian and inefficient school system. Lack of qualified teaching staff, lack of equipment and other facilities are constant complaints from the schools. In recent years the rate of failure in the Forms IV and VI National Examinations have been astoundingly high, as shown in the Table on page 93.

This has resulted in real discontent and frustration on the part of the secondary school students. This is the contradiction which cannot easily be eased without radical overhaul of the whole educational system which is in any case inseparable from the whole question of neo-colonial structures.

These secondary contradictions make the lower sectors of the petty bourgeoisie one of the most volatile sections. Given its instability and unreliability it can easily provide a social base for reactionary forces. But at the same time, if led by a correct ideology, it can become a most useful ally of the exploited classes.

The further development of these contradictions is tied up with the development of the 'bureaucratic bourgeoisie' and the workers' struggles.

In analysing a process which is still going on, one can only talk about trends. We have indicated a strong trend towards the formation of the 'bureaucratic bourgeoisie', which was consolidated particularly with the 1967 nationalizations. This has been possible in Tanzania (as contrasted

[67] 'Workers call for unity', *Maji Maji*, No. 14 (February 1974).

[68] The decentralization measures create District and Regional Development teams consisting of Planning, Financial, and Personnel Officers, together with 8 Functional officers led by District and Regional Development Directors. 'This means that we shall have in each District and in each Region an organization like the existing organization of central Government in Dar es Salaam.' (President Nyerere's Speech on 'Decentralization', May 1972, p. 5.)

The State Trading Corporation, a commercial parastatal has now been decentralized into some 18 regional companies and its various Departments too have been turned into independent companies – all these companies with their usual paraphernalia of directors, managers, etc.

TABLE 4

RATE OF FAILURES IN FORM IV AND FORM VI NATIONAL EXAMINATIONS

(a) FORM IV SUBJECTS	EACE*	(*in percentages*) NATIONAL EXAMINATIONS	
	1969	1972	1973
Political Education	–	13·6	23·7
History	59·0	25·1	39·2
Geography	36·7	19·9	38·9
English Language	35·2	15·8	20·4
Kiswahili	23·8	21·9	16·6
Mathematics (modern)	52·4	65·8	79·4
Mathematics (traditional)	41·4	74·4	79·8
Biology	34·2	44·3	38·1
Chemistry	14·7	61·1	53·3
Physics (syllabus N)	20·7	61·3	51·6

(b) FORM VI SUBJECTS	EACE*	(*in percentages*) NATIONAL EXAMINATIONS	
	1969	1972	1973
		(*Failures + subsidiary combined*)	
History	41·3	65·8	65·3
Geography	50·8	51·7	62·1
Economics	46·7	73·0	89·7
Mathematics	46·9	40·0	66·1
Physics	68·2	33·8	44·3
Chemistry	70·1	55·6	58·0
Biology	69·1	46·5	49·9

* (EACE = East African Certificate of Education).
Source: Institute of Education Teachers' Seminar, April 1974.

with, say, Kenya) because of the relative weakness of the petty bourgeoisie as a class, which has made its ruling section relatively powerful. However, we cannot say that the 'bureaucratic bourgeoisie' as a class is an accomplished fact. In fact it still faces resistance and opposition from the various sectors of the petty bourgeoisie who would like least interference of the state and straight 'private' enterprise system. These sectors may be said to be on the right of the 'bureaucratic bourgeoisie' with possible connections with the right wing of the 'bureaucratic bourgeoisie' itself and may be even supported by the racist sub-imperialist and colonial powers.

The development of the 'bureaucratic bourgeoisie' is a dialectical process. Its further consolidation gives rise to intense contradictions which will dominate future struggles and determine the movement of this bourgeoisie. All development is contradictory and the development of the 'bureaucratic bourgeoisie' is no less subject to this as will become clear in the subsequent discussion of the *Mwongozo*. However, for the purpose of understanding immediate contradictions and their movement, it is important to identify the conditions of reproduction of this class. All these conditions may not be fully developed indicating that the 'bureaucratic bourgeoisie' itself is not yet a fully-fledged class.

8.3.1 *Conditions of reproduction*

Political control of the state apparatus is one of the most important conditions for the continued existence and reproduction of the 'bureaucratic bourgeoisie' especially in the initial stages when its grip over the economy has not yet been fully established. It is not necessary to elaborate on this as we fully discussed the central role of the state power in the very rise of the 'bureaucratic bourgeoisie' and in the class struggle with the commercial bourgeoisie.

The class control of the neo-colonial territorial economy through the state is the second important condition of its reproduction. [Private control of the economy in an underdeveloped African country (Cf. Kenya) is a condition for the existence and reproduction of the petty bourgeoisie, which would be a ruling class in the classical sense of the word, in which case there would be no need to identify separately the 'bureaucratic bourgeoisie'.] It is the state ownership of the means of production which distinguishes a neo-colony of the 'bureaucratic capitalist' type from the 'neo-colony *par excellence*' – to use the terminology of *The silent class struggle*.[69]

The third condition is the continued reproduction of the system of underdevelopment within the world-wide capitalist system. For this is what makes the 'bureaucratic bourgeoisie' both a *dependent* – and at the same time a bourgeoisie. Without that, it would either be a full-blown national bourgeoisie or merely a *bureaucracy*, in the strict sense of that word. There is no need to stress that the reproduction of the class and the reproduction of the structures are interlinked, mutually reinforcing and inseparable.

In so far as the neo-colonial economy is basically a capitalist economy, it obeys its fundamental laws of motion, one of which is the accumulation of capital, the driving force of capitalism. A large part of the actual

[69] I do not think Szentes, in his discussion of 'State Capitalism' in his comment on my paper, introduces radical innovations to make me reject this terminology. Impliedly, Szentes appears to assume that state capitalism, by definition, is anti-imperialist in the sense of being against the world capitalist system. This is precisely not the case as was argued in my paper. When coming to the analysis of state capitalism, concretely in the 'third world' countries, Szentes wants to forget their being part of the world capitalist system and therefore neo-colonies. This is unacceptable. The world capitalist system provides a panorama, and the concrete analysis of state capitalism of a country which is part of it, cannot be done separately from it.

accumulation takes place in the imperialist metropolis from the surplus[70] drained from the neo-colony. Irrespective of the *character* and the sectoral distribution of the capital accumulated in the neo-colony, accumulation is necessary for the system to reproduce itself. In a situation of 'bureaucratic capitalism', it is not the 'bureaucratic bourgeoisie', which does private accumulation, but the state. Thus the function of accumulation is carried on by the state and state institutions; the 'bureaucratic bourgeoisie' only does the consumption! This may be one of the factors, among others, responsible for the conspicuous consumption, lack of thrift and zeal of saving among the members of the 'bureaucratic bourgeoisie'.

The accumulation of capital by the state is an important characteristic of this system. But it demands a restraint on the part of the 'bureaucratic bourgeois' class in terms of consumption so that the state may be left with enough for accumulation. Secondly, the individual members of the class cannot be allowed to accumulate because it is the function of the state to accumulate on behalf of the *class as a whole*. The 'leadership code' was objectively a recognition of precisely this fact. It placed a restraint· on the part of the individual members of the 'bureaucratic bourgeoisie' not to compete with the state in the function of accumulation. The leaders as defined are not allowed to have two incomes which means they cannot participate in any private business. The only income they can have is their official salary. This does not mean that the Code has been very successful. It shows that it takes a long time before the individual members of a class can evolve and internalize an ideology (in this case not to compete with the state) in the long-term interests of its class. Thus there have been numerous breaches of the Code and a number of leaders continue to participate in private business (transport, for instance). Of course, they cannot do this openly because of the Code. They have to employ all sorts of indirect means.

Apart from the important conditions of reproduction of the 'bureaucratic bourgeoisie' mentioned above, we may note other subsidiary

[70] In a situation obtaining in Tanzania where parastatals and public companies go into partnership with private foreign capital, the drained surplus may take varied *forms*, besides profits and dividends: management and technical assistance fees; payment of royalties; over-invoicing; unfavourable 'terms of trade' between the Tanzanian subsidiary and its foreign parent based 'in the metropolis, and so on.

The surplus of the parastatals and the public companies, on the other hand, takes the characteristic form of the balance sheet profits. The surplus so realized is under the control of the Board of Directors of such companies – i.e. the economic section of the 'bureaucratic bourgeoisie', who decide on its utilization within, of course, the limits imposed by the neo-colonial socio-economic system.

It will be realized that besides the typical criteria of the 'form' of surplus and the 'manner of its disposal', we make the *class character of the state* part (even a decisive part) of the *differentia specifica* of a system. Actually, these are interlinked and should not be separated. cf. The exchange of letters between Sweezy and Bettelheim, *On transition . . .*, op. cit.

conditions deriving from them. As a result of the historical circumstances under which the 'bureaucratic bourgeoisie' developed and its current domination of the state, and high income levels, it is the members of this class who disproportionately benefit from various services – education, medical facilities,[71] etc. The educational system, through its examination system, urban location of schools, entry qualifications, etc., is heavily biased in favour of the petty bourgeoisie, especially the upper echelons. The common background helps in sharing common values; values which are further reinforced at exclusive social gatherings and parties, attendance at the same bars and hotels and, most important of all, sharing exclusive residential areas,[72] formerly occupied by the colonial representatives. Admittedly, these things look insignificant when compared to the age-old exclusive social and cultural class-institutions of the bourgeoisies of the developed countries. But then the 'bureaucratic bourgeoisie' has neither the historical past nor the present capability of the European and North American bourgeoisies. Even as a class it is a *caricature* of the developed bourgeoisie, and this is reflected in its ideology and institutions.

Finally, there appears to be some trend, though by no means conclusive until some empirical evidence is collected, towards 'endogamous' marriages within the 'bureaucratic bourgeoisie' and the upper sector of the petty bourgeoisie. It is not, however, uncommon that one of the partners – usually the female – is from the 'middle' or 'lower' sectors of the petty bourgeoisie (but, rarely, I believe, from the workers or peasant classes) in which case the marriage itself acts as a channel for 'instant' upward mobility for the female partner.

8.3.2   The ideology of the 'bureaucratic bourgeoisie'?

The 'bureaucratic bourgeoisie' being very much in the process of formation, it has hardly evolved any distinct ideology. Nor can it really have any independent ideology given that its very material base is a dependent one. Thus its basic political ideology is petty bourgeois. However, its approach and method of work are so much characterized by bureaucratic decision-making and technocratic implementation that these may be said to be the particular features of the 'ideology' of the emerging 'bureaucratic bourgeoisie'.

In this 'ideology' the problems are seen as the problems of administering things rather than *involvement* of the people. Decision-making is

[71] cf. M. Segal's article on 'The politics of health in Tanzania', in Uchumi Editorial Board, *Towards socialist planning* (Dar es Salaam: Tanzania Publishing House, 1972).

[72] Estate development by NHC's (National Housing Corporation) (parastatal) associate, NEDCO in Oyster Bay, Msasani, Kurasini, Kinondoni etc., is a good example. These are all built under the pretext of providing houses for 'workers'. How many workers can afford to buy sh. 38 000 houses and how many of them earning a minimum of sh. 380 or so per month will be given loans to buy these houses, are questions that only NHC can answer.

typically a process of movement of files and orders through the hierarchy of officials. In the absence of a national bourgeoisie, even the notions of bourgeois democracy do not exist. The bureaucratic method of decision-making finds its counterpart in the technocratic method of implementing the decisions so made. Again the problems of implementation are seen as technical problems: in terms of correct 'expert advice', 'efficient' organization and 'planning' of *things* and use of qualified manpower. People are just another statistic in the plan who should implement the instructions.

This is very well illustrated in Tschannerl's study[73] of the rural water-supply programmes in Tanzania. As he notes:

> The staff of the Water Ministry tends to have a technocratic and bureaucratic attitude, putting primary emphasis on the establishment of technically sound structures, rather than close co-operation with the peasants.
> The *peasants' participation* in the creation of a scheme is very limited. Projects are designed, constructed, and maintained by the engineers and technicians of the water department. Some consultation with the peasants (mostly with the local leaders) usually takes place at the planning stage, but the staff maintains control over all phases of the scheme, from early planning to maintenance. Self-help, where it has taken place in the past, was nearly always limited to a contribution of free labour under the supervision of the water department staff.[74]

The transformation of the people themselves through struggle, in the eyes of these qualified 'experts' would be 'politics' unnecessarily interfering with their work: probably even a 'constraint' hindering development.

Thus the bureaucratic method of decision-making and the technocratic method of implementing are two sides of the same coin. They in fact reflect in ideology the very material conditions of reproduction of the 'bureaucratic bourgeoisie': The control of the state, on the one hand, and the state control of the economy, on the other.

The dependent and underdeveloped nature of the class is reflected in the fact that, in practice, despite its 'ideology', there is neither bureaucratic efficiency nor sound technocratic expertise. This 'ideology' is false consciousness *par excellence*!

---

[73] G. Tschannerl, 'Rural water-supply in Tanzania: Is "politics" or "technique" in command?'. Paper presented to the Annual Social Science Conference of the East African Universities, 1973.

[74] ibid., pp. 4–5.

8.4 CONCLUSION:
THE PROGRESSIVE NATURE OF
THE 'BUREAUCRATIC BOURGEOISIE'

Politically, the 'bureaucratic bourgeoisie' has played and, to some extent, continues to play a progressive role.* We may briefly mention some of the important areas where it clearly played a politically progressive role.

Firstly: the very class struggle between the petty bourgeoisie (led by the 'bureaucratic bourgeoisie') and the commercial bourgeoisie was not only inevitable but historically necessary as much as political independence was necessary for the conduct of this class struggle. In a way, this struggle is helping to clear the way for further struggles unencumbered by the obfuscation of the racial divisions. Thus the liquidation of the inherited *racial* structures was *conditio sine qua non* for 'purifying' the class struggles. The adoption of non-racial ideology for this struggle was in itself a contribution towards the process notwithstanding the fact that it has now and again surfaced here and there.[75]

Secondly, the most important role played by the 'bureaucratic bourgeoisie' has been in the sphere of ideology. The vigorous 'anti-imperialism' (defined and explained supra p. 65) and support for the liberation movements have had their effects on the internal dynamics of the country. The very question of the meaning of anti-imperialism and the discussion of its scientific nature within Tanzania are a by-product of the official 'anti-imperialism' – at anti-colonial and foreign policy levels.

Thirdly, the historical necessity for expanding the 'public sector' through the Arusha Declaration put socialism on the agenda for the first time in a concrete way. Discussion and debates about socialism are bound to contribute to the consciousness of the people. Bureaucratic ideological obscurantism notwithstanding, the workers and peasants and conscious elements in their own practical way have not been slow to point out inconsistencies. This has considerably limited the area of the freedom of action of the 'bureaucratic bourgeoisie' even if only for the purposes of good 'public relations'.

---

* 'Progressive' only in the *political* sense within the context of the concrete conditions in Tanzania, but not in the epochal sense. For at the epochal level it is only the proletariat which is the progressive class in the present era.

[75] With the disintegration of the commercial bourgeoisie the objective-material base for a racial ideology is considerably weakened. Since these processes cannot be instant and are bound to be drawn out, it would be unrealistic to dismiss completely the possibility of the racial ideology intensifying occasionally before its final death. In a long-term perspective, the very disintegration of the commercial bourgeoisie – the physical running away, and the export of resources, etc. – may give temporary credence to racial prejudices.

The leadership code, too, has acted as a brake on the members of the 'bureaucratic bourgeoisie' to conduct some of their anti-Arusha activities *openly*. This may have other implications, however: what cannot be conducted *privately* may be increasingly conducted *publicly* through the state institutions. This is reflected in the 'conspicuous consumption' of the State itself: state parties and celebrations; posh parastatal residential estates and headquarters; increasing use of public vehicles for private use; large number of big delegations leaving almost every day to represent Tanzania at all sorts of conferences. This appears to have, more than adequately, substituted for private holidaying abroad.

Whatever progressive role this class may have played politically at a particular juncture it is being fast exhausted as the contradictions with the exploited classes, the workers and peasants, intensify. It is the development of these contradictions that we discuss in the next two parts.

PART FOUR

Ujamaa Vijijini and Class Struggle

Outside the class struggle, socialism is either a hollow phrase or a naïve dream.   LENIN

NINE

Ujamaa Vijijini *without Cadres and Class Struggle: the Dilemma of Metaphysics*

9.1 THE POLICY AND THE ECONOMIC RATIONALE

Ujamaa Vijijini, the policy which was adopted together with the Arusha Declaration for rural development, is the successor of the villagization programme that was put into effect immediately after independence. The economic rationale justifying the villagization scheme assumed the problems of agriculture to be mainly twofold:

(1) Scattered living and therefore difficulties of providing expert agricultural advice and other services;
(2) Low level of technology and the dominant use of the 'traditional' methods of cultivation resulting in low productivity.

In his Presidential Inaugural address, President Nyerere put it thus:

The first and absolutely essential thing to do, therefore, if we want to be able to start using tractors for cultivation, is to begin living in proper villages. So if you ask me what our Government is planning to do during the next few years the answer is simple. For the next few years Government will be doing all it can to enable the farmers of Tanganyika to come together in village communities. And if you ask me why Government wants us to live in villages, the answer is just as simple: unless we do we shall not be able to provide ourselves with the things we need to develop our land and to raise our standard of living.[1]

The strategy that was adopted for agricultural development was divided into the 'improvement approach' and the 'transformation approach'. These 'approaches' had in fact been pushed by the colonial government as well. The improvement approach was supposed to raise progressively the productivity of the peasant by improving his methods of crop and animal husbandry 'without any radical

---

[1] *Hansard*, 10 December 1962. Reprinted in his *Freedom and unity*, op. cit., pp. 183–4.

changes in traditional social and legal systems'.[2] The transformation approach on the other hand meant selecting a few areas and concentrating resources for intensive production with 'modern' methods.

The implicit aim behind the whole strategy was of course to raise production for the world market. Thus the question of the structure of the economy and its being part of the world capitalist system was not even raised, let alone challenged.

The economic rationale and the aim behind the villagization programme, which utterly failed,[3] are also the implied assumptions of the policy of *Ujamaa Vijijini*, albeit in a radically different ideological framework. The policy paper 'Socialism and Rural Development'[4] makes no global analysis of Tanzania's economy and its integration in the world capitalist economy. It only sees a 'slight' threat in the 'embryonic' agriculture capitalism which it hopes can be arrested by the development of the Ujamaa Villages. That, what appears to be an 'embryonic' capitalism is in fact not embryonic at all but an *under-developed* one, cannot be grasped within the analysis of the policy paper given its complete lack of understanding of capitalism as a system. *Ujamaa Vijijini*, therefore, is not conceived as part of an overall strategy to transform the *colonial, vertically integrated economy* (see Chart I p. 35) to a *nationally integrated economy* (see Chart III p. 105). Thus even if the Ujamaa programme raises the *volume* of production of the primary crops, this in the long run does not help for *inter alia*, the terms of trade have been deteriorating drastically. For instance, Tanzania's exports in 1964 amounted to 1600 million shillings, and in 1971 1988 million shillings. But owing to the rising import prices what Tanzania could buy in 1971 was less than 1600 million (1590) shillings-worth of goods.[5] Thus even if the primary producers *run*, they can never catch up with the rich countries because the latter are neither *walking* nor running, but flying!

Low level of the productive forces in the agriculture sector too cannot be remedied by the *Ujamaa Vijijini* strategy alone. Productivity whether in the industrial or agriculture sector, is basically the function of the level of *industrial* development. In absence of an industrial sector providing the requirements (producer goods and consumer necessities) of the agriculture sector, the productivity in agriculture is not likely to rise substantially. The policy paper says hardly anything about a programme for simultaneous industrial development and of course nothing about

[2] The First Five Year Development Plan, p. 21.

[3] For a more detailed discussion see H. Mapolu, *The social and economic organization of Ujamaa villages*, M.A. Thesis presented to the University of Dar es Salaam, September 1973.

[4] (Dar es Salaam: Government Printer, 1967).

[5] Figures cited by John Loxley in a lecture to the TANU Youth League Ideological Class, University of Dar es Salaam.

CHART II

NATIONALLY INTEGRATED ECONOMY

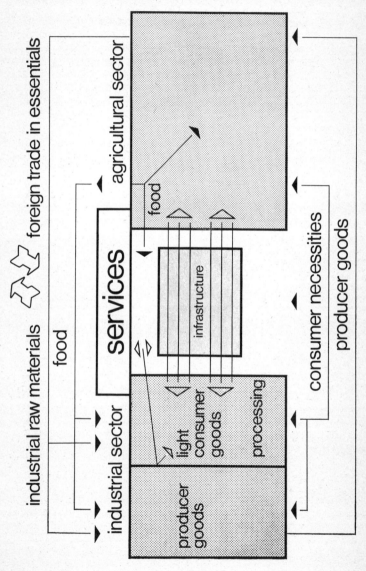

agricultural sector

foreign trade in essentials

food

services

infrastructure

industrial raw materials

food

consumer necessities

producer goods

industrial sector

light consumer goods

processing

producer goods

the *type* of industrial development. In fact, the policy paper sees Tanzanian socialism as being 'firmly based on the land and its workers' (p. 10). Elsewhere the paper asserts: 'it should not be our purpose to convert our peasants into wage-earners . . .' (p. 15). But then the *reproduction* of agriculture as the dominant economic sector and the peasantry as the numerically dominant class is precisely one of the most marked characteristics of underdevelopment. It is a well-known fact that the process of development – both in the capitalist and socialist countries – was accompanied by the increasing preponderance of the industrial sector and the working class. This is illustrated in the case of some 'socialist' countries in the table below:

TABLE 5

*CHANGING AGRICULTURE STRUCTURE
IN SOME SOCIALIST COUNTRIES*

COUNTRY	NATIONAL INCOME				LABOUR FORCE			
	% Industry		% Agriculture		% Industry		% Agriculture	
	1950	1969	1950	1969	1950	1969	1950	1969
Bulgaria	36·8	50·4	42·1	24·4	11·4	37·9	79·5	37·6
Hungary	48·6	43·6	24·9	20·5	23·3	41·2	50·6	29·1
GDR	47·0	60·7	28·4	11·6	43·7	50·0	27·3	13·3
Poland	37·1	53·4	40·1	19·2	26·2	35·1	54·0	37·4
Rumania	43·4	56·6	27·3	24·4	14·2	29·2	74·3	51·2
USSR	57·5	54·6	28·8	19·7	27·5	36·4	47·6	28·7
CSSR	62·5	60·7	16·2	13·3	36·3	46·4	38·6	18·8

Source: H. J. Wienhold 'On socialist transformation of agriculture', (mimeo.).

But then the very policy of *Ujamaa Vijijini* reflects its petty bourgeois class character. As Mapolu has put it:

. . . [I]t has always been a characteristic of petty bourgeois socialists that industry and the proletarian class are feared like the plague. The nineteenth-century utopian socialists in Europe actually argued for the dismantlement of industrial organization so as to fit into their conception of small scale co-operative units. Again, such notions are most reactionary for they seek to move history backwards: historical trends are inevitably towards the enlargement of scale and the concentration of resources.[6]

In sum, the objective effect of the *Ujamaa* policy, like its predecessor, the villagization programme, is to integrate the non-monetarized (or the so-called 'subsistence sector') within the cash economy. Given the overall

[6] *The social and economic organization of Ujamaa villages*, op. cit., p. 37.

neo-colonial structures of the territorial economy this means integration within the world capitalist system. Cliffe has noted that almost all existing ujamaa villages have been formed in what he calls 'marginal subsistence areas', that is areas which are as yet 'only marginally involved in the cash economy'.[7]

The integration of the economy within the world capitalist system was begun by colonialism though the extent to which this was done varied from country to country and even areas within the same country. Tanzania was one country where there remained large areas still outside the monetary economy, though not necessarily outside the system of underdevelopment as we argued in Part One. In this respect the function of the post-independence government has simply been to accelerate this process of monetarization,[8] and the attendant peasant differentiation. In this respect the *Ujamaa* rural policy is a continuation of the preceding agriculture policies. This continuity is not an accident but derives from the very class base of *Ujamaa*. A real transformation of agriculture as part of an overall strategy of disengagement from the world capitalist system and building of a nationally integrated economy is not simply a technical question of changing economic structures. Above everything else, it involves political struggle – class struggle against the internal and external classes with vested interests in maintaining and perpetuating the existing relations of production. *Ujamaa*, as would be expected, does not conceive the question as primarily a *political* question involving class struggle. This is amply illustrated by the way in which its implementation has been approached.

9.2 THE IMPLEMENTATION

Most studies[9] of the *Ujamaa* Villages done recently have consistently noted two important features with respect to its implementation:

[7] 'The policy of *Ujamaa Vijijini* and the class struggle in Tanzania', in Saul and Cliffe, *Socialism in Tanzania*, Vol. II, op. cit., p. 195.

[8] I am by no means advocating that large areas should be left out of the *cash* economy. The question is how should the integration be done. If the overall existing structures remain untouched, the integration takes place within the world capitalist system and is not necessarily a movement towards a nationally integrated economy.

[9] Among others see M. Von Freyhold, 'Rural development through *Ujamaa Vijijini*: questions of economic and technical strategies', (mimeo.); P. Raikes, '*Ujamaa Vijijini* and rural socialist development', Paper presented to the Annual Social Science Conference of the East African Universities, 1973; J. Sender, 'Some preliminary notes on the political economy of rural development in Tanzania, based on a case-study in the West Usambaras' (University of Dar es Salaam: Economic Research Bureau, 1973); M. J. Mbilinyi, 'The transition to capitalism in rural Tanzania' (University of Dar es Salaam: Dept of Education, 1974); J. Angwazi and B. Ndulu, 'Evaluation of Operation Rufiji, 1968' (University of Dar es Salaam: Bureau of Resource Assessment and Land use Planning, 1973);

(1) Complete lack of any analysis of the differentiation among the peasantry in the area concerned and which sections can be potentially mobilized to effect the programme and which sections are likely to oppose it.

(2) Bureaucratic (as opposed to democratic) and technocratic (as opposed to political) methods in implementing the programme.[10]

As noted earlier most ujamaa villages have been established in areas where there are no strong kulak elements. Thus, 'There has been a reluctance to face up to the necessity of confrontation with those elements who are already exploiting the labour of others.'[11] On the other hand, in a number of areas the rich peasants have managed to occupy leadership positions in the ujamaa village committees or forge links with the local bureaucracies thereby using ujamaa in their own interest.[12] In other areas, like Hanang, Kilimanjaro, and Mbulu Districts and the Usambaras, rich peasants have formed ujamaa villages on their own initiative as a method of getting more land and access to credit and other facilities provided by the government.[13]

It should hardly be surprising that the lack of a discriminatory attitude towards the different strata of the peasantry has only resulted in the control of the ujamaa villages by the rich peasants or the so-called government 'staff'. In either case the poor and the middle peasants remain politically dominated and economically exploited.

So far as the mobilization of the peasants to form the ujamaa villages is concerned, it is the bureaucratic and technocratic methods which have dominated. This is true even in areas where there is no substantial class of rich peasants. Freyhold notes outright use of force to move people into the ujamaa villages – 'ranging from threats to forced transport from old homes to short prison sentences under the pretext of tax arrears or minimum acreage violations'.[14] In other cases, the bureaucrats have typically held out government 'aid' as an incentive to the peasants to move into the villages.[15] Thus *Ujamaa* does not come to the exploited as a process of political struggle in which they themselves are involved but as something imposed from the above.

In the case of Ismani, Iringa Region, where Dr Klerru, the late Regional Commisioner (he was shot dead by a rich peasant) attempted

---

H. Mapolu, 'The social and economic organization of *Ujamaa* villages', op. cit.; H. U. E. Thoden Van Velzen, 'Staff, kulaks and peasants', in Saul and Cliffe, *Socialism in Tanzania*, Vol. II, op. cit., p. 153, A. Awiti, 'Class struggle in rural society of Tanzania', op. cit.

[10] In fact we discussed earlier that this appears to form the kernel of the 'ideology' of the 'bureaucratic bourgeoisie'. See *supra* p. 96.

[11] L. Cliffe, 'The policy of *Ujamaa Vijijini*. . . .', op. cit., 205.

[12] P. Raikes, '*Ujamaa Vijijini*. . . .', op. cit., p. 19.

[13] See P. Raikes, ibid., and J. Sender, 'Some preliminary notes . . .', op. cit.

[14] Quoted by M. Mbilinyi, 'The transition to capitalism . . .' op. cit., p. 35A.

[15] A. Awiti, 'Class struggle . . .', op. cit., p. 34.

to mobilize the peasants on the basis of struggle, Awiti notes that 'he did it only as a single person'. 'The rank and the file of the Party were not involved, in fact the majority of the high ranking officials opposed him for being radical. Secondly, the workers and peasants in a ward – people were not mobilized to struggle against the capitalist by themselves. For example, if they had difficulties of any sort, they had to send somebody to Iringa Town to ask the Regional Commissioner or the Area Commissioner what to do. In short, mobilization, though meant to implement socialism and self-reliance, did not seem to be a consciously planned political strategy aimed at transforming the whole foundation of the society.[16]

More or less similar observations are made by Angwazi and Ndulu in their study[17] of 'Operation Rufiji', which was initiated as some sort of an emergency project to resettle the people in villages on higher ground and later convert these villages into *Ujamaa* villages. The researchers noted the two important problems of the Rufiji villages to be:

> The second problem which hampers the execution of *Ujamaa* activities in these villages is the fact that in all these villages decision-making is bureaucratic. The leaders carry out the function of passing out orders from above. They attend district meetings which brief them with the development directives for the coming period, then they (top leadership) with the lower leadership sit and decide for the villagers (p. 17).
>
> The third but greatest problem of *Ujamaa* is the absence of political consciousness all the way from village leaders to the villagers (p. 18).

A planned political strategy 'aimed at transforming the whole foundation of the society', that Awiti talks about would involve political (class) struggle guided by the correct ideology and implemented by a party of politically committed, ideologically sound and trained ('red and expert') cadres. None of these preconditions is satisfied. In fact the rule of the 'bureaucratic bourgeoisie' ensures the failure of even a few individual good cadres and leaders. In any case, building of socialism is not a question of a few conscientious leaders, either. It is the question of class struggle. As Lenin puts it: 'Outside the class struggle, socialism is either a hollow phrase or a naïve dream.'[18]

But then dreaming about utopia has always been a classical preoccupation of the petty bourgeoisie!

· · · · ·

[16] ibid.

[17] 'Evaluation of Operation Rufiji . . l', op. cit.

[18] 'Socialism: petty bourgeois and proletarian' (Moscow: Foreign Languages Publishing House, n.d.). (This small pamphlet was written by Lenin in 1905 against the Narodniks who believed they could build socialism based on the peasant commune. In fact they considered the Russian peasant as the man of future in Russia.)

This brings us to the whole complex question of peasant differentiation and class struggle. A number of studies already cited have attempted to discuss the question of class struggle on land, so to speak. This is not an attempt to integrate them in any coherent form, though this is an urgent task requiring attention on its own. Nevertheless, in the ensuing section I shall offer a few thoughts on what appears to me to be a confusion over some basic theoretical issues.

TEN

Peasant Differentiation and Class Alliances: Some Thoughts

10.1 ON PEASANT DIFFERENTIATION

The introduction of cash crops to the Tanganyikan economy by colonialism set into motion the process of differentiation within the peasantry. While it is true that 'commercial agriculture for a territorial or international market offered new opportunities for inequality within African societies', as Iliffe[19] has noted, it must be remembered that commodity-production although a necessary condition for, is not in itself, *the* distinguishing feature of capitalist relations. As Bettelheim[20] has vigorously argued one must always investigate the class relations behind the market- or plan-forms to determine the nature of systems. Secondly, the commercial agriculture that was initiated and developed during colonialism (and even after independence) was part of the process of integration of the colonial economy into the metropolitan capitalist structures. In this fundamental respect the development of agrarian capitalism in Tanganyika has to be distinguished from the kind of capitalist development in the European countries that Marx described. This was not that youthful capitalism all out to destroy the pre-capitalist relations and set into motion an unprecedented development of the productive forces. It cannot be compared even to the development of agrarian capitalism in Russia, that Lenin welcomed. Both the internal structures of Russia and the international capitalist structures of that time are qualitatively different than what one finds in the underdeveloped countries today. In this regard, Marjorie Mbilinyi in her paper 'The transition to capitalism in rural Tanzania' (op. cit.), appears to accept too enthusiastically not only Lenin's method (which is a legitimate exercise) but even his *conclusions* about the progressive nature of agrarian capitalism in Tanzania.

[19] *Agricultural change in modern Tanganyika*, op. cit., p. 26.
[20] *On transition to socialism*, op. cit.

111

Capitalist development means the breaking down of traditional pre-capitalist relations of production and modes of production – is that a bad [sic!] thing? Most affirmatively, no (p. 47).

And in a footnote on commodity-exchange she says:

I would argue, however, that the development of commodity-exchange is a necessary step, on whatever basis [!], in the transformation of pre-capitalist production systems into capitalist *or* socialist ones (p. 49).

The problem with these statements is that they are 'lifted' above the very process of history and the stage of development of particular societies and turned into universal (ahistorical) truths: something which would have never occurred to either Marx or Lenin. As Lenin once put it: 'The whole spirit of Marxism, its whole system, demands that each proposition should be considered (*a*) only historically, (*b*) only in connection with others, (*c*) only in connection with the concrete experience of history.'[21]

Taken *historically* the development of capitalism and widespread commodity-exchange in the now developed capitalist countries was no doubt progressive both as opposed to the previous mode (feudalism) and because it revolutionized the very process of production thereby enabling the development of the productive forces by leaps and bounds. By an increase in the overall productivity it freed the labourer from the land to work in the factories: it proletarianized the peasantry. But this was (and is) precisely not the case in Africa because of the very *historical* situation under which capitalism came to Africa and the nature of its contemporary relations with the developed capitalist countries.

In many African and other 'third world' countries the so-called capitalist development has in fact meant the conservation of the old forms – in some cases feudal and semi-feudal – to serve the new ends. In a number of them, agrarian capitalism has in fact failed to 'free' labour from land in the classical sense, to any appreciable extent: rather it has resulted in greater pressures on land and disguised unemployment and underemployment. The following description by Sweezy still remains largely true:

Under the domination of imperialism, industrialisation advances very slowly, too slowly to absorb the steady flow of handicraft producers who are ruined by the competition of machine-made products from the factories of the advanced regions. The consequence is the swelling of the ranks of the peasantry, increased pressure on the land and the deterioration of the productivity and living standards of the agricultural masses who constitute by far the largest section of the colonial

[21] In a letter to Inessa Armand, 30 November 1916, reprinted in T. Deutscher, *Not by politics alone – the other Lenin* (London: George Allen & Unwin, 1973), p. 113.

populations. Imperialism thus creates economic problems in the colonies which it is unable to solve.[22]

As for the development of the productive forces it is well-known that colonialism thwarted and completely distorted this. This is seen in the low level of productivity so characteristic of the underdeveloped economies. In the case of Tanzania, Rweymamu observes that the suggestion that 'colonial imperialism was beneficial because it introduced new method of production . . . is not supported by available evidence. The acreage for cotton for example increased from 142 000 acres in 1945 to 582 000 in 1960. During the same period, cotton output rose from 7512 long tons to 34 241 long tons, thus revealing insignificant change in labour productivity during the period, if we assume a labour force rising proportionately to acreage.'[23]

Finally, in hardly any of the black African countries can it be said that a genuine independent rural bourgeoisie has developed. Certainly not in Tanzania. In fact, Mbilinyi herself notes elsewhere in her paper, that unlike Lenin's rural bourgeoisie, who managed to 'accumulate both merchant and industrial capital and were owners of large factories and large commercial enterprises', the so-called Tanzanian 'rural bourgeoisie' are 'more likely to invest in trade or shops or buses' (p. 41).

The accumulation of capital as commercial capital is in fact the distinguishing characteristic of many underdeveloped economies, and brings out the basic dependent nature of an underdeveloped bourgeoisie. The externally oriented, commercial economy acts like a 'sucking pump' for all capital, in whatever sector it may originate. Thus the studies of Tanzania cited above invariably note that petty trade, transport, and shops, real estate, etc., are the economic activities that the rich peasants immediately enter into as soon as they have made some cash in the agricultural activity.

On the other hand, the national bourgeoisies in the developed countries played a crucial role in the development of capitalism there. This is precisely what is absent in many underdeveloped countries.

In short, therefore, the progressive effects of the development of capitalist relations cannot simply be transposed from the developed capitalist societies to the underdeveloped ones. As we have seen colonial (and now neo-colonial) capitalism in Africa had all the 'evils' but hardly any 'benefits' of capitalist development. Paul Baran has put this succinctly:

> Thus in most underdeveloped countries capitalism had a peculiarly twisted career. Having lived through all the pains and frustrations of childhood, it never experienced the vigour and exuberance of youth,

[22] P. M. Sweezy, *The theory of capitalist development* (New York: Monthly Review Press, 1956), p. 326. (It should perhaps be noted that even where there is an overall increase in the non-agricultural labour-force, it is much more in the non-productive sectors (services) than in manufacturing.)

[23] J. Rweymamu, *Underdevelopment and industrialization* . . . , op. cit., p. 27.

and began displaying at an early age all the grievous features of senility and decadence. To the dead weight of stagnation character- istic of pre-industrial society was added the entire restrictive impact of monopoly capitalism.[24]

Similarly one has to analyse the effects of commodity-exchange in the context of a 'historically determined system of production', to use Lenin's phrase. Thus whether or not the development of commodity- exchange is a 'necessary step . . . in the transformation of pre-capitalist production systems into capitalist *or* socialist ones' is a non-issue in this context. The truth is that the society that Mbilinyi is analysing is neither pre-capitalist, nor capitalist (developed) or socialist; nor is it being transformed from pre-capitalist to either capitalist or socialist. It is an *underdeveloped* capitalist society within the World Capitalist System. The question therefore should be: what is the role of the development of commodity-exchange in this underdeveloped society? (The answer most probably would be that it in fact results in the development of under- development!)

The consequence of the failure to frame the question in some such way is the failure to relate the whole question of rural differentiation and the so-called emergence of capitalist relations into both the terri- torial and the international class structures and the respective systems of production. This is quite common among many researchers of *Ujamaa Vijijini* in Tanzania. In some cases agrarian capitalism as such is held out as the enemy[25] and the policy of Ujamaa is seen as a *socialist* attempt against it. In this type of analysis the failures of the *Ujamaa* programme at the level of implementation become 'mistakes' or bureaucratic blunders[26] rather than an integral part of the very system. Such analyses also fail to grasp the global class structure and the nature of the class in power. Worse still, in some cases it is taken for granted that by showing the 'presence' of rich peasants (kulaks) in the village committees it is proved that they also control the state at the national level. But as I argued earlier, this may not necessarily be the case. On the other hand, it is a matter of specific investigation and analysis as to the extent of links between the members of the 'bureaucratic bourgeoisie' and the kulaks and as to what sections within the 'bureaucratic bourgeoisie' represent the interests of the kulaks. These interests may find greater or lesser expression in terms of national policies depending on the stage of the general class struggle and the balance of forces among the various factions of the ruling class at a particular time. But these are concrete questions which have to be analysed in terms of the on-going process of short-term political developments, a task beyond our present purposes. Suffice it to mention that all the recent studies show that the process of

[24] P. A. Baran, *The political economy of growth*, op. cit., p. 177.
[25] See, for instance, '*Ujamaa* v. capitalism', in *The Standard*, 3 and 4 July 1970.
[26] Happily this tendency appears to be changing. cf. P. Raikes, '*Ujamaa Vijijini* . . .', op. cit.

peasant differentiation has marched apace, the policy of *Ujamaa* notwithstanding. In the most commercialized areas like Kilimanjaro there is even a substantial landlessness. It is interesting to note that the recently taken-over farms in that area belonged almost exclusively to the white settlers and the majority of the farms were handed over to the co-operative societies virtually controlled by the African kulaks.[27] The sisal estates around Geita and Morogoro which were taken over were all, except two, handed over to the Tanzania Sisal Authority. Among the two exceptions, one was converted into an *Ujamaa* village while the other was given to the University Faculty of Agriculture.

Given the official policy of *Ujamaa*, it is not surprising that the interests of the kulaks do not find *open* recognition in the national policies; not even in terms of encouragement for the 'progressive farmers'. In practice therefore, the kulaks protect their interests by fraternizing with the bureaucracy and controlling the local level organizations.[28] But of course that does not make the exploitation and domination of the poor peasant less worse. He finds himself at the exploited and the oppressed end of both the internal and the external dominating classes. It is this objective situation that makes the African peasant potentially the most reliable ally of the working class in their struggle against the local dominating classes and imperialism. To quote Nga Tabiso:

. . . [The] African peasant does not exist in isolation; his mode of production is integrated in the world capitalist system. The African peasant who has undergone colonialism and now is part of the world capitalist system, is therefore, different from the classical peasant, though at the same time sharing many characteristics with the latter because of his mode of production. The classical small-owner was the predecessor of the capitalist: his aspirations were to become a capitalist and therefore he found himself the ally of the bourgeoisie. In the African case, on the other hand, he is objectively exploited by the international bourgeoisie: this begets a limited solidarity among peasants. Therefore, the peasantry forms a *reliable ally* of the working class, albeit its mode of production does not allow it to seek for an *alternative* system, based on radically opposite relations of production. This is what limits the revolutionary potential of the peasantry, whose most radical ideology cannot transcend the bounds of populism based on private ownership: ('land to the tiller!'). Hence, it cannot be a *leading* revolutionary force but only the *main* force in alliance with the working class, the only class which can fight for revolutionary goals.[29]

That brings us to the question of the worker–peasant alliance.

[27] See the *Daily News*, issues of 25/10/73; 9/11/73, 26/11/73 and 4/12/73. Also cf. G. Fimbo, 'Land, socialism . . .' op. cit., pp. 22–3.

[28] cf. H. U. E. Thoden Van Velzen, 'Staff, kulaks and peasants', op. cit.

[29] Nga Tabiso, 'Revolution and class alliances: a short comment', *Maji Maji*, No. 12 (September 1973).

10.2 THE WORKER–PEASANT ALLIANCE

The question of the worker-peasant alliance has been thoroughly misunderstood, distorted, and misinterpreted by radical academic writers. Since it is a very important *political* question, some of these misconceptions starting with the 'labour aristocracy' theorists, have to be dealt with, however briefly.

The 'labour aristocracy' theorists who have argued that the peasantry rather than the working class in Africa constitute the revolutionary class have misconceived both the theory of labour aristocracy and the nature of the African working class. The revolutionary potential of the African working class is not based on their income but on the role they play in the process of production. In the given neo-colonial situations in Africa, the working class not only plays an important role in the process of production but a very strategic one too, notwithstanding their small numbers. To be sure, even in the independence struggle the workers were in the forefront.[30] And certainly since independence and particularly after the *Mwongozo*, the Tanzanian workers, for instance, have waged the most political struggles. We shall have occasion to discuss this in greater detail in Part Five. Suffice it to say that this thesis is not based on any concrete historical experience. There has been no example in Africa where the peasants have played a leading revolutionary role while the workers have sided with the dominating classes. It is a complete confusion therefore to identify the whole working class (as Arrighi[31] does) as a labour aristocracy. In Arrighi's formulation even the 'élite and sub-élite', who should be included in the petty bourgeoisie, become part of the labour aristocracy.

Another novel argument put forward lately to throw doubts on the possible worker–poor peasant alliance has been to show 'strong links between that minority of the Tanzanian population which has had access to wage employment and the proto-kulaks in the rural areas'[32] thereby suggesting that the workers, who are supposed to be the ally of the poor peasants are in fact linked with the peasants' exploiters, the kulaks. This question requires dealing with at some length.

The authors of this are talking of at least two *types* of 'links' which they do not appear to distinguish: hence much of the confusion in their thesis. Firstly, there is the question of the historical link as a result of the

---

[30] See J. Woddis, *New theories of revolution*, (London: Lawrence and Wishart, 1972).

[31] G. Arrighi, 'International corporations, labour aristocracies, and economic development in tropical Africa', in I. Rhodes, (ed.), *Imperialism and underdevelopment*, (New York: Monthly Review Press, 1970). [In many other respects this paper is an excellent piece of work.]

[32] J. Sender, 'Some preliminary notes . . .', op. cit., p. 32. See also M. Mbilinyi, 'The transition . . .', op. cit.

origin of the kulak-capital and *secondly* the question of the link because of the place occupied and the role the social groups play in the on-going systems of production. Let us consider each one of these in turn.

Several Tanzanian studies already referred to definitely establish one thing: that the *original* capital for kulak-farming come largely from outside the agriculture sector, mostly petty trade, transport, or wage employment. This is quite understandable. The structure of the colonial economy meant that substantial amounts of accumulated 'cash' could only come from those sectors predominantly integrated in the cash economy – wage employment (in the plantations, mining, commerce, etc.) and trade being the more important ones. Secondly (and this is a less important reason) large farmers or kulaks almost by definition would mean those producing for the market and in particular agricultural cash crops for export; coffee, cotton, tea and so on. But as Iliffe has argued, producing for the market necessitated a certain amount of 'innovation' and understanding of the market-relations. This would readily come from 'three sorts of people in African society in the early twentieth century . . . its leaders, who often had greater political awareness and more knowledge of the outside world than most other members of society; those who had travelled widely as traders, migrant labourers, or in other capacities; and those who in one way or another had detached themselves partly from the society, perhaps through education or conversion to Christianity.'[33]

The fact that wage-employment was one of the sources of kulak-capital does not therefore mean that in the existing system of production kulaks and workers have *identical class interests*. The argument is fallacious. The origin of developed capitalism, for example, lay in the small-commodity producer, the classical petty bourgeois.[34] But this was precisely the class of people who were crushed and increasingly proletarianized by the development of capitalism. The fact that today's capitalist arose from yesterday's petty bourgeois (so to speak) does not make him an ally of the today's proletarianized petty bourgeoisie! Nor does the fact that today's African bureaucrat can trace his class origin to yesterday's African peasant make him the poor, exploited peasant's bosom friend.

The second limb of the argument which asserts that 'in many cases' (Sender's phrase) the people in wage employment are also the so-called proto-kulaks is more serious. Here there are a number of questions at both the empirical and theoretical levels, that have to be answered and clarified. Firstly, what is the *extent* of the wage-earners who are also kulaks, that is rich peasants employing labour? Secondly, what is their predominant activity – working for wages or as rich peasants employing labour? Thirdly, what is meant by wage-earners here: are the salariat

[33] Iliffe, *Agricultural change in modern Tanganyika*, op. cit., p. 21.
[34] There is some debate on this: See M. Dobb, P. Sweezy, *et al.*, 'The transition from feudalism to capitalism. A symposium', *Science and Society*, 1967.

or the petty bourgeoisie included? Sender's formulations (p. 30) appear to suggest that this distinction between the bourgeoisie and the workers is not always maintained, and that can be very misleading. Again there is no satisfactory answer to the first question, phrases like 'in many cases', 'some proportion' (Mbilinyi, p. 40) are not very useful. As for the second question it is not even posed. In the absence of more studies, I do not think 'far reaching' (à la Sender) with respect to the question of the identity of class interests between workers and kulaks can be drawn.

More crucial then even the lack of adequate empirical data are the theoretical questions. Let us for instance look at this problem of 'overlap' between workers and kulaks that Mbilinyi mentions:

> We are . . . led to the problem of class or stratum categorisation – is a blue collar semi-skilled worker who runs his farm on the basis of hired labour, all at the same point of time, a member of the proletariat or the rural bourgeoisie (assuming he is among the rich peasant strata at the rural location of his farm)? . . .
> The existence of such overlap is an indication of the degree of uneven development found in underdeveloped economies. It would appear to be crucial to understand the complexity of class and strata formation in Tanzania in order to act properly *to arrest* [sic!] *the development of capitalism and transform the economy along a socialist path*.[35] [Emphasis supplied.]

In a class society, classes are hardly ever very clearly demarcated and there are all sorts of what appear to be intermediate groups, and strata and even the 'overlaps'. Rather than expect the classes to be clearly demarcated, the better way of looking at them would be in terms of the 'core' and 'fringes' of the various classes.[36] However, it must be remembered that these overlaps are not the *links* between classes or 'bridges' giving identity of material interests to the two different classes. Identity of interests or contradiction arise from the *role* the 'cores' play in the production process and are part of the very system of production.

Thus when the contradictions between the large social groups (classes) become most intense and the class struggle is at its highest stage of open struggle for state power, these 'fringes' are forced to take *political* positions in favour of one or the other important classes which *characterize* the system as a whole. It is in fact the existence of these fringes and overlaps which the petty bourgeois sociologists use to assert that there are no fundamental contradictions between the exploiting and the exploited classes and that there is merely a continuum or a continuous hierarchy of interests without any qualitative break. In the so-called

---

[35] 'The transition . . .', op. cit., p. 40. The words underlined show the complete confusion between arguing about the progressive nature of capitalism *à la* Lenin, on the one hand, and wanting (?) 'to arrest' it for socialist transformation, on the other. (See my earlier discussion *supra* pp. 111-13.)

[36] See P. M. Sweezy, 'The American ruling class', in P. M. Sweezy, *The present as history* (New York: Monthly Review Press, 1953).

'peaceful' stages of class struggle this type of views gain ascendancy but, as I have tried to show, it is only a partial truth which becomes a complete lie in a revolutionary situation when the opposed classes are locked in fierce political battles.

As regards the specific question of the overlap between the workers and the rich peasants (and peasants generally) in Tanzania one has to determine its extent so as to find out if this is merely a remnant of a dying tendency having historical roots or in fact a tendency which is *reproduced* by the very logic of the system. As is well known, Tanzania had the system of migrant labourers which was both produced and encouraged by colonialism in its own interests. Immediately after independence, various measures were effected to abolish the system of migrant labour. Nevertheless, one would expect that it lingers on to some extent. Freyhold's study appears to indicate that increasingly the trend is against migrant labour and towards the formation of a permanent proletariat. She argues that the 'workers are no longer migrants, that they are unlikely to leave their urban jobs to return temporarily or permanently to farming and that they do no longer rely on rural areas to supplement their incomes and feed their wives and children.'[37]

In the neo-colonial situations in Africa the migrants to town from land on failing to secure a job join the 'lumpen-proletariat' rather than resuming their lives as poor peasants.

Finally, the most crucial and the central aspect (explicit or implied) of the arguments we have discussed above is its *political* conclusion. Both the 'labour aristocrats' and the 'kulak-worker-link' theorists are challenging either the revolutionary potential of the African working class ('proletarian messianism'!) or the possibility for worker–poor peasant alliance under the leadership of the proletarian ideology, or both. It is here that they completely fail to grasp the essentially *political* nature of both the class struggle and class alliances. In this respect, the analysis of the working class and the poor peasants in *relation to other classes*, the place they occupy and the role they play in the system of social production reveals that they objectively stand opposed to the interests of imperialism and its local class allies.[38] This of course does not mean that either the workers or the poor peasants would simply spontaneously embrace each other. Such spontaneity has certainly nothing to do with the theories of Marxism–Leninism. It is here that the leadership of the proletarian ideology embodied in the proletarian party becomes most crucial and decisive. For the proletarian ideology does not exist in vacuum. It is the proletarian party which is the *seat* of the proletarian ideology. The proletarian party therefore is the very organizer and developer of the *class instinct* of the exploited classes into their *class consciousness*. It can therefore be seen that the leadership of the

[37] M. Von Freyhold, 'The Workers, the Nizers and the peasants' (mimeo.) (n.d.) (Summary of her research, p. 1.)

[38] See Nga Tabiso, 'Revolution and class alliances', op. cit.

proletarian ideology is an indispensable factor in the political alliance of the workers and poor peasants.

Those who have attempted in practice to participate in the struggle have clearly found that the workers more than the peasants have been in the forefront providing leadership. Again Guinea's example is most illustrative. Cabral sums up the Guinean experience as follows:

> Many people say that it is the peasants who carry the burden of exploitation: this may be true, but so far as the struggle is concerned it must be realized that it is not the degree of suffering and hardship involved as such that matters: even extreme suffering in itself does not necessarily produce the *prise de conscience* required for the national liberation struggle. In Guinea the peasants are subjected to a kind of exploitation equivalent to slavery; but even if you try and explain to them that they are being exploited and robbed, it is difficult to convince them by means of an unexperienced explanation of a technico-economic kind that they are the most exploited people; whereas it is easier to convince the workers and the people employed in the towns who earn, say, 10 escudos a day for a job in which a European earns between 30 and 50 that they are being subjected to massive exploitation and injustice, because they can see.[39]

It is the lack of *political* understanding of the theory of class struggle and class alliances which is responsible for the confusion of the labour aristocracy and the worker-kulak-link theorists. However, such confusion has to be cleared for it has more than *academic* interest. For as I said in Part One: 'What theories reign in academic circles is of course not simply of academic interest.'

[39] *Revolution in Guinea*, op. cit., pp. 51–2.

PART FIVE

The Beginnings of the Proletarian Class Struggle

For a Tanzanian leader it must be forbidden to be arrogant, extravagant, contemptuous and oppressive.   *MWONGOZO*, CLAUSE 15

We are ready to work night and day if allowed to take over the factory.

For 21 years now from 1952 to 1973, there has been no improvement at the factory.

This factory belongs to the workers. It is in Dar not in Persia.

WORKERS' PLACARDS AT THE TIME
OF MOUNT CARMEL TAKE-OVER

ELEVEN

Background to the Workers' Struggles I: the Mwongozo

11.1 WHY *MWONGOZO*?

On 26 January 1971 President Obote of Uganda was overthrown by a military *coup* while he and other African leaders were attending the Commonwealth Conference in Singapore. Less than two months before that the Republic of Guinea had been invaded by mercenaries from Portugal with the help of local dissident elements. Both these events and particularly the Uganda *coup* were condemned vigorously and bitterly by the Tanzania leadership.[1] The progressive sector of the powers-that-be rightly saw in this a mirror-reflection of the threat to its own security. Guinea and Uganda had too many parallels with Tanzania to be ignored. Guinea, like Tanzania, is in the forefront in its support of the liberation movements. This makes both of them immediate targets for South African and Portuguese plots and intrigues, sometimes in alliance with the extreme right-wing elements of the local petty bourgeoisie. (Ironically, just at the time of the Uganda coup, Tanzania's first treason trial, in which a number of prominent leaders were charged with plotting to overthrow the government, was in session.)

Moreover, Obote's government, just before its overthrow, had adopted the 'Common Man's Charter' (equivalent of Tanzania's Arusha Declaration), announced its 'move to the left', and nationalized a number of enterprises including the banks. Since then the relations between Tanzania and Uganda had become openly very warm.

Thus the invasion of Guinea and the overthrow of Obote were the strongest possible warnings to Tanzania itself. President Nyerere drew the parallels very vividly:

When President Obote set for the control of the economy, naturally he angered some of the Ugandan Africans who wanted to mass wealth

---

[1] See, for example, the Comment in the Government owned daily, *The Standard*, 27 January 1971, and the Government statement on the *coup* (*The Standard*, 29 January 1971) which described it as 'an act of treason to the whole cause of African progress and African freedom'.

and they branded him as their enemy and will work hard to slow the process of his return. When we in Tanzania nationalized the major means of production, we basically angered the British and even some of our leaders and to those aspiring for wealth we laid down a code of behaviour. President Obote was working for a similar goal to define the function of the leader and that was why some of these Ugandan Africans are enthusiastic towards the rebel régime in Kampala.[2]

He went on to explain that the *coup* was 'directed against progressive African countries in a desperate move to blow up the bridge between Sudan, Uganda, Tanzania, and Zambia'. This was the theme which Ngombale-Mwiru, the then Secretary-General of the TANU Youth League had been repeatedly emphasizing in his public speeches since the Uganda *coup*. He argued that the *coup* was a strategic move on the part of imperialism aimed at surrounding Tanzania to conquer her easily. 'Mr Ngombale-Mwiru said that the imperialists wanted to build a fence around Tanzania so that they could easily attack her. This could only be possible if all countries around us were in their favour.'[3] The TANU Youth League statement issued on the next day warned 'that the imperialists had already decided to liquidate the progressive régimes of Uganda, Zambia, and Tanzania', and called for 'Tanzanian Youth and people [to] be on alert and prepare for popular armed defence against imperialist attack.'[4]

Thus the situation immediately after the Uganda *coup* and just before the adoption of the *Mwongozo* was tense. The threat was felt to be real. It was under these circumstances that the document was adopted by the National Executive Committee of the Party at a session which had been called to deliberate the Uganda *coup*.

11.2   THE TANU GUIDELINES: THE CONTENT

In the 'Introduction' to the Guidelines the Guinea and Uganda events are discussed as the central theme and the following lessons are drawn:

8. The Portuguese invasion of the Republic of Guinea is a big lesson for us. Guinea was invaded by the Portuguese imperialists firstly because of its policy of equality and its opposition to exploitation, and secondly because of its genuine stand in supporting the freedom fighters in Guinea Bissau and Africa. For similar reasons the imperialists may attempt to attack Tanzania one day. But Guinea has

[2] In an interview with Mustafa Amin, a visiting Sudanese journalist. Reported in *The Standard*, Tanzania, 16 February 1971.
[3] *The Standard*, 28 January 1971. This was at a mass rally held just before the arrival of the President from India which he was visiting after the Commonwealth Conference.
[4] *The Standard*, 28 January 1971. [Newspaper's words.]

also taught us that when the people and the army stand solidly together, no imperialist will be able to subvert their independence.

9. The lesson we draw from Uganda is one of treachery and
counter-revolution. It shows that, instead of invading the country to
overthrow the revolutionary government, imperialism prefers to use
local puppets to overthrow the legitimate government and replace it
with a government of 'foremen' or puppets. Such a government will
allow the imperialists to exploit national wealth in partnership with
the local bourgeoisie.

The people must learn from the events in Uganda and those in
Guinea that, although imperialism is still strong, its ability to topple a
revolutionary government greatly depends on the possibility of getting
domestic counter-revolutionary puppets to help in thwarting the
revolution (page 3).

These paragraphs then are the *raison d'être* of the next two sections,
'Politics' and 'Defence and security'. They emphasize the need for the
Party to control its instruments, including the army, and the need to arm
the people – that is to form Militias 'in co-operation with our regular
army' (p. 8). Both of these aims require involving the people in decision-
making and scrutinizing the habits of some leaders who 'must be forbidden to be arrogant, extravagant, contemptuous, and oppressive'
(para. 15).

The section on 'Economics and progress' emphasizes the importance
of savings; conserving of foreign reserves, and the control of the surpluses. The concern with these issues reflects the precarious foreign
exchange situation[5] that Tanzania found herself in at this time and also
the very unsatisfactory performance of a number of parastatals.

It is submitted, therefore, that the events that preceded the *Mwongozo*,
which made the powers-that-be immediately very insecure, explain its
adoption. In other words, it was a result of the contradiction between the
'bureaucratic bourgeoisie' and the right-wing sectors of the petty bourgeoisie, who posed a potential threat, possibly even with the backing of
colonial and racist powers like Portugal and South Africa. Not surprisingly therefore the *Mwongozo* does not consider the imperialist system
as such as the long-term enemy of the exploited classes. 'For Tanzania,
it must be understood that the imperialist enemies we are confronting
are *British imperialism, Portuguese colonialism, the racism and
apartheid of South Africa and Rhodesia*' (page 3). [Emphasis supplied.]

To be sure, in terms of its rhetoric and vocabulary, the *Mwongozo* is
qualitatively different from the documents of the Arusha period. This
suggests that it may have been the work of the most left-wing members
of the Party. At the same time, the issues dealt with in the *Mwongozo* –
like the involvement of the people in decision-making 'habits of the

[5] See, for example, *The Standard*, 9 January 1971 reporting the Bank's 'concern'
over the dwindling foreign exchange holdings.

leaders', etc. – touched not only on the intra-petty bourgeoisie contradictions, but also on the general social contradictions. If the Arusha Declaration was the document primarily reflecting the contradiction between the petty bourgeoisie and the commercial bourgeoisie, and the 'leadership code' a self-restraint imposed on the individual members of the emerging 'bureaucratic bourgeoisie' in the long-term interests of the class, the *Mwongozo* reflected primarily the contradiction between the rising 'bureaucratic bourgeoisie', on the one hand, and some sectors of the petty bourgeoisie and some imperialist powers on the other.

By referring to the 'oppressive habits' of some 'leaders', the *Mwongozo* provided an immediate opening for the fundamental contradiction between the workers and the 'bureaucratic bourgeoisie' to come to the fore, albeit wrapped in the ideology of the *Mwongozo*.

These are the famous continuing struggles of the workers following the *Mwongozo* which we discuss in the ensuing pages.

TWELVE

Background to the Workers' Struggles II: the Formal 'Industrial Relations Machinery'

The *Mwongozo* acted like a vehicle to carry the contradiction between the workers and the 'bureaucratic bourgeoisie' to the fore. As Mihyo put it: 'on the freedom train *Mwongozo* is just a fuel not the locomotive. It is not the cause of the widespread protests but is used as an ideological weapon to attract sympathy from the government and the Party and to legalize or give ground for charges made.'[6]

Immediately following the *Mwongozo* there was a spate of workers' strikes, popularly called 'downing of the tools'. This was, of course, not expected, much less intended, by the 'bureaucratic bourgeoisie'. However, the *Mwongozo* provided the necessary *legitimate* ideological outlet for the struggles of the workers. The nature of the struggles has been described rather concisely in none other than the employers' monthly bulletin:

> This month has been characterized by a wave of labour unrest in several industries where workers have either gone on strike or decided to go slow. The favourite theme is once more the famous clause 15 of the TANU Guidelines (Mwongozo) establishing a code of conduct for Managers [sic!]. A characteristic style is that workers stop working immediately when the unwanted Manager enters the compound of the firm, and work resumes again when the victim steps out of the fence. In some cases in Dar es Salaam, workers decided to evict the Management and ignored appeals from their NUTA representatives and even from Government officials to negotiate along established legal channels.[7]

Before we consider the various phases of the struggle it may be useful to recount very briefly the formal machinery of so-called 'industrial relations' and in particular the structure of the workers' participation.

[6] P. Mihyo, 'Labour unrest and the quest of workers' control: three case studies' (tentative title). Student undergraduate dissertation to be published in the *Eastern Africa Law Review*.

[7] The Federation of Tanganyika Employers, Monthly Bulletin, May 1973, p. 2.

12.1 THE INDUSTRIAL RELATIONS MACHINERY: SOME ASPECTS

As noted earlier, the Tanganyika Federation of Labour (TFL) which had become the base of a faction of the petty bourgeoisie opposed to the government was banned in 1964 and, instead, the National Union of Tanganyika Workers (NUTA), the only legal trade union, was established by an Act of Parliament. NUTA came virtually under the control of the government and was also affiliated to the Party. The General Secretary of the Union and his Deputy are appointed by the President of the Republic. In practice the General Secretary has almost always been also the Minister of Labour. The other members of the leadership including the directors of the various departments and the heads of the various industrial sections are appointed by the General Secretary in consultation with the General Council. The Regional and Branch Chairmen and secretaries are appointed by the Executive Council, all of whose members are *appointed* officers. Basically, the Union has a double hierarchy: a hierarchy of appointed officials heading the hierarchy of committees of elected union members at various levels: Branch, Regional, Headquarters.

Clearly this type of structure did not augur well for the control of the union by its members. The Presidential Commission on NUTA, appointed in 1966 to look into the workers' complaints against NUTA, observed that the present union structure did not provide 'adequate and visible means of democratic expression'.[8]

Be that as it may, in 1967 the National Assembly passed more legislation which further circumscribed even the economic role of NUTA. As a result of Professor Turner's Report on 'Wages, Incomes and Prices Policy'[9] in which he recommended a watchdog institution to supervise the rise in wages, a Labour Tribunal was set up under the Permanent Labour Tribunal Act of 1967. This Act, like its predecessor, the Trade Disputes Act of 1962, made strikes virtually illegal and no agreement between the Union and the employers is binding unless it is registered by the Tribunal. The Tribunal also acts as the highest organ for settling industrial disputes. Thus the Permanent Labour Tribunal regulates *collective* disputes between the employers and the workers besides supervising the 'national' wage policy on behalf of the state.

The Security of Employment Act of 1964, on the other hand, is intended to regulate *individual* disputes between the employer and the workers. It sets out rules and procedures for the imposition of punish-

[8] *Report of the Presidential Commission on the National Union of Tanganyika Workers* (Dar es Salaam: Government Printer, 1967), p. 8.

[9] *Report to the Government of the United Republic of Tanzania on Wages, Incomes and Prices Policy*, by the International Labour Office. Government Paper No. 3 of 1967.

ments on the workers by the employers for breaches of the disciplinary code provided in the Act. In this process of disciplining 'his' workers, the employer is provided with the assistance of the workers' committee, also established by the Act.

These committees have played an important role in the post-*Mwongozo* struggles of the workers. It may be useful therefore to consider their composition and functions as provided in law.

12.1.1 *The Workers' Committees*

The Workers' Committees are required to be established in every enterprise employing more than ten union members. The committee members are elected by the union members themselves, the only qualification being that they must be members of NUTA. The functions of the committee are two-fold: It *advises* the employer on such matters as efficiency; safety and welfare arrangements; work rules; redundancies, etc. Secondly, it has to be consulted by the employer before he imposes any punishment on a worker for a breach of the disciplinary code, though the employer is not bound by the opinion of the committee. Thus it helps to administer the disciplinary code.

The objective effect has been succinctly described by Mihyo:

. . . [The] Security of Employment Act, 1964, only secures employment for the employer. It imposes a stringent disciplinary code which if strictly enforced can only be observed by angels. It creates a system of indirect rule by leaving the employees themselves to enforce the disciplinary code through the workers' committee whose other function is to advise on efficiency. It goes on begging the employer to soften his iron rule as a token of appreciation of the committee's functions and achievements in enforcing discipline and increasing efficiency. Given all responsibility without power, the Security of Employment Act is itself a misnomer and the workers' committee its major creation, a high-sounding nothing.[10]

That may be so: but even the ruling class rules within the framework of the objective conditions and its power is circumscribed by historical circumstances. Thus when the contradictions sharpen, its own instruments are turned against it. That is an inevitable dialectical process, which asserted itself in case of the workers' committees, which became important instruments of the workers' post-*Mwongozo* struggles.

There are three important features deriving from the very official composition and functions of the committees which enabled the workers to turn what was meant to be an employers' instrument against them.

Firstly, the workers' committee is the only official organ of the workers at the level of the production-unit whose membership is *wholly elected* by the workers.

Thus it is the workers' committee which is closest to the workers,

[10] Mihyo, op. cit.

129

much more so than any organ of the trade union, NUTA, and it is the committee which they know and recognize. The membership being wholly elected, the militant workers were able to get elected to the committees and thereby provide the necessary leadership in the post-*Mwongozo* period. In the case of the Rubber Industries takeover in 1973, the unofficial 'Revolutionary Council' formed by the militant workers was able to overthrow the reactionary workers' committee and form a new one with militant workers in it.[11]

Secondly, the only relation the workers' committees have legally with NUTA is that their members should be union members and that union officials supervise the elections. Apart from this, the committees are not at all integrated in the union structure. In fact, the union's grass-roots organ is the Branch Committee and not the workers' committee. But as the Branch Committees are not based on particular enterprises the workers' committee does not come under the direct day-to-day supervision of the union officials or the union organs. Since the committees have very little power and only deal with discipline the union bureaucracy would not be bothered. This is precisely what made the committees potentially independent of the domination of the union bureaucracy and paradoxically it was this that was exploited by the workers in *their* struggles. It is not surprising therefore that there have lately been 'suggestions' from various quarters that the workers' committees who were the cause of indiscipline in the factories, should be abolished and replaced by NUTA Branches. 'The Government would no longer tolerate workers' committees which instead of maintaining discipline created disputes and misunderstandings', Mr Mwanjisi, the Principal Secretary in the Ministry of Labour and Social Welfare was reported to have said.[12]

Thirdly, the Security of Employment Act, passed in 1964, applied only to employees earning 700 sh or less per month. In 1969, significantly, the Act was amended.[13] Now, the Act applies only to those employees who in the opinion of a labour officer are not employed in the management of the business of the employer. This meant that before 1969, members of largely the petty bourgeoisie and after 1969, those of the 'bureaucratic bourgeoisie' were effectively excluded (or rather excluded themselves) from the membership and control of the workers' committees. Nor, of course, were they interested. The committees after all were only advisory and dealt with disciplinary matters which did not apply to them in any case. As a result, the committees, unlike the Workers' Councils to be discussed below, came to be controlled by the workers themselves rather than the enterprise management. This is what enabled the committees to assume leadership in the workers' struggles against the 'bureaucratic bourgeoisie'.

[11] For a detailed study of this see Mihyo, op. cit.
[12] *Daily News*, 19 January 1974.
[13] Act No. 45 of 1969.

Whereas the workers' committees were a recognition of the contradiction between capital and labour and were meant to discipline the latter so as to maintain capital's supremacy, the workers' councils were meant to be an ideological palliative to smoothen this contradiction. The councils present an interesting contrast to the committees which is worth considering in some detail.

12.1.2 *The Workers' Councils*

The workers' councils are required to be established in every public corporation, enterprise, firm, or parastatal organization.[14] The composition of the councils is as follows:

Permanent Members:

1. (*a*) A TANU Chairman of the Branch established at the business;
(*b*) The Chief Executive of the enterprise, e.g. General Manager, Chairman, or Managing Director;
(*c*) All Heads of Departments or sections;
(*d*) All Members of the Workers' Committee.

Other Members:

2. (*a*) Additional workers' representatives elected in proportion to the number of workers in different departments or sections, provided that the number of these representatives added to the number of members of the Workers' Committee does not exceed three-quarters of the total of the permanent membership;
(*b*) Co-opted members from outside the business selected for their expertise;
(*c*) A NUTA representative.

The basic function of a council is to *advise* the Board of Directors on such matters as wages and incomes policy; productivity; marketing; planning, and such other matters connected with the running of the enterprise. The Board of Directors is the final competent authority to lay down policy.

With the workers' councils are established executive committees consisting of:

(*a*) The Chief Executive of the enterprise;
(*b*) Heads of Departments or Sections;
(*c*) Workers' representative members of the Workers' Council, provided their number is not more than one-third of the total membership of the Executive Committee.

The executive committee advises the Chief Executive of the enterprise on the execution of the policy as laid down by the Board of Directors and scrutinizes production estimates; marketing, finance, productivity, etc. programmes.

[14] See Presidential Circular No. 1 of 1970.

It is not difficult to see that both these bodies are top-heavy with bureaucrats and no doubt controlled by them. Roughly, categories 1 (*a*), (*b*), and (*c*), and 2 (*b*) and (*c*) of the Council may be said to represent the 'bureaucratic bourgeoisie' while the rest represent the workers, assuming that those elected as the workers' representatives are themselves workers and not members of the petty bourgeoisie. In his study of Ubungo Farm Implements, Mapolu[15] found that out of 27 members of the Council only 11 were workers' representatives.

In the executive committees, it is worse still because workers by 'law' cannot be more than one-third of the total membership. In effect the executive committee is simply a meeting of the General Manager with his departmental heads.

In sum, the workers' councils and executive committees, institutions established *officially* to effect workers' participation, are composed in such a way that they are effectively controlled by members of the 'bureaucratic bourgeoisie'. Not surprisingly, any employee of the enterprise concerned regardless of his rank or salary can stand for election as a workers' representative to the council. On the other hand, as we have already seen, the membership of the workers' committees which are officially established as organs for disciplining workers and not participation, is exclusively confined to the workers.

Thus it was that the workers' committees (for reasons already discussed) rather than the councils, played a leading role in the post-*Mwongozo* struggles.

12.2   SOME CONCLUDING REMARKS

The 'industrial relations machinery' discussed here very briefly shows beyond doubt in whose class interest it was established. It is not surprising therefore that during the post-*Mwongozo* struggles the bureaucrats kept on harping that the workers should exhaust the so-called 'established machinery'. Through their accumulated experience, however, the workers knew that the established machinery was the *establishment* machinery in which their voices would be drowned and which would keep them subservient.

One of the most important class functions of industrial relations machinery in a bourgeois society is to *individualize* the workers and their grievances and attempt to destroy their class solidarity. The hierarchy of institutions set up with token workers' representation has the ideological function of appeasing the workers, on the one hand, and robbing the working class of its best elements by making them representatives in the established machinery, on the other. The institutionalization of *class*

[15] H. Mapolu, 'The organization and participation of workers in Tanzania', *The African Review*, Vol. 2, No. 3 (1972).

opposition in the form of *individual grievances* is one of the leading functions of bourgeois law and the bourgeois legal system.

But in the post-*Mwongozo* era the workers have begun to blow off this lid of ideological false consciousness. The workers' councils, the official organs of workers' participation, represent the 'ideology' – the false consciousness – that the 'bureaucratic bourgeoisie' would have workers internalize. The councils are neither controlled by the workers nor do they allow the workers to participate effectively in decision-making. The workers' committees represented the real social relation of domination between the two classes. Their function was to use the workers' representatives to discipline their fellow workers.

When the time came, the workers by their very action began to expose the 'ideology'. They ignored the workers' councils and turned the committees against their own creator. The process of class struggle is dialectical and has no respect for the *intentions* of individuals or classes. Mr Mwanjisi, the Principal Secretary in the Ministry of Labour and Social Welfare, vigorously complained against this dialectic:

> Following . . . uneasiness in industrial relations, the Government would very soon redesign the roles of the workers' committees, workers' councils and Tanu branches based in industrial premises. The workers' committees were originally set up to handle disciplinary problems but they were now sacking managers, he said.
>
> The workers' councils, intended to be boards of governors from the inside, were now handling disciplinary matters. They should, he went on, confine themselves to over-all planning and management.[16]

[16] *Daily News*, 19 January 1974, p. 1. (As reported in the newspaper.)

THIRTEEN

The Post-Mwongozo *Proletarian Struggles*

13.1 THE STRUGGLE

The post-*Mwongozo* 'downing of the tools' or strikes by the workers have been the most intense on the industrial scene in Tanzania since the establishment of NUTA in 1964. Table 6 is an indication of the various phases of class struggle. The strike figures correspond to these various phases remarkably accurately.

As noted earlier, the workers' strikes in the late 1950s played a crucial role in the struggle for independence. In the three years (1958–60) just before independence, there were 561 strikes involving 239 803 workers with 2 194 212 man-days lost, the greatest number to be recorded. But soon after independence the struggle between the different sectors of the petty bourgeoisie – based in the government and the trade union – broke out. The high number of strikes between 1961–64 bears this out (362 strikes involving 99 382 workers with 613 778 man-days lost). The demands as before revolved around wages and conditions of work mainly. In its attempt to curb TFL opposition the government passed the Trade Disputes Act 1962, which prohibited strikes unless the established machinery was exhausted. This made strikes virtually impossible. Although the number of strikes in 1963–64 went down to half that of the previous two years, the trade-union opposition to the government continued. The decisive step in this intra-petty bourgeois struggle was the banning of TFL and the establishment of NUTA in 1964. NUTA came virtually under the government control. The post-1964 strike figures consequently show a drastic fall. In the six-year period, 1965–70, there were 74 strikes involving only 9308 workers with 26 518 man-days lost. The few strikes were sporadic and spontaneous without NUTA leadership. The NUTA Act itself prohibited strike action unless sanctioned by the General Council which is under the leadership of government appointees. Moreover, in terms of class struggle, it was the contradiction between the petty bourgeoisie and the commercial bourgeoisie which was being ironed out during this period.

Meanwhile, although subdued some NUTA leaders continued to pose

TABLE 6

INDUSTRIAL DISPUTES INVOLVING STRIKES 1958–73

	YEAR	NUMBER OF STRIKES	NUMBER OF WORKERS INVOLVED	NUMBER OF MAN-DAYS LOST
PETTY BOURGEOISIE- +WORKERS V. METROPOLITAN BOURGEOISIE (1)	1958	153	67 430	296 746
	1959	205	82 878	402 693
	1960	203	89 495	1 494 773
	Total	561	239 803	2 194 212
INTRA-PETTY BOURGEOIS STRUGGLES (2) (a)	1961	101	20 159	113 254
	1962	152	48 434	417 474
	Total	253	68 593	530 728
GOVERNMENT BASED V. TRADE UNION BASED (2) (b)	1963	85	27 207	77 195
	1964	24	3 582	5 855
	Total	109	30 789	83 050
PETTY BOURGEOISIE V. COMMERCIAL BOURGEOISIE (3)	1965	13	884	1 825
	1966	16	2 062	8 845
	1967	25	3 224	7 224
	Total	54	6 170	17 894
RISE OF 'BUREAUCRATIC BOURGEOISIE' DISINTEGRATION OF COMMERCIAL BOURGEOISIE (4)	1968	13	1 906	5 757
	1969	4	876	2 141
	1970	3	356	726
	Total	20	3 138	8 624

embarrassing questions to the government as at the same time the membership complained about their organization.[17] The year 1967 saw the passing of the Permanent Labour Tribunal Act making strikes virtually illegal and establishing compulsory arbitration by the Tribunal for solving trade disputes. The number of strikes between 1968–70 was

[17] See generally, L. R. Patel, *East African labour régime*, op. cit., Ch. 11.

Table 6—*continued*

	YEAR	NUMBER OF STRIKES	NUMBER OF WORKERS INVOLVED	NUMBER OF MAN-DAYS LOST
WORKERS V. 'BUREAUCRATIC BOURGEOISIE'	1971 (From Feb.)	‹15	11 043	31 915
	1972	10	8 360	17 030
	1973 (Until Sept.)	6	3 305	14 701
	Total	31	22 708	63 646

Sources: L. R. Patel, *East African labour régime*, op. cit., p. 412 and the same author's personal files.

Mapundi, 'Post-*Mwongozo* downing of the tools' (unpublished), p. 39 for 1971–73 figures.

Notes:
(1) Independence Struggle.
(2) (*a*) Trade Disputes (Settlement) Act, 1962 making strikes virtually illegal.
    (*b*) NUTA (Establishment) Act, 1964 requiring General Council's sanction before going on strike. Banning of the TFL.
(3) Permanent Labour Tribunal Act, 1967, establishing compulsory arbitration procedure for settling disputes.
(4) Adoption of the TANU Guidelines. (*Mwongozo*).

only 20, involving 3138 workers with 8624 man-days lost. But by 1971, having cleared all the ground, the fundamental contradiction between the 'bureaucratic bourgeoisie' and the workers came to the fore and asserted itself in a dramatic way in the post-*Mwongozo* 'downing of the tools'. This time, unlike the strikes before, the leadership was generally not in the hands of organized trade unions or even of the petty bourgeoisie, but of the workers themselves through, in many cases, the workers' committees. Between February 1971 and September 1973 there were 31 'downings of tools' involving something like 28 708 workers with 63 646 man-days lost. In terms of workers involved and man-days lost, this is over twice the figures for the previous six-year period, from 1965–70. Incidentally, these figures do not even include the numerous disputes against bureaucratic managers (to be discussed below) not resulting in strike.

It is the latest phase that we now propose to discuss in some detail.

The post-*Mwongozo* workers' struggles may be divided roughly into three phases, *à la* Mapolu.[18] The first phase was dominated by *downing tools*, i.e. stoppage of work. Later, in the second phase, the workers increasingly began to *lock-out* the officials whom they did not want, meanwhile continuing to work. The beginning of the third phase was the factory *take-overs* which elicited the harshest response from the government – *en masse* dismissal of workers as in the case of the Mount Carmel Rubber Factory.

In practice these phases overlapped. Besides, the workers also used other methods, such as resorting to protest marches to the offices of the Prime Minister, the President, or TANU.

Jack Sperling and Sri Nimpunoo[19] have recorded these disputes as reported in the daily newspapers. Of course, all the disputes do not get reports in the newspapers and therefore the figures calculated from their tables are likely to be rough estimates. But they do bring out the essential features of the struggle.

Their tables show that between the period July 1971 and March 1974 there were roughly 45 industrial disputes affecting both the private and the public sectors. About two-thirds of the disputes were in the state sector, i.e. the wholly state-owned enterprises and others where the state directly, or through state corporations, has some ownership interest. The fact that a particular enterprise was publicly owned did not deter the workers: as we noted earlier, class relations have little to do with legal relations.

In the majority of these disputes the trade union, NUTA, was not involved. In fact it came to the scene more as a conciliator than as a workers' representative. The workers have tended to look upon NUTA with suspicion. As early as 1966, one of the major complaints recorded by the Presidential Commission[20] against NUTA was:

A number of leaders enter into suspicious associations with employers. Business is conducted in privacy, through telephones or in English, a language which most members do not understand.[21]

And in the Rubber Industries case (1973) the workers said:

We do not want NUTA officials because the firm's director has told us time and again that the whole of the NUTA organization is in his control and that therefore we would never be listened to by that organization. We have also proved that his words are very true for we have been requesting the NUTA official to come and deal with our problems since April 9th but all in vain. They have not even answered the three letters we wrote to them.[21]

[18] H. Mapolu, 'The workers' movement in Tanzania', *Maji Maji*, No. 12 (September 1973), op. cit.

[19] Unpublished.

[20] *Report of the Presidential Commission on the National Union of Tanganyika Workers*, op. cit., p. 1, para. 5.

[21] *Uhuru*, 26 May 1973. Quoted in H. Mapolu, 'The workers' movement . . .', op. cit., p. 40.

The institution which the workers used most was the workers' committees and in some cases the TANU branches. (We have already discussed the reasons why the workers' committees assumed leadership and need not repeat them here.) In a few cases where the workers' committees had obviously become puppets of management the workers demanded the resignation of the committee members and even organized to overthrow them (Rubber Industries). Thus, the post-*Mwongozo* disputes clearly brought out the trade union as an instrument of the 'bureaucratic bourgeoisie'.

The immediate causes or reasons which were publicly put forward by the workers for either downing tools or locking-out management may be put under two broad categories: (1) those connected generally with remuneration; and (2) non-wage demands revolving around the treatment of the workers by the management. It is the second category which was predominant. The management was accused of being oppressive, indifferent to workers' grievances, disregarding them, contemptuous, and so on. The workers accused the management of breaching the *Mwongozo* and in particular clause 15, which states that 'a Tanzanian leader . . . must be forbidden to be arrogant, extravagant, contemptuous, and oppressive.' Clause 33 which states that the Party must ensure that parastatals do not use surpluses extravagantly, was also cited against the managements accused of being corrupt, misusing the funds of the enterprises, etc. In short, the workers enthusiastically quoted the *Mwongozo* as their ideological weapon in the struggle. But the bureaucracy of course would not oblige. It was one thing to issue a declaration for mobilizing the masses in the interest of their own class security, but quite another to implement it.

The response of the bureaucracy became increasingly harsher. It accused the workers of being irresponsible, misinterpreting the *Mwongozo*, and undermining the economy. But let us see whose economy was being undermined? The following recent case of the Tanganyika Motors dramatically illustrates the issue. Tanganyika Motors Ltd which mainly repairs the Peugeot cars is a privately owned company. The workers of the company locked out its four top officials on the grounds that they were indifferent to their grievances and looked down upon the African workers. The manager retaliated by closing down the enterprise. A NUTA official, trying to get the workers back to work, 'reminded the workers that Peugeot motor vehicles for which their company is agent were very much used by individuals and Government institutions'.[22] True, the Peugeot car is a status symbol for the members of the petty bourgeoisie: it was therefore the economy of the Peugeot owners and the comfort of the Peugeot users which were being undermined. No wonder, a representative of the workers said that human dignity was more important than the economy of the country.[23]

[22] *Daily News*, 16 January 1974.
[23] ibid.

The climax of the bureaucracy's reaction was the mass expulsion of the workers in the case of Sungura Textile Mill and Dar es Salaam Motor Transport (DMT). Between June 1970 and August 1972 the workers at Sungura Textile stopped work over eight times. In August 1972, the government picked on 31 workers as ringleaders and instigators. They were taken into the policy custody and dismissed from their jobs. The government statement issued at the time strongly condemned 'downing tools' as harmful to the economy. It harped on the figures of losses incurred in the privately owned Sungura Textile as a result of the work stoppages and warned that strong measures would be taken against instigators and agitators.[24]

Between 27 November 1972 and 4 January 1973, the drivers and the conductors of Dar es Salaam Motor Transport (DMT) went on strike twice. DMT is the government owned passenger transport service in the country. Because of these strikes the city public transport came to a complete standstill. When the workers went on their first strike on 27 December 1972, four of them were arrested and prosecuted. The workers were promised that their grievances would be looked into and settlement reached by 1 January. On 4 January, having heard nothing from the authorities, they again stopped work. This time the government dismissed all the 676 drivers and some 452 conductors.[25] The government statement issued at the time reads:

This act now means that there is no negotiating but competing between the Government and the workers concerned. The Government has no need for competing with a person or persons. Therefore the decision of the Government is that as from the time those drivers and conductors decided to strike to the present, the Government no longer recognizes them as works of DMT. . . . If there are some who went on strike because of being instigated or threatened, yet they would like to continue with their work wholeheartedly, those are given this chance. Special orders are being made in writing and any one who would like to continue with work should from 12 this afternoon to 6 this evening report to the DMT office in the Pugu-Msimbazi Street; he will be given these orders; if he accepts them he should sign them: thereafter he will be allowed back to his work. If not so, then he should quit.[26]

What alternative did the drivers and the conductors have but to rejoin the company. The large majority of them signed the forms.

The full story of the struggles in the various enterprises following the

---

[24] *Tamko Rasmi la Serikali kuhusu migomo* (mimeo) (n.d.).
[25] See the *Daily News*, from 28 December 1972, to 9 January 1973.
[26] Quoted in K. F. Ileti, 'Workers' disputes', Unpublished student Course-work (1974), Faculty of Law, University of Dar es Salaam.

Mwongozo has still to be told. Research[27] on these issues by a number of people has just begun but it will be some time before results become known. The following brief accounts of two famous disputes bring out some of the important features discussed in the foregoing sections.

13.1.1 *Manager Locked out: The BAT Case*

The British American Tobacco Co. Ltd (BAT) of Tanzania is a subsidiary of the National Development Corporation (NDC) which owns 60 per cent of the shares. The company has a general management and technical consultancy contract with BAT Ltd. BAT is a British company ranking fifth among the British firms and with capital employed of B£461 106 000 (1967) on which a net profit (before interest and tax) of B£103 033 000 was made. The company has 100 factories in 50 countries including South Africa. It has a virtual monopoly of the East African market.[28]

On the 23 May 1973[29] when the Personnel Manager of the company, one Mr Kashaija, came to the factory, a fire alarm bell was sounded and all the workers stopped work. Some workers walked to his office and threatened to pull it down if he did not leave the premises. 'Peace' was not restored until police armed with guns and tear gas arrived at the scene at the request of the management.

The workers refused to work until some decision was taken on the fate of Mr Kashaija. Finally, as a result of a meeting between NUTA and the management the workers' complaints were forwarded to the Permanent Labour Tribunal.

At the hearing of the case before the Tribunal Mr Kashaija was helped by Mr P. Hayward, BAT's secretary and an advocate provided by the state-owned Tanzania Legal Corporation, they being BAT's legal advisers. One of the witnesses who consistently defended Mr Kashaija was the expatriate General Manager of the company, Mr MacDonald. The alignment of the forces could not be clearer.

The stoppage of work was a result of the accumulated grievances of the workers against Mr Kashaija, which were voiced for the first time as early as 1971. The main complaints of the workers were as follows:

(a) That Mr Kashaija used the company's resources extravagantly in breach of the TANU Guidelines paragraphs 15 and 33. The two of the more important incidences cited were that Kashaija used the com-

[27] Some of the Course-work Papers done by the Undergraduates in Labour Law (1973–74) at the Faculty of Law, University of Dar es Salaam will be published in the forthcoming issues of the *Eastern Africa Law Review*.
(I am indebted to Messrs Mihyo, Kalokora, Ileti and Mapundi for letting me use some of the material from their papers.)
[28] National Christian Council of Kenya, *Who controls industry in Kenya?* (Nairobi: East African Publishing House, 1968), p. 106.
[29] This account is based on Kalokora, I. Bwesha, 'Labour disputes in Tanzania: a case study of selected incidents' (1974) (unpublished).

pany's Range Rover to attend his father's burial in Bukoba. This cost
the company as much as 5820Sh. Secondly, Mr Kashaija used
6100Sh of the company to throw a grand party to which something
like 194 people were invited.

The party enraged the workers very much. It was held at the Kunduchi
Beach, a tourist resort area. The invitation card from Mr and Mrs
Kashaija gave the duration as follows: On the 3rd March, any time after
8.00 p.m. 'The party started at 8.00 p.m. on the 3rd ran throughout the
night, and ended on the 4th at around 1.00 p.m.' No workers or even
their representatives were invited. In his evidence the General Manager
said that the purpose of the party was to strengthen the relations existing
between the company and the general public. Kalokora has given a
cross-section of the invitees which constituted the 'general public' at this
party:

Guest of Honour:
Minister for Economic Affairs and Development Planning.

Others:
Minister for Communications
Minister for Agriculture
The NDC General Manager
The Managing Chairman, National Bank of Commerce
The General Manager, National Housing Corporation
The General Manager, National Insurance Corporation
The Chairman, Pyrethrum Board
The Chairman, Civil Service Commission
Gynaecologist, Muhimbili Hospital
A Senior Medical Officer, Muhimbili Hospital
The Manager, Cooper Motor Corporation
The BAT Wholesale Manager
(Someone) from the Army Headquarters
The Manager, Development Bank
The Personal Assistant to the President
The Principal Secretary, Ministry of Information
The Director, Ministry of Foreign Affairs
The ex-Ugandan Foreign Minister and his 5 friends
An important Dar businessman (African)
The Commissioner for Lands
A Professor of Economics, University of Dar es Salaam
The General Manager, NATEX
The General Manager, TANESCO
An accountant from Cooper Brothers
A Police Public Prosecutor
The General Manager, State Trading Corporation
The Tanzanian Ambassador to the Peoples' Republic of China.[30]

There could not be a better cross-section of the representatives of the
international bourgeoisie (managers of foreign companies); members of

[30] The full list, according to Kalokora, was attached to the BAT statement of
Defence.

the Tanzanian 'bureaucratic bourgeoisie' and the upper sector of the petty bourgeoisie. Surely, it was to strengthen the relations among the dominating classes, if not the 'general public'!

(*b*) The other set of complaints accused Mr Kashaija of tribalism and favouritism. It was alleged that Mr Kashaija tended to employ people from his own area, i.e. Bukoba.

The Tribunal found that 12 per cent of the overall work force were *Wahaya*. Comparing it with *Wachagaa*, who constituted only half the *Wahaya* at the factory, the Tribunal concluded that the only way such a large proportion of *Wahaya* could be explained was that they had been employed through tribalism.

(*c*) Thirdly, the workers accused Mr Kashaija of practising segregation and discrimination. For instance at one time or another he was alleged to have encouraged separate canteens for workers and top bureaucrats.

At the hearing one worker witness said that while the Junior BAT staff were given 'prison food' the senior management members took 'delicious dishes of tourist standards'.[31]

In its decision the Permanent Labour Tribunal found that a number of allegations against Mr Kashaija were justified and recommended that he should be removed from the company.

Meanwhile the workers had voluntarily worked overtime – *unpaid* – to compensate for the losses incurred as a result of the strike.

13.1.2 *Factory Taken over: The Mount Carmel Case*

'The Rubber Industries Limited workers scratched the first match, the curtain raiser; they were followed by the five hundred nightwatchmen who refused to watch other people's property while theirs was being pillaged; then came the Mount Carmel Rubber tragedy where the Carmel having locked its master out of the tent was removed from the tent by super-powers and condemned for ever to suffer in the blizzard and the harmattan, because it refused to be mounted! The tradition at Mount Carmel is that the "Carmel" must always be mounted.' MIHYO

The highest stage after downing of the tools and the lock-outs in the workers' struggles was reached with the takeover of the factories.

The first successful takeover was at Rubber Industries Ltd. This factory was owned by a group of Tanzanian Asians in partnership with Industrial Promotion Services (IPS), which is dominated by the Aga Khan and is NDC's partner in a number of Tanzanian enterprises. The story of how the takeover was organized by the militant workers has been competently told by Mihyo in great detail and I need not repeat it. This was a successful takeover supported by the government.

[31] Quoted in Kalokora, op. cit.

The second takeover was that of the Night-Watch Security Company whose owner had in fact left the country.

The third takeover, which resulted in the workers' dismissal, was that of the Mount Carmel Rubber Factory, situated just opposite Rubber Industries.

The Mount Carmel is owned and managed by one Mr Yadzani. The conditions at the factory were deplorable. 'When on the 17th of March, 1971, the factory inspector visited the Mount Carmel Rubber Factory, he found that it was in a terribly unhealthy situation. The set up of the factory was itself a violation of the letter and spirit of the . . . Factories Ordinance. This inspection report has revealed that contrary to section 13 of the said ordinance the factory was not kept clean – that indeed it was stinking. Dirt was lying about in heaps as if it was a raw material or a commodity for sale.'[32] The boiler was not adequately housed; it constituted a danger to human life. There were no adequate drinking facilities for the workers. When asked about this by Mihyo, the employer replied that there was shortage of water in Dar es Salaam and added cynically: 'I am of course not a rain maker!'

Out of the 70 or so workers employed at the factory, 20 or more were casual employees. They were in even worse conditions, because they would not be entitled to any terminal benefits nor was their employment secure. Thus the working conditions at the factory were as bad as could be.

There was no workers' committee at the factory until 1971. NUTA had hardly done anything for the workers. It was only after the formation of the committee that a collective agreement was drafted. However, it was never enforced. In January 1972, the workers, led by their committee, had threatened to go on strike. A meeting of the workers was called but nothing substantial came of it.

It was under such circumstances that the workers finally decided to take over the factory. In this they were encouraged by the neighbouring factory.

Thus, sometime in June 1973, when the factory's personnel manager tried to enter the factory gates he was met by the workers, shouting and booing. He was told by the Chairmen of the TANU branch and the workers' committee that the workers did not want him or the Managing Director, Mr Yadzani. The workers had taken over the factory. While some of them kept guard at the gates, others continued production. Some of the placards posted at the factory read:

'Long live Mwalimu and Mwongozo.'

'We are ready to work night and day if allowed to take over the factory.'

'For 21 years now from 1952 to 1973, there has been no improvement at the factory.'

[32] Mihyo, op. cit. The account that follows is also based on Mihyo, op. cit., Mapolu, 'Workers movement . . .', op. cit. and newspaper reports.

'The factory belongs to the workers. It is in Dar not Persia'
[reference to the employer's origin].

The workers refused completely to see the NUTA or other labour
officials despite a warning by the Labour Commissioner that refusing to
meet officials 'was very serious and would lead to punishment'. The then
Regional Commissioner, Mr Kisumo, who had approved the Rubber
Industries takeover a few days ago, vehemently opposed this takeover.
He tried to persuade the workers to allow their employer in, but
they would not budge from their decision. Next day the regional
commissioner again appeared at the factory, this time with a contingent
of policemen, but the workers remained adamant:

'The workers told the regional commissioner who advised them yesterday to abide by the Party's ruling that they were prepared to leave
the firm any time if they would be provided with transport and land
to establish their own *Ujamaa* village, rather than accept their employer as the leader of the firm. (Mr Kisumo told them): "TANU
advises you to allow your employer to enter the firm's premises and
wants you to work together with him." Amid applause a worker
assured Mr Kisumo that their decision was firm and that all workers
in the firm were members of TANU, therefore their decision was still
in line with Party policies.'[33]

The workers accused their employer of being a neo-colonialist and
involved in importing raw materials which were obtainable locally.

Meanwhile, the workers of the Hotel Afrique were reported making
preparation to take over their 'factory'. Mount Carmel was setting a bad
precedent. This could not be allowed. Next day, at 11 a.m. a labour
officer accompanied by police and trucks appeared at the factory gates.
Let the *Daily News* report take up the story in full: 'An official from the
Ministry accompanied by a number of policemen called at the factory in
Chang'ombe and issued to all the workers what he called a Government
order. He said that those workers who were not ready to work under Mr
Yadzani should stay apart from those who accepted his leadership. All
workers who refused to accept their employer's leadership were ordered
to enter packed vehicles. Sixty-two were driven away to the Central
Police Station leaving the industry with only 15 workers.'[34] All the
members of the workers' committee and the TANU Branch Committee
including their Chairmen were among those arrested.

Having had their finger-prints taken, and after staying in the police
custody for a few days, the workers were repatriated to their respective
'home' (!) areas.

The government statement issued on the occasion warned the workers
against 'the habit of unilaterally taking over factories' and that it would

[33] *Daily News*, 20 June 1973. Quoted in Mapolu, op. cit.
[34] *Daily News*, 21 June 1973.

not 'tolerate such unruly behaviour on the part of the workers'. The statement triumphantly declared that 'early yesterday morning the Government re-instated the owner of the firm in his factory and opposed the workers' demands to take it over'.[35] And, as usual, the Government daily, the *Daily News* joined in the celebration. The editor in his *Comment* on the dismissal, had a 'brilliant brainwave':

> 'Socialism is coming,' he wrote,
> 'This no one can prevent. . . .
> The action was not meant for
> the benefit of a capitalist or a group
> of capitalists. In the final analysis
> it was for the benefit of the workers
> of Tanzania themselves.'[36]

The state thus asserted its class character regardless of the ideology. But in so doing it laid bare the fundamental contradiction between the exploited and the exploiter. It is this contradiction which is going to be the dominant one henceforth. True, the workers' struggles we have described have been sporadic and not necessarily couched in conscious class ideology. The reaction of the workers has been more a consequence of their class instinct, rather than because of definite class consciousness. But class consciousness does not come spontaneously. It is the role of proletarian ideology to develop class *instinct* into class *consciousness*. Meanwhile, the workers have definitely declared that the stage of history when they were used as cannon fodder in the intra-petty bourgeois struggles to be fast coming to an end. This time it will be their own struggles – their own class war – and the struggle of their fellow exploited class, the poor peasants that they will fight, not to replace one exploiter with another but to begin to replace the very system of exploitation.

[35] *Daily News*, 21 June 1973.
[36] *Daily News*, 22 June 1973, quoted in Mapolu, op. cit.

APPENDICES*

Underdevelopment and Relations with International Capitalism

In the text I argued that the essential features of the economy – its underdeveloped structures – did not change fundamentally either after independence or the Arusha Declaration. The purpose of the present Appendix is to give further empirical data on the economy and, in particular, to show its economic relations with international capitalism.

* This Appendix is partly based on my previous papers, 'The silent class struggle', in *The silent class struggle* (Dar es Salaam: Tanzania Publishing House, 1973) and 'Capitalism unlimited: public corporations in partnership with multi-national corporations', *The African Review*, Vol. 3, No. 3 (1973). I am grateful to the editors of *The African Review* for permission to use this material. Some of the empirical data are either taken from or based on G. Tschannerl's paper, 'Periphery development and the working population in Tanzania' (University of Dar es Salaam: May 1974, mimeo). I am grateful to Tschannerl for letting me see and make use of the very first draft.

ONE

The Nature of the Economy

1.1 SECTORAL DISTRIBUTION

As is typically the case with the underdeveloped economies and more so those of Africa, Tanzania's economy is based on primary production with a narrow industrial sector and a large, 'parasitic' services sector. This is brought out by both the sectoral distribution of the GDP and employment. Table B.1 gives figures for the underdeveloped world as a whole for comparison purposes.

TABLE A

GDP BY INDUSTRIAL SECTOR 1962–72 (At current prices)

Sector	1964	1967	1972
MILLION SHILLINGS			
1. Agriculture & mining	2924	3053	4080
2. Industry & construction	581	967	1581
3. Services	2089	2772	4189
Total	5594	6792	9850
PERCENT			
1. Agriculture & mining	52	45	41
2. Industry & construction	10	13	16
3. Services	38	42	43
Total	100	100	100
PRODUCTIVE ACTIVITIES[a]			
Million shs	3337	3711	5160
Percent of total GDP	60	55	52

[a] Productive activities consist of agriculture, mining, manufacturing, and public utilities.

Source: G. Tschannerl, 'Periphery development and the working population in Tanzania', op. cit., Table 4·1, p. 35.

APPENDIX: UNDERDEVELOPMENT AND INTERNATIONAL CAPITALISM

It is interesting to note that between 1962–72, the share of productive activities (taking agriculture, mining, manufacturing, and public utilities) fell by 8 per cent. At the same time, between 1962–70, the rise in employment in the services sector was biggest – 12 per cent, and overall employment in *productive* activities again also *fell* by 12 per cent.

TABLE B

EMPLOYMENT BY INDUSTRIAL SECTOR 1962–70
(Including casual labourers, excluding Zanzibar.)

Sector	1962	1964	1967	1970
NUMBER				
1. Agriculture & mining	202 500	171 400	130 400	113 500
2. Industry & construction	79 400	62 000	80 200	109 600
3. Services	115 100	117 900	136 200	152 600
Total	397 000	351 300	346 800	375 700
PERCENT				
1. Agriculture & mining	51	49	38	30
2. Industry & construction	20	18	23	29
3. Services	29	33	39	41
	100	100	100	100
EMPLOYMENT IN PRODUCTIVE ACTIVITIES[a]				
Number	n.a.	199 600	168 700	168 500
Percent of total employment	n.a.	57	49	45

[a] As in the Table above.
Note: Domestic servants in private households, seasonal workers in peasant agriculture and those employed in the military forces are not included.

Source: G. Tschannerl, op. cit., Table 4·2, p. 37. and The Economic Survey, 1971-72.

TABLE B.1

EMPLOYMENT BY INDUSTRIAL SECTOR IN THE
UNDERDEVELOPED WORLD 1970

SECTOR	ASIA*		AFRICA†		LATIN AMERICA		TOTAL	
	%	millions	%	millions	%	millions	%	millions
Agriculture	66	277	67	77	34	30	61	384
Industry & construction	12	50	12	14	27	23	14	87
Services	22	93	21	24	39	34	25	151
Total	100	420	100	115	100	87	100	622

* Excluding People's Republic of China.
† Excluding Southern Africa.

Source: International Labour Office, *The employment prospects for the 1970s,* reprinted in, R. Jolly, *et. al.,* (ed), *Third world employment* (London: Penguin, 1973), p. 79.

1.2 EXPORT-ORIENTED PRIMARY PRODUCTION

Tanzania's economy is crucially dependent on the export of primary products mainly agricultural and to some extent mining. In 1962, the four main crops – sisal, coffee, cotton from the mainland, and cloves from the island – constituted 56 per cent of the total exports and, if diamonds are added, it comes to 66 per cent as shown in the Table below.

The export-pattern has not changed much since independence except that sisal has fallen from its leading place owing to a drastic fall in the sisal prices in the world market. None of these exports (as was discussed in the text, see p. 34) has a substantial domestic market.[1] They are primarily for export, thus conforming to what Professor Thomas[2] called one of the 'laws' of underdevelopment: Divergence between domestic resource use and domestic demand.

The export-orientation of the economy as a whole is further illustrated in Table D where the value of the exports is expressed as a percentage

[1] See Table 2 in the text.
[2] C. Thomas, 'The transition to socialism: issues of economic strategy in Tanzanian-type economies' (University of Dar es Salaam) (mimeo).

TABLE C

VALUE IN PERCENT OF MAIN PRIMARY EXPORTS 1962–72
(Per cent of total exports, including exports to East African Countries.)

COMMODITY	1962	1967	1972
Coffee (unroasted)	11	14	18
Cotton	13	15	17
Sisal (fibre & tow)	28	12	7
Cloves	4	12	7
Total (agriculture)	56	5	11
Diamonds	10	13	6
Total per cent exports of main primary products	66	59	59

Source: G. Tschannerl, op. cit., Based on his Table 3·1, p. 13.

of the total gross domestic production in the main productive sectors. It can be seen from the table that both in the pre-Arusha and the post-Arusha periods there was an upward trend in the export-orientation rising at 3·07 per cent and 2·7 per cent respectively.

TABLE D

*EXPORT-ORIENTATION IN
THE PRODUCTIVE SECTORS OF THE ECONOMY 1964–72**

(Value of total exports expressed as a percentage of the total GDP in the productive sectors† – both the export-values and GDP at 1966 prices.)

PRE-ARUSHA			POST-ARUSHA					
1964	1965	1966	1967	1968	1969	1970	1971	1972
77·22	79·52	83·35	70·99	65·01	65·48	65·46	77·45	82·43

* Productive sectors consist of agriculture, hunting, fishing, forestry; mining and manufacturing. Public utilities, almost fully *domestic* (and constituting a very small percentage), are left out.

† I am indebted to Hasan Fazel for computing these figures for me.

Sources: UR of Tanzania, *The Annual Economic Surveys.*
For export-price indices, J. Rweyemamu, 'Basic information on Tanzania's International Trade' (University of Dar es Salaam: January 1974) (mimeo).

As is typically the case with figures, these are only rough indications but there is no doubt that the economy is heavily dependent on the narrow range of primary products almost exclusively for export, slight shifts in the proportions since independence notwithstanding. As a matter of fact when a few attempts at the so-called diversification are made, they are usually within the same pattern. Thus, lately, much emphasis has been placed on the production of tobacco and cashew nuts, again for export. The value of tobacco exports rose from nothing in 1962 to 3 per cent of the total exports in 1972. The respective figures for cashew nuts are: 4 per cent (1962) to 7 per cent in 1972.

The commercial primary sector forms the very base of the economy for even the secondary sector and the *necessary* services are geared mainly to serve this sector.

1.3 CONSUMPTION-ORIENTED SECONDARY SECTOR

The narrow industrial sector is again a familiar phenomenon in the underdeveloped economies. Lately in Latin America this sector has been showing considerable growth owing to the multinational corporations transferring their processing, assembly and packaging, and a few capital-goods industries to this area. This is basically to take advantage of regional markets and the tariff protection afforded by various regional economic groupings as well as to forestall competition from rival oligopolies. This trend may be picking up in Africa as well. The parent multinational corporations continue to retain control over the local plants by essentially keeping their monopoly over science, technology, and research[3] and controlling both the markets and the supply of essential machinery and equipment.

This new strategy of the multinational corporations has been well described by none other than the organ of the international bourgeoisie, *Fortune*.

International Corporations originally invested in resource-based production – mines and plantations – for export to their home markets. . . . As [this] placed foreigners in . . . control of basic natural resources, it was . . . hated and in some cases nationalized.

In the era of import substitution, foreign investment began to assume an entirely different character. To protect infant local industries, governments had erected high tariff barriers or imposed stringent controls on a wide range of imports. Since foreign industrial companies could not export to developing countries over these barriers, they moved inside them. Foreign investment in extractive industries was supplemented by extensive outlays in, among other things, chemicals, pharmaceuticals, paper, automobiles, and farm

[3] cf. T. Szentes, '*Status quo* and socialism', in *The silent class struggle*, op. cit.

machinery. Like the first wave . . . into extractive industries – the third-wave investment will be specifically export-creating. Unlike investment involving ownership of natural resources, however, it probably will not elicit violent nationalistic reaction. The developing countries' contribution to this activity will be reserves of low-cost and teachable labour. The international corporation's input will be capital, of course, but also technical knowledge, global commercial intelligence, and marketing expertise.

With products where labour is a substantial part of total production costs and economies of scale are not especially great, the combination can be commercially successful. Such goods would include canned and frozen fruits and vegetables, textiles, clothing, leather products, furniture and other wood products, sewing machines, component and spare parts, forged hand tools, small motors, electrical parts and assemblies, and lathes and other simple machine tools.[4]

We shall see in subsequent sections that this is precisely the strategy borne out by the pattern of investments of the public corporations in Tanzania in partnership with the multinational corporations.

The Table below gives the detailed breakdown of the industrial divisions in the secondary sector.

TABLE E

THE SECONDARY SECTOR BY INDUSTRIAL DIVISIONS 1964–72
(Per cent of total GDP at current prices.)

INDUSTRIAL DIVISION	1964 %	1967 %	1972* %
Manufacturing & handcrafts	6·6	8·7	9·9
Electricity & water (public utilities)	0·8	0·9	1·1
Construction	3·0	4·6	5·1
Total	10·4	14·2	16·1

* Estimates.

Source: '*Hali ya Uchumi wa Taifa Katika Mwaka, 1972-73*', Table 2, p. 6.

Out of the six per cent growth between 1964 and 1972, one-third was in construction. More than half the employment is also in construction (Table F). A large percentage of so-called construction in fact consists of residential and non-residential buildings while the rest is basic in-

[4] Sanford Rose, 'The poor countries turn from buy-less to sell-more', April 1970, pp. 90–1.

TABLE F

EMPLOYMENT IN
THE SECONDARY SECTOR BY INDUSTRIAL DIVISION 1962–71

INDUSTRIAL DIVISION	1964		1968		1971*	
	Numbers	%	Numbers	%	Numbers	%
Manufacturing	23 583	38	35 359	38	54 714	46
Public utilities	4 637	8	9 601	11	10 618	9
Construction	33 740	54	47 305	51	52 658	45
Total	61 960	100	92 265	100	117 990	100

* Provisional.

Source: UR of Tanzania, *The Economic Survey, 1971–72*, p. 39.

frastructure building – roads, bridges, ferries, etc. In 1971, building construction was 54 per cent of the total construction, only one-fifth of
which could be considered for productive (i.e. *parastatal* and private
non-residential buildings) purposes.[5]

Manufacturing too has to be analysed further. It is virtually that of
consumer and intermediate goods while little capital goods – only 16
million shs in 1970.[6] The intermediate goods consist mainly of items
which go to the construction industry (building materials; saw milling;
wood products, etc.) and as inputs to the primary sector (cordage, rope
and twine, insecticides, etc.).[7]

The manufacture of consumer goods constituted 59 per cent of the
total gross domestic production in the manufacturing sector (1970).
Consumer goods production itself is heavily biased in favour of luxury
consumer goods. Mass consumption goods, on the other hand, consist
mainly of the processing of basic food-stuffs: Grain milling, sugar refin-
ing, and vegetable oil production alone in 1970 constituted over 70 per
cent by value of the total gross value of output of the mass consumption
goods.[8] (See Table below.)

Failure to provide the basic capital and producer goods to the agricultural sector, which in turn is not directed to the domestic but external
market, results in the small secondary sector only reinforcing the
external-orientation of the economy.

[5] *The Economic Survey, 1971–72*, Table 72, p. 102.
[6] G. Tschannerl, op. cit., p. 31.
[7] J. Rweyemamu, *Underdevelopment and industrialization* . . . , op. cit., pp.
244–5 for classification.
[8] See G. Tschannerl, op. cit., Table A.1, p. A.3.

TABLE G

VALUE ADDED BY CATEGORY OF CONSUMER GOODS, 1970

TYPE OF COMMODITY	VALUE ADDED (MILLION SHS)	PER CENT OF TOTAL
Export	87·4	20
Luxury consumption	140·9	33
Mass consumption	200·3	47
Total consumer goods	428·6	10·0
*Total consumer goods as per cent of total GDP in manufacturing**	59	–

* Computed from *The Economic Survey, 1971–72* (GDP at current prices).
Source: G. Tschannerl, op. cit., p. A3.

1.4 DISPROPORTIONATE (NON-PRODUCTIVE) SERVICES SECTOR

As Table A shows, this sector constitutes the largest percentage of the GDP. Again it was this sector which recorded the largest employment growth (Table B).

TABLE H

THE SERVICES SECTOR BY INDUSTRIAL DIVISIONS, 1964–72
(Per cent of total GDP at current prices.)

INDUSTRIAL DIVISION	1964	1967	1972*
Wholesale & retail trade, restaurants & hotels	11·8	12·7	13·0
Transport, storage & communications	6·2	7·9	8·8
Finance, insurance, real estate & business services	9·2	10·7	10·7
Public administration & other services	10·6	11·0	11·6
Total per cent of GDP	37·8	42·3	44·1

* Estimates.
Source: The Economic Survey, 1971–72, and 72-73, p. 6.

TABLE I

EMPLOYMENT IN
THE SERVICES SECTOR BY INDUSTRIAL DIVISIONS, 1964–71

INDUSTRIAL DIVISION	1964		1968		1971*	
	Numbers	%	Numbers	%	Numbers	%
Commerce	17 341	15	21 415	15	22 508	13
Transport & communications	25 670	22	31 764	22	39 984	24
Finance	—		—		5,681	3
Services (public administration & other)	74 662	63	90 933	63	100 505	60
Total	117 673	100	144 112	100	168 678	100

* Provisional.

Source: The Economic Survey, 1971–72, p. 39.

The large services sector in an underdeveloped economy has to be distinguished from a large tertiary sector in an economy like that of the United States. In the latter case, the tertiary sector is based on a strong secondary sector and therefore forms part of an integrated economy. This is not the case with underdeveloped economies as we have already seen.

The structure of the economy we have discussed is the internal *reflection* of the economy's external 'links' with international capitalism. It is this that we briefly consider in the next two sections.

TWO

Relations with International Capitalism I: Trade and 'Aid'

2.1 TRADE AND TRADING PARTNERS

We saw in section 1.2 that the principal exports of the economy are primary products, mainly agricultural. Its imports have been changing the pattern since independence from a consumer goods bias to an emphasis on capital and intermediate goods.

TABLE J

COMPOSITION OF IMPORTS 1967–71 (Per cent of total value of imports includes E.A. countries)

CLASS OF ITEM	1967	1971
Consumer goods	35	27
Intermediate goods	41	43
Capital goods	24	30
Total	100	100

Source: G. Tschannerl, op. cit., Table 3.3, p. 21.

The fall in consumer goods imports are due mainly to import-substitution in such areas as textiles, beverages, and tobacco. Thus the imports of beverages and tobacco fell from 53 million shs in 1962 to 11 million in 1971, while textiles fell from 169 million shs in 1962 when they constituted roughly one-sixth of the total imports, to 77 million in 1971.[9] On the other hand the imports of such non-consumer goods as mineral fuels, and lubricants, and transport equipment have gone up considerably. For example, the imports of cars and other transport equipment rocketed from 93 million shs in 1962 to 371 million shs in 1971.[9] In recent years because of the food shortages, the import of food has also

[9] The Economic Surveys, 1971–72; 1968; and 1972.

gone up. (For example: 183 million shillings in 1971 to 312 million shillings in 1972.)[9]

The pattern of imports presents the familiar picture of a former colony, becoming independent and indulging in a spate of import-substitution industrialization to 'save foreign exchange.' Since most of these import-substitution activities have very high import-content – not to mention the high costs of production – it is soon discovered that this type of activity does not help *even* to save foreign exchange. The next stage usually is to try and stimulate *exports* again to earn foreign exchange. But the manufactured exports from the 'third world' countries fail to penetrate the markets of the developed countries: they are not competitive and in any case are kept out by the high tariffs that the developed countries impose on *manufactured* goods from the under-developed countries. Failing both, temporary reliefs are sought in loans and aid from the capitalist countries and the World Bank only to be burdened with debt-servicing and repayments. The vicious circle is complete and continues to be worse.

TABLE K

SOURCES OF IMPORTS 1962–72
(Per cent of total value of imports.)

AREA	1962	1967	1972
Developed capitalist countries, of which	54	59	48
... UK	(26)	(24)	(16)
... EEC	(11)	(21)	(21)
Socialist countries	1	7	18
of which ... China	(0)	(4)	(17)
'third world'	26	20	12
of which ... Kenya & Uganda	(21)	(17)	(11)
Other*	19	14	22
Total	100	100	100

Source: G. Tschannerl, op. cit., p. 27. (Based on his Table 3.)

Note: Developed capitalist countries = UK, EEC, N. America; Japan and Hong Kong. (Hong Kong, though not a developed capitalist country basically serves that area.)

* The large percentage in the 'other' category includes some developed capitalist countries and some 'third world' countries. Therefore, this is only a rough indication, though the dominance of the capitalist world as sources of imports is clear.

[9] *The Economic Surveys, 1971-72*; 1968; and 1972.

APPENDIX: UNDERDEVELOPMENT AND INTERNATIONAL CAPITALISM

As for the trading partners Tanzania since independence has been increasingly moving away from the United Kingdom to other capitalist countries, in particular the European Economic Community with which it has an Association Agreement. In recent years China has come to occupy an important place as a supplier of imports. This is mainly because of the Tanzania–Zambia Railways (TAZARA) whose local costs are paid by 'buying' commodities from China. Thus the fall in the capitalist countries' share as a source of imports is made up by China. In the case of exports too the share of the capitalist countries has fallen. The shares of the socialist countries to some extent and the 'third world' have risen. Actually, it is only two or three 'third world' countries (India and Zambia in particular) which import substantial amounts from Tanzania. India for example is the sole importer of Tanzania's cashew nuts.

Overall, the capitalist countries still constitute the most important trading partners of Tanzania.

TABLE L

DESTINATION OF EXPORTS 1962–71
(Per cent of total value of exports).
(Excluding East Africa.)

AREA	1962	1968	1971
Developed capitalist countries	88	64	61
Socialist countries	–	6	7
'Third World' countries	10	27	25
Others	2	3	7
Total	100	100	100

Source: E. A. Customs & Excise, *Annual Trade Reports*.

2.2 'AID'

Since independence Tanzania has been borrowing and receiving grants from foreign countries. Table M, which gives figures for the so-called foreign 'aid' in each year since 1962, illustrates the importance of 'aid' in the economy.

It is interesting to note that the total foreign aid after the Arusha Declaration to 1973 was almost three times the previous six-year period.

Together with increased loans, debt servicing has also been going up. In 1971, it stood at 8 per cent of the export earnings.[10]

[10] *The Economic Survey*, 1971–72, p. 28.

TABLE M

FOREIGN AID 1962–72
(Million shs)

PRE-ARUSHA PERIOD

	1961–62	1962–63	1963–64	1964–65	1965–66	1966–67
External loans	79·4	5·8	27·8	59·1	75·7	119·9
External grants	63·6	98·6	23·6	19·5	7·8	7·4
Total foreign aid	143·0	104·4	51·4	78·6	83·5	127·3

Total foreign aid in the Pre-Arusha period (6 years), 588·2.

POST-ARUSHA PERIOD

	1967–68	1968–69	1969–70	1970–71	1971–72*	1972–73*
External loans	81·5	122·7	121·5	269·7	347·4	635·9
External grants	2·5	0·1	0·4	0·1	37·8	110·7
Total foreign aid	84·0	122·8	121·9	269·8	385·2	746·6

Total foreign aid in the Post-Arusha period (6 years), 1730·3.

* Estimates.
(Excluding TAZARA).

Source: The Annual Economic Surveys.

The following table shows the 'aid donors'. Again the developed capitalist countries and the capitalist-dominated world agencies dominate the scene. (In 1962, the 'aid' donor was almost exclusively the United Kingdom.)

Apart from trade and 'aid', the other most important relationship with international capitalism is in terms of investments. Before the Arusha Declaration, these were under the direct ownership of the multinational corporations and, after the Declaration, in joint ventures or other forms of partnerships with the public corporations. It is this that we consider next.

TABLE N

SOURCE OF EXTERNAL LOANS 1962–72

AREA	1962		1968		1972*	
	Million shs	%	Million shs	%	Million shs	%
Developed capitalist world (including US dominated world agencies)	105·6	100	380·9	81·5	991·9	81·5
Socialist countries of which China	–	–	76·3 (75·1)	16·3	207·5 (207·5)	17·0
Others	–	–	10·0	2·1	17·9	1·5
Total	105·6	100	467·2	100	1217·3	100

* As at 31st March.
(Excluding TAZARA.)

Source: The Annual Economic Survey, 1971–72, p. 31 and 1966–67, p. 66.

THREE

Relations with International Capitalism II: Investments and Partnerships with Multinational Corporations

3.1 BEFORE THE ARUSHA DECLARATION

The strategy adopted by the post-independence government typically involved inviting foreign investments. The First Five-Year Plan allocated something like 80 per cent of investments to foreign sources.

Table O shows the sectoral distribution of foreign investments in Tanzania in 1964, which conforms to the pattern of foreign investments in the 'third world' generally.

TABLE O

SECTORAL DISTRIBUTION OF DIRECT FOREIGN INVESTMENTS IN 1964

SECTORS	£000	%
Raw materials	7 352	60·1
Consumer goods	2 393	19·0
Services	1 782	14·6
Intermediate goods	86	0·7
Producer goods	613	5·0
Total	12 226	100·0

Source: J. Rweyemamu, 'The political economy of foreign investments in the underdeveloped countries', *The African Review*, Vol. I, no. 1 (March 1971), p. 108, Table I.

Table P shows the capital inflow and the profit outflow. Thus within this period of eight years the outflow exceeded the inflow by 373·2 million shillings – a net loss to the economy. Of course, this is not the

TABLE P

OUTFLOW OF INTERNATIONAL INVESTMENT INCOME (GROSS)
AND INFLOW OF PRIVATE LONG-TERM CAPITAL (NET) 1961–68

YEAR	PROFIT OUTFLOWS	CAPITAL IN FLOW
	(Million shs)	(Million shs)
1961	−71·2	+50
1962	−73	+58
1963	−123	+155
1964	−93	+79
1965	−110	−6
1966	−114	+138
1967	−159	−66
1968	−114	+76
Total	−857·2	+484

Source: J. Rweyemamu, 'The political economy . . .,' op. cit., Table 2, p. 115.

whole picture for there are many other ways by which the foreign
corporations drain away surplus from the underdeveloped economies.

The few important industrial projects initiated during the period all
illustrate the fact that foreign investments only reinforce the dependency
relations of the host economy.

Thus the oil refinery (TIPER) was established by the Italian government firm, ENI, which was interested in getting a foothold in the market.
It was trying to ward off a potential threat from its rival consolidated
Petroleum Company (a consortium of Shell, British Petroleum, Caltex,
and another American company) which had built a two-million-ton
capacity refinery in Mombasa.[11]

The second project, the Kilombero Sugar Plant, was built by British–
Dutch interests and managed by HVA International NV of Holland.
This was to take advantage of the rise in world sugar prices in the early
1960s as a result of the ban imposed by the United States on imports of
sugar from Cuba.

The Associated Portland Cement Company together with Cementia
Holding from Zurich, invested in a cement plant in the third major
project. Associated Portland is a London company with 43 subsidiaries
and associated companies with a capital of B£142 068 000. It is listed
at no. 34 in *'The Times* 300'. White's South African Portland Cement
Co. Ltd, and the Salisbury Portland Cement Co. Ltd, are its subsidiaries in Southern Africa. In 1967 its world sales totalled
B£122 500 000 with Group profits over B£12 000 000.[12] Its Kenya

[11] J. Rweyemamu, *Underdevelopment and industrialization*, op. cit., p. 125.
[12] *Who controls industry in Kenya?*, op. cit., pp. 51–2.

interests include both important cement companies – the East Africa Portland Cement Company Ltd, and the Bamburi Portland Cement Company Ltd. It is linked with Mackenzie–Dalgety and with A. Baumann & Co. Ltd, through interlocked directorships. The Bamburi Cement Co. and Smith Mackenzie, in fact, provided loans for the establishing of the Dar es Salaam plant. 'Thus, using Tanzania's own raw materials, the new cement company ensured its position in the rapidly expanding Tanzanian market – in 1967, Tanzania consumed almost 20 per cent more cement than Kenya – while avoiding the cost of the long haul from Kenya.'[13]

A number of textile firms were also set up during the period either by former Indian businessmen or as joint ventures with multinational corporations. This was typical import-substitution industrialization.

3.2 AFTER THE ARUSHA DECLARATION

Following the Arusha Declaration, the National Development Corporation, NDC, acquired majority ownership in some seven large, foreign-owned companies. The Government also took over outright a majority of the food processing firms. Thus the public sector was substantially expanded. But nationalization does not necessarily mean socialization of the economy. In fact, it did not even loosen the grip of the multinational corporations for the NDC immediately went into a variety of partnership arrangements with them. Thus they continued to manage their former companies. Although changes in details have been since taking place, it is still useful to discuss in some detail these partnerships with the multinational corporations which constitute an important aspect of the economic relations with international capitalism.[14]

3.2.1 *Forms of partnership*
The partnership between the public corporation and a multinational corporation (MNC) takes various forms. The MNC may participate with the public corporation in the equity of a subsidiary established to carry out a particular project. In most cases it is in fact satisfied to be a minority shareholder. In many of the subsidiaries of the National Development Corporation (NDC), the foreign partner owns anything from 10 to 45 per cent of the equity. An interesting form of partnership taken by a finance corporation is illustrated by the Tanganyika Development Finance Ltd. The NDC, the Commonwealth Development Corporation of Britain, the Netherlands Finance Company for Developing

[13] A. Seidmann, *Comparative development strategies in East Africa* (Nairobi: East African Publishing House, 1972), pp. 113–14.
[14] The discussion that follows is largely taken from my paper 'Capitalism unlimited . . .', op. cit.

Countries of Holland, German company for economic co-operation of West Germany hold shares in equal proportion in this company. Its main function appears to be to act as a catalyst fishing out and stimulating new projects in which foreign monopoly capital can combine with local state or private capital.[15] Here is an example of an economic partnership between the states of three developed capitalist countries and that of an underdeveloped country to provide, what is, basically, an infrastructural service in the modern financial world, to foreign and local private capital. The historical drama of the capitalist state ultimately serving the interests of the capitalist class appears to be re-enacted on the world stage!

The third and probably the most important form of partnership is where a public corporation, its subsidiary or its associate, enters into a Management–Service Agreement with a multinational corporation. The Management–Service Agreement embraces General Management Agency Agreement; Consultancy Agreement; Licensing Agreement; Marketing and Sales Agreement; Purchasing Agreement, etc. These agreements are not mutually exclusive and in practice they are found in varied combinations. In each case, it is possible that the Management Agent also participates in the equity of the company in which case we would have Partnership–Management Agreement, Partnership–Consultancy Agreement, and so on. The duration of the management contracts depends on the mutual agreement of the parties and may be automatically renewable. Remuneration of the Managing Agents also varies. It may take, among others, any of the following forms, singly or in combination:

(1) commission fees;
(2) percentage of net sales or turnover;
(3 percentage of profit before taxes;
(4) percentage of profit after tax and depreciation;
(5) fixed fee;
(6) purchase of machinery, equipment, etc.;
(7) payment for travelling, board, and lodging expenses;
(8) royalty for patent, trade mark usage, etc.

Again it is quite common to provide in such agreements that the payment will be made wholly or partly in foreign, named currency.

In a number of cases the agreements stipulate the governing law and in a substantial number, this is foreign law. In certain cases, the Arbitration Clauses provide for the venue (London, Paris, etc.), and even the Tribunal (International Chamber of Commerce, Paris, etc.).

The case of the BAT (Tanzania) Ltd, illustrates some of the points discussed above. BAT was one of the seven companies in which the NDC acquired majority shareholding as a result of the Arusha Declara-

[15] See TDFL Annual Reports.

tion nationalizations. The BAT was a wholly owned subsidiary of the EA Tobacco (UK) Limited, which itself is the subsidiary of the BAT Limited of London. By virtue of the nationalization (with compensation), the NDC acquired 60 per cent shares while the EA Tobacco retained the rest. Immediately, BAT Tanzania entered into a Management Agreement with BAT (UK). The duration of the Agreement is for 12 years presumably because the compensation is to be paid over that period and the original owners would like to control the company meanwhile to safeguard their compensation payment. The remuneration was to be 5 per cent of the net profit after deduction of taxes and depreciation.

These partnership arrangements allow the multinational corporations to serve the old ends of exploitation through new forms.

During the era of formal colonialism, the metropolitan companies had the fullest support of their respective states and were free to exploit the resources of the 'third world' through the typical form of absolute capitalist private ownership. But even during this period where local private capital was relatively strong foreign capital quickly entered into partnership with it. Such examples are to be found in a number of Latin American and Asian countries, especially India. Thus, for instance, the Management Agency contracts between foreign and local private capital developed very rapidly in India in the 1930s.[16] But as the wave of nationalism began to rise, and the formal colonialism began to withdraw the form through which the resources of the 'third world' were to be exploited had also to be changed. Furthermore, the newer forms had become necessary also because of the important changes in the international economic and political order. The expanding socialist world provided the 'third world' with an example and the alternative of public state ownership to private ownership. The monopoly of technology and science in the hands of the MNCs plus the large size, relative financial autonomy, and long-term horizon, not to mention the military might and the political leverage of their powerful states, meant that the MNCs commanded a very strong position (bargaining or otherwise) *vis-à-vis* the underdeveloped countries. Hence, complete ownership of the means of production in the 'third world' was not absolutely necessary. What was important was to retain control of the means of production so as to ensure the supply of important raw materials, expanding markets and good profits. As William H. Beatty, the Vice-President of the Chase Manhattan Bank remarked in January 1965:

Most successful projects have been achieved without hard and fast requirements for certain rigid percentages of stock ownership. The important element is that there be a meeting of minds at the beginning as to who does what – *who manages and controls*. Under

[16] cf. M. Kidron, *Foreign investments in India* (London: Oxford University Press, 1965).

167

these circumstances, a minority shareholder can in fact functionally not only manage but control the enterprise.[17] [Emphasis mine.]

In fact, the initial hostile reactions notwithstanding, the spokesmen of the imperialist big finance have taken the African nationalizations rather calmly. In some cases the companies themselves offered participation to the governments. Paul Semonin, in his article 'Nationalizations and Management in Zambia' cites the spokesmen of Shell–BP who claimed that initiative for the government's newly announced 51 per cent participation in their operations came from the Company and was 'a good business deal'. *The Economist*,[18] following the Zambian nationalizations, cautioned its investor readers to analyse the move rationally. It said:

> It will be a pity if the realities of President Kaunda's move last week to nationalize Zambia's copper mines are overlooked in a useless debate on the ethics of it. It will be a tragedy if potential investors in Africa are mistakenly led to believe that there is no longer a place for them there. Although doing business in independent Africa now calls for a high degree of political acumen, the opportunities available to those who possess it are good. The risks are greater than in more settled parts of the world but so are the returns.

The article continues:

> The questions that anyone either possessing or contemplating a financial stake in Zambia ought to be asking have to do with the future political and economic stability of the country, rather than with the principles of nationalization or the mechanics of compensation. The shrewdest businessmen in that part of the world have argued for some time that 49 per cent stake in a business whose success is underwritten by government participation may be more valuable than 100 per cent of a concern exposed to all the political winds that blow. Companies (like Booker Brothers) that have anticipated the direction of events and invited the government into partnership have no reason to regret Zambian investment so far.

A. H. Ball, the Chairman of Lonrho Ltd one of the most important MNCs in Africa said:

> We welcome Government participation in these businesses for, in our view, the very fact that Government will be a substantial shareholder should assist in their future stability and expansion.[19]

These assessments by the spokesmen of the MNCs are not very far from the truth for they stand to derive a number of benefits through these partnerships.

[17] Quoted in P. Semonin, 'Nationalizations and management in Zambia', *Maji Maji*, No. 1, 1971, p. 23.
[18] 'A stake in Zambia', 23 August 1969, p. 56.
[19] Quoted in Semonin, op. cit., p. 19.

3.2.2 Benefits of Partnership

Mobilization followed by denationalization of local capital: With a relatively small equity capital and a management contract, a multi-national corporation can mobilize and use substantial amounts of local capital. By associating with local private or public capital and retaining day-to-day control through a management–service agreement, it is able to effectively *denationalize* local capital. Thus, for instance, the Tanganyika Development Finance Company, which we have already mentioned, had something like Shs 226 million invested in its 42 or so projects at the end of 1971. Out of this, total local capital constituted about 63 per cent (Shs 141·95 million) and the foreign capital the remaining 37 per cent (Shs 84·05 million). Large portions of so-called foreign capital may in fact be part of the profits made during the period of the company's existence (i.e. 1962–71), and ploughed back, thereby increasing the assets of the company without net foreign exchange gain for the national economy. As Pierre Jalee, citing the Moroccan case, has pointed out:

> [Foreign capital] knows that the enterprise is viable only on the basis of foreign patents, foreign materials and supplies, and foreign technical capital. Although in the majority, the indigenous capital is the prisoner of its foreign partner. Mixed investment is, perhaps, the worst form of neo-imperialist exploitation for it ties up the indigenous capital of the host country and denationalizes it.[20]

Retaining the old and capturing the new markets: By associating with public capital, the foreign partner retains his previous market or, if he is new, gets a foothold in the new market with all the protection and backing of the state. I have already cited the example of the oil refinery. Another case is that of the radio assembly plant, established by the Philips Electronics (EA) Ltd, a subsidiary of Philips of the Netherlands. This plant was established because after 1962 Philips began to lose its radio market to Matsushita of Japan. Philips was able to break down this competition only by establishing the assembly plant and getting a 50 per cent tariff protection. Matsushita retaliated by setting up a battery factory in Dar es Salaam.[21]

In addition, the foreign partner, most likely a member of a global multinational group, is able to collect market and economic intelligence for the group as a whole and establish necessary contacts.

Thus when the mismanagement of the Mwananchi Engineering and Construction Company (MECCO) by its managing agent the OCC (Overseas Construction Company of Holland) was discovered, it was also revealed that OCC was using MECCO at cheap rates as sub-

---

[20] P. Jalee, *The pillage of the third world* (New York: Monthly Review Press 1968), p. 82.

[21] J. Rweyemamu, *Underdevelopment . . .* , op. cit., p. 125.

contractors.[22] Similarly, Mlonot, an Israeli company formerly managing the Kilimanjaro Hotel, used to divert the clients of Kilimanjaro to its own hotel, The Africana – a Vacation Village.[23]

Tariff protection, duty, and tax concessions: One of the important immediate advantages that the foreign partner derives from the partnership is the tariff protection, which is quite high for locally produced goods in many African countries. This considerably reduces the competition that the foreign firm would otherwise have to face from the rival oligopolies. (See the Philips case above.) On top of that, in many African countries the foreign firm, by virtue of having brought in new investment and especially when the local company participates with public corporation and is considered a public enterprise, is entitled to all sorts of tax and import duty concessions.

Priority in government contracts, etc.: Being considered a public enterprise means it gets priority in government contracts, tenders, etc. It would also be easier to get work permits for its expatriate staff, guarantees that a certain portion of its remuneration may be repatriated, not to mention the fact that the state bureaucracy as a whole looks favourably and would give priority to public enterprise, and thereby the foreign partners in the public enterprise.[24]

Outlet for the products of the group: The foreign partner who is a managing agent is in a very good position to encourage the sale of the products of the parent company; to hire out patents, trade marks, etc.; to make use of the R. & D. programme already developed by the Group, at a fee-even to push obsolete machinery on to the local subsidiary. Most important of all, and the common feature of the partnership relation, is the manipulation of inter-corporate prices thereby enhancing the profits or reducing the costs and taxes of the parent company or the Group as a whole.

Pressuring the government: Partnership with state capital substantially facilitates the use of infrastructural activities, such as loans from the nationalized banks, by the foreign partner. Where the public corporation is a partner, the government does all the pressuring necessary to get things done.

This is very well illustrated in the recent example of the Tanzania Fertilizer Factory, the subsidiary of NDC in which Kloeckner of West Germany holds 40 per cent of the shares and also has a management contract. In this case it was necessary to build a jetty for transporting the raw materials for the factory. It was the NDC which exerted all the

[22] A. Coulson, 'Blood sucking contracts' (University of Dar es Salaam: mimeo).

[23] ibid.

[24] See, for instance, R. Hutchison, 'How UK firm exploited Tanzania', in *Daily News*, 26 and 27 July 1973. These articles expose the actions of the UK's Macmillan Co. which was in partnership with the NDC in the local company, the Tanzania Publishing House. The TPH case once more illustrates all the points we have made about the 'results' of partnership with MNCs.

pressure necessary for the jetty to be built.[25] (Notwithstanding the fact that Kloeckner, as Andrew Coulson has shown, are likely to be the net beneficiaries of this whole project rather than Tanzania's economy.)

Political security, security against high wage demands, strikes, etc.: Political security is probably one of the most important benefits that a MNC derives by associating with public capital. The state, with all its vigour and under the guise of encouraging economic development, passes all sorts of legislation – anti-strike laws, ceiling on wages – which ultimately benefit the MNC. In both Tanzania and Zambia strikes are virtually illegal and if and when the workers go on strike, they are accused of economic sabotage. President Kaunda banned the strikes and froze the wages of the mineworkers simultaneously with the partial nationalization of the mines.[26] The trade unions and the political party, too, are likely to be reluctant to back workers of a company whose majority shareholder is a public corporation, notwithstanding the fact that day-to-day management is in the hands of a foreign firm.

The above is not an exhaustive list of the numerous benefits derived by the MNCs from the partnership. Nevertheless, it is formidable, for we shall now try to show that what is beneficial to an MNC is detrimental to the underdeveloped economy.

3.2.3 *Losses to the public corporations*

Siphoning off surplus: The historical relation of the underdeveloped countries with the developed countries has, besides many other things, meant the drain of a large portion of the economic surplus generated in the 'third world' to the metropolitan countries. This has been well-documented,[27] and it is not necessary to go into statistical details here. If this was true during the colonial times, it is still truer today. The large income from the 'third world' is one of the most important reasons behind foreign investment. Profits and other revenues which are repatriated by the MNCs represent a net loss to the host economy. The size of this loss is difficult to estimate, especially after the nationalizations where association with foreign capital takes such forms as Management–Service Agreements. The profits and interests on loans, etc., made by the MNCs as equity holders and shown officially in the accounts in themselves are substantial but this does not give the true picture. Most of the companies that enter into partnership with the NDC, for instance, are members of some global group. This means that the company concerned is in an excellent position to manipulate inter-corporate prices, over-invoicing, etc., thereby enhancing the profits of the Group as a

[25] A. Coulson, 'The fertilizer factory', *Maji Maji*, No. 8 (1972), p. 26.
[26] Semonin, op. cit.
[27] cf. Ernest Mandel, *Marxist economic theory* (New York: Monthly Review Press, 1969). Jalee, *The pillage of the third world*; op. cit., Harry Magdoff, *The age of imperialism* (New York: Monthly Review Press, 1969).

whole. For example, when President Kaunda announced that the foreign companies would not be allowed to repatriate profits in excess of 50 per cent, the giant Anglo-American changed its accounting procedures so as to increase the apparent profits from which dividends (and remissions) were declared. As Zulu, the Governor of the Bank of Zambia declared: 'Before Mulungushi they minimized profits in order to pay less taxes. Now they maximize profits to get them out of the country.'[28]

One economist has estimated that before the nationalizations Tanzania may have lost as much as 80 million shillings per year through various manipulations, some forms of which we have discussed above.[29]

Besides the profits made on equity holding, one must take into account the drain of surplus through the Management/Service Agreements, increasingly the more important form of capital export. We will illustrate this by a few examples.

The Overseas Construction Company, the former managing agent of MECCO, was charging the latter 1 per cent of the overall turnover as its management fees. When they found that the company was not making profits they artificially tried to maximize the turnover by taking on large contracts even when they knew that they would make losses on them. They over-invoiced (a tower crane was purchased from Europe for much above its cost price); they used MECCO to do subcontracting work for OCC (who were the main contractors for new berths in Dar es Salaam harbour) 'at below cost rates – some of the rates for earth-moving were so low that they did not even cover the running costs of the machinery'[30] and, when the mismanagement of MECCO by OCC was revealed, they had to be paid 2 million shillings for their virtually worthless shares before they left.

The Kilimanjaro Hotel, which was managed by an Israeli firm, Mlonot, is another such example. The management agreement provided that Mlonot would pay the Government two-thirds of the net operating profits of the hotel, or $6\frac{1}{2}$ per cent on the Government investment, whichever was greater. The balance would be kept by Mlonot. 'The net operating profit was carefully defined to exclude payments of rent and provision for depreciation. To cover the expenses of running the hotel Government would pay Mlonot a "group management fee" equal to 3 per cent of the turnover.'[31] Mlonot organised its accounts to ensure maximum return for itself.

All three of these case studies show the enormous loss in surplus incurred by a host country through countless ways by which the foreign partner manipulates the management agreements. Since the statistics are

[28] Quoted in Semonin, op. cit.

[29] Aart J. M. van de Laar, 'Foreign business and capital-export from developing countries', in J. Saul & L. Cliffe, Socialism in Tanzania, Vol. 1.

[30] Coulson, 'Blood sucking contracts', op. cit., p. 9. The information on MECCO and the Kilimanjaro Hotel is taken from this source.

[31] ibid.

'top secret' in this area, it is difficult to compute the amount of the loss involved. Van de Laar, in the study already cited, estimates that Tanzania may have lost over 25 million shillings in 1966 through fees for management agents, payments for patents, trade marks, etc. This figure is certainly an underestimate. If one were to arrive at even a rough approximation of the total costs, one would have to take into account, besides the management fees, such other costs as: overpricing of raw materials, machinery, and equipment supplied by the foreign partner; fees for patents, trade marks, licences, fees for feasibility surveys, market research, inflated salaries, and such facilities as housing for the expatriate staff and so on.

While, therefore, it is difficult to estimate exactly the extent of surplus drainage or capital-export resulting from the exploitation by foreign capital, there is no doubt that this is substantial. Based on Van de Laar's estimates, one can safely say that this may be anything between 30 and 50 per cent of the gross national investment. This is by no means a small figure. In fact, the retention of such an amount of the economic surplus within the country and its productive investment could decisively and critically affect the rate of economic development. Thus partnership with foreign capital substantially reduces the size of economic surplus available for investment.

Next we propose to discuss how this association with foreign capital effects the *mode of utilization* of the economic surplus.

Pattern of investment: The main criterion by which private investors make their investment decision is, of course, profit; if not in the short-run definitely in the long-run. Public corporations in most underdeveloped countries are no different in this respect. Their investment decisions too are based on the criterion of profit as is clearly illustrated in the case of the National Development Corporation. In fact, they can hardly do otherwise. Most of these public corporations function in the overall unplanned liberal economy. Therefore, their project evaluation and investment decisions which are not based on profit would in fact be irrational. What is irrational therefore is not so much the investment decisions (based on profit) made at micro-level, i.e. at the level of each individual project or individual public corporation, but the system (i.e. the macro-economy) itself. And this overall economy is what we call, the colonially structured, externally oriented economy. Economic development on the other hand, requires a structural reorganization to lay the foundations for a nationally integrated or internally oriented economy. This in turn requires a planned generation and utilization of the economic surplus. The use of the economic surplus based on the profit criterion, given the structures of the economy, only reinforces the two important characteristics of an underdeveloped economy described by Professor Thomas:

(1) Divergence of domestic resource use and domestic demand; and
(2) Divergence of needs with demand. (This, in fact, succinctly ex-

presses the essentials of what we have called the colonially structured economy, which is characterized by a cumulative divergence between domestic resource use and domestic demand and between demand and needs.)

The investment pattern as we saw in the earlier section has a double bias: against capital goods and against mass consumption goods production. This pattern only perpetuates the two characteristics described by Thomas.

There are many ways by which association with foreign private capital leads to investment decisions by the public corporations resulting in the pattern just discussed. Some of the more important of these are:

(1) *The control of the enterprise by the managing agents:* The managing agents not only make day-to-day decisions but also exert decisive influence on the Board of Directors. It is they who advise, produce board papers, and generally argue out the case for a particular investment. The director-representative of a public corporation – who may be representing his corporation on several boards – has neither the time nor the expertise to argue successfully against this. (And in any case, in the absence of any overall strategy, the assumptions of the local director are unlikely to be very different from those of the foreign partner.) Besides, being the supplier of machinery or raw materials, patent or trade marks, or a marketing agent and probably a substantial lender as well, the foreign partner is in an overwhelmingly strong bargaining position.

(2) *Initiation of projects:* In many cases the original ideas for a particular project in fact come from a potential foreign partner. It is not uncommon that an aggressive foreign salesman who has some machinery to sell sets the ball rolling and probably also offers to do the feasibility survey.

(3) *Leverage of the home state:* The foreign partner – the MNCs – do not stand alone but in various ways are backed by their home states. Thus, besides the political leverage that the home state exerts, it is often the case that a loan from the foreign partner is secured by the home government, or the purchase of machinery and equipment is backed by suppliers' credit. In these cases, there is every reason to believe that the foreign state can in important ways affect the destination of the particular investment. In fact reliance on foreign finance from such institutions as the World Bank and the International Finance Corporation very much affect the pattern of investment of the recipient countries. These institutions have their own ideas about the types of investments that should be made in the 'third world' no different from those of the MNCs.

All in all, association with MNCs plays a decisively influential role in structuring the pattern of investment, i.e. the mode of utilization of the economic surplus – thereby deciding the direction of development. And as we have shown, this is in the direction of reinforcing the externally oriented economy. Therefore whatever 'development' that takes place is in fact the development of underdevelopment.

Technological Underdevelopment: One of the chief arguments of the protagonists of partnership with foreign MNCs in Tanzania has been that it helps the underdeveloped country to get the necessary technology and train skilled manpower and managerial personnel. We propose to deal with the question of the importation of technology through partnership with an MNC from two important aspects: (1) What is the *extent* of technology imported, and the technical skills imparted; and (2) the *type* of technology imported, and the technical skills imparted.

The extent of the imported technology: The sectoral bias of the multi-national corporations' investment against capital goods means that not much technology is imported. In fact, absence of capital goods production means that the local plant has to rely almost exclusively on foreign sources for spare parts and maintenance. This greatly hinders the development of the integrated technology in the host economy. Technical consultancy agreements under foreign experts introduce a further bias against using anything available locally by way of spare parts and maintenance.

Secondly, the extent of skilled training imparted too is minimal. The foreign partner prefers to employ expatriates rather than to train local personnel. In fact, more often than not the number of expatriates employed is more than necessary. Thus in both the case studies we have referred to – the MECCO, where OCC were the managing agents, and the Kilimanjaro where Mlonot were managing – the foreign partner openly flouted the training provisions. The MECCO management agreement provided that OCC would undertake to train skilled craftsmen and technicians at all levels of industry, and would draw up a plan for a technical institution to be established within the organization of MECCO. Two and a half years later virtually nothing had been done in this direction. Instead it continued to employ expatriates. As Coulson has pointed out:

> The expatriate staff did not show any capacity for passing on their knowledge to Tanzanians and virtually no training was done, so that when OCC left Mr Tara Singh had to be called out of retirement to run the company again for a period.[32]

The Kilimanjaro case was worse. After nine years and shs.400 000 paid by the Government for training purposes, 'Mlonot was admitting that no steps to train middle and top level management had been taken, and that the training programme had been confined to junior staff'.[33] Even some two secretaries, a laundry manager, and the chief of reception were expatriates. When the agreement was terminated and Mlonot thrown

[32] A. Coulson, 'Blood sucking contracts', op. cit., p. 6.
[33] ibid.

out, the Chief of TTC had to rush to Europe to recruit new managers – there was no Tanzanian to take over! These cases are not exceptions but appear to be the rule. Often in the joint ventures, local personnel is employed in such areas as public relations, personnel matters, local marketing and sales, while technical areas are headed by the expatriates, thus depriving the local personnel of technical know-how.

The type of imported technology: The type of technology necessary at a particular stage of development in a particular economy depends on a number of factors, some of them specific to the economy and society concerned. Therefore technology cannot simply be imported but has to be adapted to the requirements of the host economy. The foreign partner is obviously not interested in such specific considerations. He is likely to import that technology which he knows best, which is cheaper and which in the final analysis gives him profit. Thus, for example, the important question of techniques – whether capital-intensive or labour-intensive – is also decided by the foreign partner. Arrighi[34] has argued that MNCs are typically biased against labour-intensive techniques and capital-goods industry. While it is wrong to say that underdeveloped countries simply need to employ labour-intensive techniques to reduce the problem of unemployment, the decision on the question of technique cannot be left to the foreign MNC. This is well illustrated by the following examples: Friendship Textile Mill and the Mwanza Textile Mill. The Friendship Textile Mill was built by the Chinese at a cost of £2·5 million with an interest-free loan, and is fully owned by the Tanzanian Government. At full capacity it employs over 3000 people and produces 24 million square yards of cloth and 1000 tons of yarn. The Mwanza Textile Mill built at a cost of £4 million, on the other hand, is 40 per cent owned by NDC, 40 per cent by the Nyanza Co-operative Union and 20 per cent by Amenital Holding Registered Trust. It is managed by Amenital's representatives Sodefra, Maurer Textiles of Geneva and Textil Consult of Vaduz. 'It is likely that the motive for Amenital's participation (which probably explains its meagre share capital participation) was to dispose of Société-Alsacienne des Constructions Mécaniques de Mulhause's (SACM) machinery. The fact that machinery was obtained with a supplier's credit of Shs.60 million, repayable over eight years, with three years of grace and an interest of 5.7 per cent per annum, may suggest that the profits of Sodefra must have accrued through over-invoicing of the machinery'.[35] Like the Friendship Mill, the Mwanza Textile Mill produces 24 million square yards annually but it is more capital-intensive and employs only 1200 local people as against 3000 of the Friendship. Whereas the Friendship Mill is being fully run by

[34] 'International corporations, labour aristocracies, and economic development in tropical Africa', in I. Rhodes (ed.), *Imperialism and revolution*, op. cit.
[35] Rweyemamu, *Underdevelopment and industrialization . . .* op. cit., p. 124.

local manpower, trained by the Chinese, who have already left, the Mwanza Textile Mill has only just initiated a programme for training.[36] Over and above that the Friendship has been making profits while the Mwanza Mill has been making losses due to, as the sixth NDC Annual Report puts it, 'heavy loan and interest payments'.[37]

Another example of an unnecessarily capital-intensive project is that of a 'semi-automatic' bakery built with the help of a Canadian loan. The machinery is bought from Canada. As one commentator pointed out, 'the project would have the effect of replacing 200 unskilled workers by a handful of skilled workers and some expatriates'.[38]

The important question of technique and the type of technology is often left to the foreign partner. Thus, in the case of the fertilizer plant where Kloeckner was to supply the machinery, the choice was left to the foreign partner: 'Kloeckner will select the most modern processes corresponding with the latest technical development in the chemical industry taking into consideration the objective conditions prevailing in Tanzania.'[39]

In some cases the technology imported is simply not suitable to local conditions. Thus, in the case of a cashew-nuts factory, Tanita Co. Ltd., the foreign partner – an Italian firm called Oltremare – supplied the machinery for which the Tanzanian Government provided the loan. The report in *Jenga* makes the following observation: '. . . the machinery for cashew processing at Tanita is what may be called "first generation" machinery and *it has taken the company time to adjust it in order to match it to the peculiar characteristics and shapes of the cashew-nuts.*'[40] (Emphasis mine.)

The other important aspect is the type of training that is imparted to local manpower. Firstly, since there is a bias for capital-intensive techniques, whatever techniques are imparted, affect only a small group of workers. Secondly, as we have already observed the expatriate staff are extremely reluctant to pass on technical know-how. Thirdly, given the fact that much foreign investment tends to be in light consumer goods as opposed to say, iron and steel or the machine tools industry, the technological knowledge or training that is imparted is not of the type which could create a large technically minded and mechanically skilled workforce. The latter is absolutely necessary for rapid industrialization. Fourthly, *how* useful and basic is the technological know-how imparted in such manufacturing industries as assembly and *packaging plants*: radio-assembling; motor-vehicle assembly; assembling electrical bulbs?

Finally, in the field of administrative training such as managerial,

---

[36] See *NDC Annual Report 1970*.
[37] *Sixth NDC Annual Report*, p. 60.
[38] 'Aid-What Aid!' in *The Nationalist*, 31 January 1971.
[39] Coulson, 'The fertilizer factory', op. cit., p. 2.
[40] *Jenga*, No. 13 (1973), p. 37.

accountants, administrators, etc., the training by the foreign partner is bound to leave behind the ethos of capitalism, thus reinforcing the ideological ties with the capitalist world.

For instance, the recent 'Operation Leapfrog' declared by NDC to train managers and administrators, is headed by a Dr David E. Emery. Dr Emery 'is on secondment to NDC from the IBM Corporation. During his two-year tour of duty, Dr Emery is sponsored by the Ford Foundation. He is now Management Development Adviser in the General Manager's Office and his primary responsibility is to establish a system [Operation Leapfrog] for training Tanzanian managers'.[41] So here is a man coming from one of the world's and America's largest corporations, sponsored by an American foundation, to train Tanzanian managers apparently to run a 'socialist' economy.

CONCLUSION

Thus Tanzania's economy continues to be part of the International Capitalist System. This is reflected in its internal structures and domestic class formations.

Economic structures do not exist in a vacuum. They exist only in terms of socio-economic relationships between the actors in the process of production. Thus the very question of the change of economic structures is inseparably tied up with the question of class struggle that I discussed in the text.

[41] *Jenga*, No 13 (1973), p. 31.

Index

Africa, classes in, 18–26
African Traders' Co-operative Society, 57
African traders, 42–3, 57
Agricultural Change in Modern Tanganyika (Iliffe), 16, 50–1, 111, 117
Agriculture, export orientation of, 39
Aid from overseas, 160–2
Akivaga, 90
Angwazi, 109
Army Mutiny (1964), 76
Arrighi, G., 19, 116, 176
Arusha Declaration (1967), 64, 76, 78, 103, 126
Asians, stratification of, 45–6
Asian dominance of commercial life, 43
Asians as commercial bourgeoisie, 41–6
Awiti, 109

Balbus, Isaac, 26–7
Baran, Paul, 70, 113–14
BAT, case of lockout at, 140–2; management agreement, 166–7
Bettelheim, 111
Bomani, Paul, 57, 67
Bottomore, 25
Bowles, B. D., 32
British American Tobacco Co. Ltd., *see* BAT, case of lock-out at
Bukoba district, 57–8
Bureaucratic bourgeoisie, 79–99; Arusha Declaration and, 79–80; economic base of, 85; international bourgeoisie and, 85; different sectors of, 88; conditions of reproduction, 94–6; ideology of, 96–7

Cabral, 22–4, 53, 55–6, 60, 120
Capital (das Kapital) (Marx), 5
Capitalism, international trade with, 158–62; trade and trading partners, 158–60; aid from overseas, 160–2

Carr, E. H., 63
Citizenship Bill (1961), 68–9, 80
Civil Service, Africanization of, 69–70
Class Alliances, 119
Class, Caste, and Race (Cox), 8
Class, concept of, 3–12; introduction, 3–4; formal definition, 4–7; dialectical concepts, 7–9; cultural revolution, theoretical; lessons of, 10–12
Class struggle, theory of, *see* Class, concept of
Colonialism and class struggle, 55
Commercial bourgeoisie, decline of, 82–4
Commercial sector, 36–7
Common Man's Charter (Uganda), 123
Compradore class, 45
Construction, 37–8
Consumer goods, table of, 156
Co-operative movement, 72–5
Co-operative Supply Association of Tanganyika (Cosata), 73, 75
Co-operative Ordinance (1932), 67
Corruption, 71, 84
Coulson, A., 170–2, 175
Cox, Oliver, 8, 46
Cultural Revolution, Chinese, 10–12

Dar-es-Salaam Motor Transport, 139
Debray, 31
Development Plan, First Five-Year, 75, 104, 163
Downing of tools, 134–7

Economic rationale (Ujamaa Vijijini), 103–7
Economic structures, 34–40
Economy, nature of, 149–57; sectoral distribution, 149–51; export-oriented primary production, 151–3; consumption-oriented, secon-

Economy—*contd.*
dary sector, 153–6; dispropor-
tionate services sector, 156–7
Elites, critique of, 24–6
Emery, Dr David E., 177
Estate development, 96
European Economic Community,
160
Exports, table of, 152, 160

Factory takeover at Mount Carmel,
142–5
Feudalism, 53–4
Field Force Unit (Paramilitary), 90
Fimbo, G. M., 81–2
Foreign Aid, tables of, 161
Foreign exchange scandals, 82
Foreign investments, table of, 163
Frank, A. G., 19, 34
Freedom and Socialism (Nyerere), 76
Freedom and Unity (Nyerere), 103
Freyhold, M. von, 108, 119

GATT, 21
GDP figures, 36–7, 40, 149, 152
Girouard, Sir Percy, 32

Historical background to class
struggles, 34–54; economic structures, 34–40
relations, ethnic or class?, 40–54;
metropolitan bourgeoisie, 45;
commercial bourgeoisie, 45–8;
petty bourgeoisie, 48–50; kulak
farmers, 50–2; workers, 52–3;
peasantry, 53–4

Iliffe, 16, 50–1, 57, 111, 117
ILO (International Labour Office),
78, 151
IMF (International Monetary
Fund), 21
Imports, table of composition of,
158–9
Indian Association (Chamber of
Commerce), 67
Industrial disputes involving strikes,
table of, 135–6
Industrial relations machinery, 127–
33, *see also* Proletarian class
struggle

Industrial sector, employment by,
table of, 150–1, 157
International investments, 164
Investment, pattern of, 173–6
Iringa district, 108–9

Kandoro, S. A., 59
Karagwe district, 58
Kashaija, Mr., 140–2
Kaunda, Kenneth, 168, 171–2
Key money, 81
Kilimanjaro district (and Hotel),
57–8, 108, 115, 170
Kilombero Sugar Plant, 164
Kisumo, Mr., 144
Klerru, Dr., 108
Kulak farmers, 50–2, 57–8, 69, 108,
114–15

Labour and Social Welfare, Mini-
stry of, 130, 133
Labour Tribunal, 128, 135–6, 142
Lake Province, 57
Land alienation, 50
Landlords, emergence of, 81–2
Latin-America, communism in, 15
Law discussed, 5–6
Leader, definition of, 79
Leadership Code, 80–1, 95
Leigh, Benjamin W., 66
Lenin, Vladimir I., 19, 109, 112
Loans, sources of external, 162
Lock-out, BAT, case of, 140–2
Lyall, A. B., 40

Maguire, G. A., 43
Mali ya Taifa (Nyerere), 51
Manufacturing industries, 37
Mao Tse-tung, 10
Mapolu, H., 106, 108, 132, 137
Mapundi, 136
Marketing Co-operatives, 42
Marx, Karl, 5, 64–5, 112
Marxism, 3–12, 13–14
Marxist orthodoxy, 27–8
Marxist theory in Africa, 13–26;
Marxism as a dogma?, 13–14;
capitalist stage, skipping the, 14–
18
classless Africa, 18–26; petty
bourgeoisie, 21–2; proletariat

INDEX

and revolution, 22–4; critique of Elites, 24–6
Mau mau, 50
Mbilinyi, Marjorie, 111–14, 118
Mbulu district, 58, 108
Meisal, 25
Michele, 25
Mihyo, 127, 129–30, 142–3
Militias, proposed formation of, 125
Mining and quarrying, 37–8
Ministers, Government, and Parastatal posts held, table of, 89
Mkello, Mr, 77
MNC, *see* Multinational Corporations
Mosca, 25
Mount Carmel case of factory takeover, 137, 142–5
Mtaki, S., 80
Multinational corporations, investments and partnerships with, 163–77; pre-Arusha Declaration, 163–5
post-Arusha Declaration, 165–77; forms of partnership, 165–8; benefits of partnership, 169–71; public corporation, losses to, 171–7
Mwananchi Engineering and Construction Company (MECCO), 169, 172, 175
Mwanjisi, Mr., 130, 133
Mwanza, 57
Mwongozo (TANU guidelines), 78, 80, 94, 116, 123–4, 124–6, 136, 138; guidelines themselves, 124–6

National bourgeoisie in Africa, 20–2
National Development Corporation (NDC), 165, 173, 177
National examinations, failure rate in, table of, 92–3
National Housing Corporation, 96
Nationalism and the Commercial Economy of Tanganyika (Iliffe), 57
Nationalist Enterprise Party, 69
National Provident Fund, 77
National Service Scheme, 76

National Textile Corporation (NATEX), 83–4
National Union of Tanganyika Workers, (NUTA), 68, 77, 127, 129–30, 134, 137, 140, 143–4
Ndulu, 109
Nga Tabiso, 115, 119
Ngombale-Mwiru, Mr., 85, 124
Non-monetarized sector, 37–8
NUTA, *see* National Union of Tanganyika Workers
Nyerere, Julius K., 51, 69, 76–7, 103, 123

Obote, Milton, 123–4
Oil refinery, 164
One-party state, 72
Operation Leapfrog, 177
Operation Rufiji, 109
Overseas Construction Company of Holland (OCC), 169, 172, 175

Parastatal posts, 89–90
Pareto, 25
Peasant Differentiation, 111–20; worker-peasant alliance, 116–20
Permanent Labour Tribunal Act (1967), *see* Labour Tribunal
Petty bourgeoisie, African, 48
Political Economy of Growth (Baran) 70
Politics of Health in Tanzania (Segal), 96
Poverty of Philosophy, The (Marx), 7
Proletarian class struggle, 123–33; workers' struggles and the *Mwongozo*, 123–4; TANU guidelines (*Mwongozo*), 124–6
workers' struggles (Industrial Relations Machinery), 127–33; the machinery itself, 128–9; workers' committees, 129–31; workers' councils, 131–32, conclusion, 132–3
Proletarian nations, 86
Proletarian struggles, 134–45; BAT case of lock-out, 140–2; Mount Carmel case of factory take-over, 142–5
Public administration, 37

181

Raikes, P., 108
Revolution in Guinea (Cabral), 22
Rodney, Walter, 31
Role of the State, 31–3
Rubber Industries take-over, 130, 137–8, 142–5
Rural development, *see* Ujamaa Vijijini
Rweyemamu, J., 32, 34, 37, 42, 78, 113, 155, 163

Security of Employment Act, 1964, 77, 128, 129–30
Settlers, European, 40–1
Sender, J., 116–18
Seven Erroneous Theses about Latin-America (Stavenhagen), 15
Shigetu Tsuru, 37
Sisal production, 36
Socialism and rural development, 104, *see also* Ujamaa Vijijini
Socialism in Tanzania (Cliffe), 107
Sperling, Jack, 137
Sri Nimpunoo, 137
State Formation and Class Formation in Tanzania (Rodney), 31
State Trading Corporation (STC), 83
Stavenhagen, Rudolfo, 15, 41–2, 43–4
Stevedores and Dockers' Union, 52
Strikes, banning of, 68; in general, 134–6
Sunguru Textile Mill, 139
Sweezy, P. M., 112–13
Szentes, T., 94, 153–4

Take-overs by workers, 136–45
Tancot Limited, 36
Tanganyika African Association (TAA), 42–3, 57
Tanganyika African National Union (TANU), 42, 49–53, 57–9, 79, 123–6, 144
Tanganyika Agricultural Corporation (TAC), 50–1
Tanganyika Development Finance Company, 169
Tanganyika Federation of Labour (TFL), 52, 68, 80, 128, 134
Tanganyika Motors Limited, case of, 138–9
TANU Youth League, 124

Tanzania Sisal Authority, 115
Tariff protection, 170
Tax concessions, 170
Technology, imported, 175–6
Ten Days that Shook the World (Reed), 9
Theory of Capitalist Development (Sweezy), 112–13
Thomas, Professor C., 151, 173–4
Toward 'Uhuru' in Sukumaland (Maguire), 43
Trade and trading partners, 158–60
Trade Disputes (Settlement) Act, 1962, 77, 128, 134, 136
Trade Unionism, 52–4, 68, *see also* National Union of Tanganyika Workers (NUTA)
Tschannerl, G., 97, 149, 155
Turner, Professor, 78, 128

Uganda, coup in, 123–4
Uhuru, the fight for, 49, 53–60
Ujamaa Vijijini (rural development), 103–10; economic rationale, 103–7; implementation, 107–10
Ujamaa na Kujitegemea (Ngombale-Mwiru), 85
Ujamaa policy, 76, 91
Ujamaa versus Capitalism (press report), 114
Underdevelopment discussed, 17–18
University Students' Union, 91
Usambara district, 108

Victoria Federation of Co-operative (VFCU), 67

Wage-earners, 52–3
Wage legislation, 77–8
Wages, Incomes and Prices Policy (Turner), 78, 128
Water supply programmes, rural, 97
Weber, 25
What is History? (Carr), 63
Worker-peasant alliance, 116–20
Workers' Committees and Workers' Councils, 129–32
Workers' struggles, 127–33
World Bank, 21, 159

Yadzani, Mr., 143–4